ZOLA AND THE ART OF TELEVISION
ADAPTATION, RECREATION, TRANSLATION

LEGENDA

LEGENDA is the Modern Humanities Research Association's book imprint for new research in the Humanities. Founded in 1995 by Malcolm Bowie and others within the University of Oxford, Legenda has always been a collaborative publishing enterprise, directly governed by scholars. The Modern Humanities Research Association (MHRA) joined this collaboration in 1998, became half-owner in 2004, in partnership with Maney Publishing and then Routledge, and has since 2016 been sole owner. Titles range from medieval texts to contemporary cinema and form a widely comparative view of the modern humanities, including works on Arabic, Catalan, English, French, German, Greek, Italian, Portuguese, Russian, Spanish, and Yiddish literature. Editorial boards and committees of more than 60 leading academic specialists work in collaboration with bodies such as the Society for French Studies, the British Comparative Literature Association and the Association of Hispanists of Great Britain & Ireland.

The MHRA encourages and promotes advanced study and research in the field of the modern humanities, especially modern European languages and literature, including English, and also cinema. It aims to break down the barriers between scholars working in different disciplines and to maintain the unity of humanistic scholarship. The Association fulfils this purpose through the publication of journals, bibliographies, monographs, critical editions, and the MHRA Style Guide, and by making grants in support of research. Membership is open to all who work in the Humanities, whether independent or in a University post, and the participation of younger colleagues entering the field is especially welcomed.

ALSO PUBLISHED BY THE ASSOCIATION

Critical Texts
Tudor and Stuart Translations • New Translations • European Translations
MHRA Library of Medieval Welsh Literature

MHRA Bibliographies
Publications of the Modern Humanities Research Association

The Annual Bibliography of English Language & Literature
Austrian Studies
Modern Language Review
Portuguese Studies
The Slavonic and East European Review
Working Papers in the Humanities
The Yearbook of English Studies

www.mhra.org.uk
www.legendabooks.com

TRANSCRIPT

Transcript publishes books about all kinds of imagining across languages, media and cultures: translations and versions, inter-cultural and multi-lingual writing, illustrations and musical settings, adaptation for theatre, film, TV and new media, creative and critical responses. We are open to studies of any combination of languages and media, in any historical moments, and are keen to reach beyond Legenda's traditional focus on modern European languages to embrace anglophone and world cultures and the classics. We are interested in innovative critical approaches: we welcome not only the most rigorous scholarship and sharpest theory, but also modes of writing that stretch or cross the boundaries of those discourses.

Editorial Committee
Chair: Matthew Reynolds (Oxford)
Robin Kirkpatrick (Cambridge)
Laura Marcus (Oxford)
Patrick McGuinness (Oxford)
Ben Morgan (Oxford)
Mohamed-Salah Omri (Oxford)
Tanya Pollard (CUNY)
Yopie Prins (Michigan)

Advisory Board
Jason Gaiger (Oxford)
Alessandro Grilli (Pisa)
Marina Grishakova (Tartu)
Martyn Harry (Oxford)
Linda Hutcheon (Toronto)
Calin-Andrei Mihailescu (London, Ontario)
Wen-Chin Ouyang (SOAS)
Clive Scott (UEA)
Ali Smith
Marina Warner (Birkbeck)
Shane Weller (Kent)
Stefan Willer (Berlin)

Managing Editor
Dr Graham Nelson
41 Wellington Square, Oxford OX1 2JF, UK

www.legendabooks.com/series/transcript

TRANSCRIPT

1. *Adapting the Canon: Mediation, Visualisation, Interpretation*, edited by Ann Lewis and Silke Arnold-de Simine
2. *Adapted Voices: Transpositions of Céline's Voyage au bout de la nuit and Queneau's Zazie dans le métro*, by Armelle Blin-Rolland
3. *Zola and the Art of Television: Adaptation, Recreation, Translation*, by Kate Griffiths
4. *Comparative Encounters between Artaud, Michaux and the Zhuangzi: Rationality, Cosmology and Ethics*, by Xiaofan Amy Li
5. *Minding Borders: Resilient Divisions in Literature, the Body and the Academy*, edited by Nicola Gardini, Adriana Jacobs, Ben Morgan, Mohamed-Salah Omri and Matthew Reynolds
6. *Memory Across Borders: Nabokov, Perec, Chamoiseau*, by Sara-Louise Cooper
7. *Erotic Literature in Adaptation and Translation*, edited by Johannes D. Kaminski
8. *Translating Petrarch's Poetry: L'Aura del Petrarca from the Quattrocento to the 21st Century*, edited by Carole Birkan-Berz, Guillaume Coatalen and Thomas Vuong
9. *Making Masud Khan: Psychoanalysis, Empire and Modernist Culture*, by Benjamin Poore
10. *Prismatic Translation*, edited by Matthew Reynolds
11. *The Patient, the Impostor and the Seducer: Medieval European Literature in Hebrew*, by Tovi Bibring
12. *Reading Dante and Proust by Analogy*, by Julia Caterina Hartley
13. *The First English Translations of Molière: Drama in Flux 1663-1732*, by Suzanne Jones
14. *After Clarice: Reading Lispector's Legacy in the Twenty-First Century*, edited by Adriana X. Jacobs and Claire Williams
15. *Uruguayan Theatre in Translation: Theory and Practice*, by Sophie Stevens
16. *Hamlet Translations: Prisms of Cultural Encounters across the Globe*, edited by Márta Minier and Lily Kahn
17. *The Foreign Connection: Writings on Poetry, Art and Translation*, by Jamie McKendrick
18. *Poetics, Performance and Politics in French and Italian Renaissance Comedy*, by Lucy Rayfield

Zola and the Art of Television

Adaptation, Recreation, Translation

Kate Griffiths

LEGENDA
Transcript 3
Modern Humanities Research Association
2020

Published by Legenda
an imprint of the Modern Humanities Research Association
Salisbury House, Station Road, Cambridge CB1 2LA

ISBN 978-1-78188-709-7 *(HB)*
ISBN 978-1-78188-402-7 *(PB)*

First published 2020

All rights reserved. No part of this publication may be reproduced or disseminated or transmitted in any form or by any means, electronic, mechanical, photocopying, recording or otherwise, or stored in any retrieval system, or otherwise used in any manner whatsoever without written permission of the copyright owner, except in accordance with the provisions of the Copyright, Designs and Patents Act 1988, or under the terms of a licence permitting restricted copying issued in the UK by the Copyright Licensing Agency Ltd, Saffron House, 6–10 Kirby Street, London EC1N 8TS, *England, or in the USA by the Copyright Clearance Center, 222 Rosewood Drive, Danvers MA 01923. Application for the written permission of the copyright owner to reproduce any part of this publication must be made by email to legenda@mhra.org.uk.*

Disclaimer: Statements of fact and opinion contained in this book are those of the author and not of the editors or the Modern Humanities Research Association. The publisher makes no representation, express or implied, in respect of the accuracy of the material in this book and cannot accept any legal responsibility or liability for any errors or omissions that may be made.

Trademark notice: Product or corporate names may be trademarks or registered trademarks, and are used only for identification and explanation without intent to infringe.

© *Modern Humanities Research Association 2020*

Copy-Editor: Charlotte Brown

CONTENTS

	Acknowledgements	ix
	Introduction: Zola and the Art of Television?	1
1	Selling Zola to Twenty-First-Century Television Audiences: Zola, Gutt and *The Paradise*	23
2	Bodies in Translation: Zola, Venuti, *L'Œuvre* and *Madame Sourdis*	51
3	Interpersonal Transactions: Zola, Nord and *L'Argent*	77
4	The Art of Deformation: Zola, Berman and *Une page d'amour*	101
5	*Germinal* and the Politics of Patronage: Zola, Lefevere and the BBC	123
	Conclusion: Zola and the Art of Television	149
	Bibliography	159
	Index	165

ACKNOWLEDGEMENTS

To my lovely Dad, John Griffiths, with more love, gratitude and pride than I can squeeze into words. Dwi'n dy garu Dad. Dwi'n dy golli di. Diolch am bopeth.

To my lovely daughters, Evie and Mari Sheppard, for, so they say, making a small Grinch's heart grow three sizes in one day. Am so proud of you both.

Much of this book is about the networks of people behind creative projects. And I need to thank the many people behind this one.

This book began life on an AHRC Fellowship and I am very grateful for the transformative support of that body at key moments in my career. It has also been supported by research leave at Cardiff University. Behind its pages lie the comments of numerous colleagues at Cardiff who read and helped shape it. Specific thanks go to Claire Gorrara and Rachael Langford for their leadership and back-up, to Liz Wren-Owens for reading, ideas and support, to Hanna Diamond for her guidance, to Cristina Marinetti, Dorota Goluch, Loredana Polezzi and Abdel-Wahab Khalifa for being mines of information on the intricacies of the landscape of translation theory, to Cathy Molinaro for being an organisational demon, to Carlos Sanz Mingo for irreverent laughter, to Luisa Tramontini for helping me track down contemporary reviews and to Catriona Noonan for sharing her television archive knowledge in exchange for coffee. The voices of successive years of Cardiff translation or multi-media students also feed into this book. Their questions nudged my writing in different and unexpected directions. You were a treat to teach.

A network of colleagues in various institutions helped this book's progress. Thanks are, as ever, due to Andrew Watts and Bradley Stephens for their willingness to let me test-drive ideas on them. So too are they due to Helen Abbott for her willingness to talk Bach and to Rob Stone for letting me tap into his television knowledge. I owe a debt of thanks to Susan Harrow for her help at the various twists and turns of my career. To Legenda and to Graham Nelson in particular I owe a debt of gratitude for asking me for the book in the first place, for supporting its progress as it was being written and bearing with me throughout as events made it a longer project. To various people working in or associated with the BBC, I owe renewed thanks: Pauline Harris for her help tracking down adaptations, the late Diana Griffiths for her generousness of thought, Miranda Emmerson for her practical insights, Dan Rebellato for pushing me to rethink how modern audiences view collectively, Billy Smart for reading suggestions, Cerian Arianrhod for friendship.

But the biggest set of thanks of all go to my family. They go to my Mum for back-up and for her endless pride in my 'vertiginous spirals'. Thanks too are due to Kathryn Collins and Siân Keepin for years of love and laughter. They're also due to Nicole Kennedy for being there no matter the distance. It couldn't and wouldn't have been written without the quiet support of Richard Sheppard, who ringfenced time for me to write. Thank you. The very biggest thanks of all go to Evie and Mari, though, who sat on my lap, coloured in successive versions of the manuscript, decorated it with chocolate fingerprints and did spelling homework on it. You made it an infinitely more beautiful thing. Caru chi'n fwy na'r byd i gyd yn grwn. Rwyf mor falch ohonch chi'ch dwy.

K.G., Cardiff, February 2020

INTRODUCTION

Zola and the Art of Television?

The frequency with which the novels of Emile Zola appear on British and French television underscores the strength of the bond between the novelist's output and this medium. But little is written about that bond. This book seeks to counter the critical silence on Zola and television by making visible the range and depth of adaptations across eras and channels in these two nations. It uses six television adaptations — four French, two British — as its case studies: *The Paradise* (BBC, 2012), *L'Œuvre* (Deuxième Chaîne, 1967), *Madame Sourdis* (Antenne 2, 1979), *L'Argent* (Antenne 2, 1988), *Une page d'amour* (FR3, 1980) and *Germinal* (BBC, 1970). It reads them through the prism of core strands in translation theory, working specifically from the translation theories of Ernst-August Gutt, Lawrence Venuti, Christiane Nord, Antoine Berman and André Lefevere as critical frames.[1] It does so not in order to elide translations and adaptations as cultural products — the two are different artefacts, resulting from different processes. It does so because when read in association, these Zola television adaptations and these theorists have a powerful revisionary impact on core debates in Adaptation Studies. Collectively, in diverse ways, they re-evaluate the critical frames and terms which have shaped the discipline. They make us rethink what we mean by the word 'fidelity', a concept which has dominated both translation and adaptation theories despite moves to pass beyond it. They do so in two key ways. First, though we may use it as such, fidelity is not a fixed, absolute term. Rather it is a shifting construction shaped by the cultural, critical, temporal, political imperatives of the person or system invoking it. It is a relative term, a term which adapts and means different things in different cultural contexts. Second, the case studies and theorists at the heart of this book make clear that fidelity, as a term, limits our reading of adaptations. It confines us to a text-to-text approach to the artefact as we seek a source text in its reproductive adaptation. The case studies at the heart of this book, though, make clear that adaptation is an interpersonal creative transaction. It is done by people for people. To seek only a source text in the Zola adaptations at the heart of this book is to bypass the layers of different subjective identities whose influence, implicit or explicit, shapes them. Thus, to hold 'fidelity' up as the absolute marker or arbiter of the success or failure of an adaptation is, first, to fail to recognise its shifting, adapting essence and, second, to ignore the innately subjective nature of art works so rooted in networks of interpersonal and intercreative exchange. Zola, the theorists in this book and the adaptations with which they are brought into dialogue, engage with and demonstrate varying visions of fidelity. They explore its creative value as a concept as well as its fault-lines, contemplating the art generated by its pursuit.

Fidelity has in many ways become something of a straw man in Adaptation Studies, its invocation and implications persuasively undercut by an increasing number of scholars. Some twenty years ago, Brian McFarlane argued of fidelity, 'No critical line is in greater need of re-examination — and devaluation'.[2] Julie Sanders concurs, persuasively seeking to locate art in the movement away from fidelity: 'Fidelity to the original? [...] It is usually at the very point of infidelity that the most creative acts of adaptation [...] take place'.[3] Fidelity, though, as a critical framework will not quite go away. McFarlane and Sanders both set out their approach to adaptation in relation to the term.[4] Robert Giddings and Erica Sheen in their 2000 work *The Classic Novel: From Page to Screen* acknowledge McFarlane's belief in the need to move beyond fidelity as an all-encompassing critical framework, whilst making clear that the essays in their collected volume 'take the question of fidelity as their critical point of reference'.[5] David L. Kranz and Nancy C. Mellerski, in *In/Fidelity: Essays on Film Adaptation*, argue for the centrality of fidelity even while pushing for the need to acknowledge a plurality of other perspectives alongside it.[6] Colin MacCabe, Kathleen Murray and Rick Warner's *True to the Spirit: Film Adaptation and the Question of Fidelity* also pushes for a need to recognise fidelity as a core concept, even while accepting its innate complexity.[7] David T. Johnson, in his overview of the evolution of fidelity as a critical concept, evaluates both fidelity's status as a critically contested topic and the ways in which it might usefully feature in future critical developments.[8] Fidelity as a concept will not be shaken off. And perhaps it is right that it should not. Adaptations which profess to adapt an earlier source will inevitably be assessed in relation to that source. The translation theorists at the heart of this volume do not stop us asking whether an adaptation is faithful to its source text, rather they push us to consider what we mean when we ask that question. They underscore the different ways in which an adaptation may be faithful, the different incarnations fidelity may have in different eras and contexts. They push us to assess fidelity as an innately subjective and multiple term, the fixity of its invocation belying the very different things which may be meant by it.

Such a reading of fidelity links Translation Studies and Adaptation Studies as disciplines. The impulse to associate translation theory and adaptation theory is not a new one. Writing in 2007, translation theorist Lawrence Venuti called for far greater dialogue between the disciplines of translation and adaptation in their theoretical discourses in his piece 'Adaptation, Translation, Critique'.[9] Venuti suggests: 'Translation theory advances thinking about film adaptation by enabling a more rigorous critical methodology'.[10] There are clear points of commonality between translation theory and adaptation theory. Both disciplines have been dominated since their inception by discourses of fidelity in various guises. Both have recognised the inherent flaws in the very fidelity debate which has shaped their existence, and the ultimate impossibility of the concept. They have, as Katja Krebs points out, worked in overlapping ways, seeking to go 'beyond discussions of equivalence, faithfulness and fidelity'.[11] Translation theory, from the time of Seneca, has offered taxonomies seeking to encompass the strategies via which one might be faithful, a trajectory which adaptation theory echoed in the twentieth century.[12] Whether taxonomies are or are not useful ways to approach translation, this time lag is far from insignificant. Adaptation theory is, in many ways, a far younger discipline than its translation counterpart. Adaptation theory, by and large, takes as its theoretical starting point George Bluestone's 1957 *Novels into Film*.[13] Translation theory, in contrast, can, in the form of prefaces, private letters and public pronouncements, trace itself back to Roman times and earlier, enjoying a rich, dialogic history in the ensuing centuries before formalising as a discipline in the twentieth century. Specific scholars have taken Venuti at his word, reading adaptations via the prism of translation theory, but they have done so on disparate adaptations and in relation to cinema and theatre. Laurence Raw's article 'The Skopos of a Remake: Michael Winner's *The Big Sleep* (1978)' reads said film via the prism of Hans Vermeer's incarnation of Functionalist theory.[14] Katja Krebs's edited volume *Translation and Adaptation in Theatre and Film* persuasively brings together academics and practitioners in a debate which draws on voices within and beyond translation theory to consider cinema and theatre. Patrick Cattrysse addresses the interstice of cinema and translation in his 1992 article 'Film (Adaptation) as Translation: Some Methodological Proposals'.[15] Each of these scholars calls on a different element, theorist or theoretical movement in Translation Studies. Each reads what translation theory has to offer Adaptation Studies differently. For Katja Krebs, for example, in addition to its fertile and contested history, translation theory forces Adaptation Studies out of its often monolingual focus.[16] Age of discipline aside, each of these articles underscores in a very different way that translation theory and its counterpart in adaptation speak powerfully to common issues.

The present monograph uses a range of translation theorists to read a diverse body of adaptations of the works of Emile Zola for television. It does so in order to generate a revisionary dialogue about how the term 'fidelity' is used and what might be meant by it. It constructs its critical frame from translation theorists from very different schools of thought who make key interventions in relation to the topic: Ernst-August Gutt, Venuti himself, Christiane Nord, Antoine Berman and André Lefevere. Berman and Lefevere in particular are compelling in their reading of fidelity as a shifting cultural construct, a term fashioned by the cultural, economic and political imperatives of the context of its use. It is, they argue, a concept which adapts over time, place and culture. The recognition of fidelity as an evolving, subjective concept often wielded with a cultural, political or economic framework in mind, has powerful implications for Adaptation Studies. It highlights cultural, temporal, political and economic contexts as formative both of the production and reception of adaptations. Berman and Lefevere resonate, to varying degrees, with the Cultural Turn in translation theory, a movement focusing on the way in which translations and their critical receptions are both fashioned by and act upon the cultures from which they stem. Fidelity, viewed through the prism of their theoretical stances, thus tells us as much if not more about the system, poetics or moment invoking it than the adaptation's relationship to its source. Lefevere writes, in lines to which this book will return:

> 'Faithfulness' is just one translational strategy that can be inspired by the collocation of a certain ideology with a certain poetics. To exalt it as the only strategy possible, or even allowable, is as utopian as it is futile. Translated texts as such can teach us much about the interaction of cultures and the manipulation of texts. These topics, in turn, may be of more interest to the world at large than our opinion as to whether a certain word has been 'properly' translated or not. In fact, far from being 'objective' or 'value free', as their advocates would have us believe, 'faithful translations' are often inspired by conservative ideology.[17]

Berman goes a stage further, citing and setting against each other multiple definitions of fidelity from famous historical voices whose polyphony on the topic enacts the innate multiplicity of the term.[18]

If Berman and Lefevere situate fidelity as a shifting cultural construct, theorists such as Gutt, Venuti and Nord require us to personalise it. One of the principal shortcomings, Nord argues, of fidelity as a construct in translation, is that it focuses on text-to-text relations, on assessments of how a source text is conveyed in the translation of it, on how faithful the translated text is to its source work. Adaptation Studies might be read in the same terms as critics have frequently asked how, why and where the source text is in its film adaptation. Nord argues, though, in relation to translation, that translation is not an intertextual process, as one text becomes another text, but rather a complex interpersonal process in which the translation is mediated by a variety of people for the people of the audience. She analyses the plurality of personalities who shape and enact the translation in starkly different ways: source authors, commissioners, translators, audiences, cultural arbiters, reviewers, editors, publishers, amongst others. Reproductive artefacts, whether they be translations or adaptations, are, Nord argues, done by people for people and there is value in unpicking the formative influence of the networks of individuals through whom translations and adaptations come into existence. Nord, Gutt and Venuti each focus on a different section of the interpersonal networks via which translative art is born. If Nord focuses on the plural identities (editors, commissioners, collaborators, etc.) who shape and form the text as it changes form, Gutt assesses the shaping influence of the audience, and Venuti concentrates on the invisible body of the translator which marks the text in visible ways. Their collective vision of translation as the product of a series of interpersonal transactions has particular purchase in the field of television adaptation, where multiple creative identities visibly mark both the television product and cultural discussions relating to its ownership/attribution: source author, screen-writer, director, producer, commissioning channel, lead actors. If the multiple creative identities involved in acts of adaptation challenge the persistent conceptualisation of artistry as integral, unitary and specific to one creative genius, then television adaptation pushes that definition still further, attributable as it is to a range of the creative identities involved. The challenge that television adaptation poses to this unitary vision of singular creative genius does not, this book will argue, mean that television adaptation is not and cannot be art. Rather it suggests that broader, more interpersonal definitions of artistry, in keeping with Nord's theory, are needed to encompass and critically assess it. Collectively Lefevere, Berman, Nord, Gutt and Venuti do not do away with fidelity as a concept. Rather they encourage us to read it in context, situating it as a shifting, contextual concept which must take into account the connected networks of creative, cultural, political and economic influence via which reproductive art works are mediated.

The re-evaluative readings of fidelity offered by these translation and adaptation theorists resonate with Zola's creative reproductive mission. They do so because Zola anticipates and speaks to many of their debates. He is an artist in and of translation and adaptation. Since their publication, his works have been translated and re-translated across time, nation and media.[19] Zola, as an artist, was involved with both the financial transactions and practicalities behind such translations. He is also an artist in and of adaptation. He both adapted himself for theatre and collaborated with those adapting him for the same medium.[20] Zola was adapted in his lifetime into a variety of art forms: painting, cartoons and caricatures, theatre plays and variety show skits.[21] Translation and adaptation, though, are not just things done to the author's fiction, rather both sit at the very core of his fiction. Great realist artistry, Zola argues, is artistry that translates reality.[22] He claimed to translate the Impressionists into prose: 'Je n'ai pas seulement soutenu les Impressionnistes, je les ai traduits en littérature, par les touches, notes, colorations, par la palette de beaucoup de mes descriptions' [I not only championed the Impressionists, I translated them into literature in the touches, notes, colours and palette of my descriptions].[23] He adapts key artists of the movement and their visual techniques of *décentrage*, cropping, series paintings and fluid analysis of light and colour in prose.[24] Zola adapts not just the visual arts, but a whole host of earlier sources in novels which position themselves as reworkings of other authors in a range of media.[25] Most importantly, though, Zola speaks to the translation theorists at the heart of this monograph as he reflects on the power and limitations of fidelity as a concept. He evaluates both his fiction's ability to capture reality in its integrity and its ability to reproduce in prose the Impressionists, gesturing in fiction to the ways in which neither of these sources may fully be captured. Fidelity is for him a flawed but very productive endeavour for it generates the fiction which enabled him to live and make his name. So too does Zola, like the theorists in this book, personalise fidelity as a concept. He contemplates the interpretive force of his own authorial body on his fictions, conceptualising the best artists as having the ability to 'traduire la réalité à travers son tempérament' [translate reality through his/her personality].[26] He writes: 'Chaque grand artiste est venu nous donner une traduction nouvelle et personnelle de la nature. La réalité est ici l'élément fixe, et les divers tempéraments sont les éléments créateurs qui ont donné aux œuvres des caractères différents' [Each great artist gives us a new and personal translation of nature. Reality is the fixed point. The different personality of each artist is the creative element which ensures that works of art are different in character].[27] He also reflects on the networks of intertextual and extratextual voices and people who fashion and shape his works, contemplating both their formative influence and their ultimate dispossession in works in which Zola's creative signature dominates. To judge realist art only in relation to fidelity to its source is, for Zola, to ignore the compellingly complex networks of creative collaboration which make its artistry possible.

If Zola's realist art was adapted multiply within his lifetime, it has found a fertile home in television, a medium which postdates the author.[28] While Zola is adapted into television across the world, television adaptations in France and Britain stand out in critical terms. They do so in four ways. First, in terms of number of television adaptations of the novelist, they are particularly prolific producers. Second, when read comparatively, they demonstrate clear national trends in British and French adaptation, trends which shape the adaptation in complex ways above and beyond the content of the source text. Third, the specific nature of the development of television in both nations enables this book to unpick the influence of television institutions on the adaptations they produce. In Britain, Zola is exclusively the preserve of BBC television and public service broadcasting. Thus, the British case studies make clear the formative, evolving and well-documented influence of the BBC on the Zola adaptations it produces. In France, Zola appears on public and private channels and the adaptive output of this nation allows for a reading of the influence of the different financial models on the adaptations they broadcast. Fourth, the comparison of adaptations between France and Britain enables this book to work at the interstice between translation and adaptation. The French adaptations adapt Zola's language intra-lingually — they may adapt his nineteenth-century French for a more modern audience but they do not move it to a new language. In contrast, the British adaptations are inter-lingual, adapting both Zola's source texts and the native language in which they are written to British contexts in different eras and reflecting on their actions in so doing. The British and French case studies at the heart of this book underscore that adaptation is always a translation of language, whether it be across national borders, across intra-lingual eras or simply across contemporary media contexts. Translation and adaptation, as processes, overlap and overlay each other. British and French adaptations of Zola are powerfully linked in their collective recognition that adaptation cannot be understood in a narrow sense as literary texts are adapted for television. The British and French Zola adaptations at the heart of this monograph visibly and consciously adapt a whole host of sources alongside their source novel. They adapt the visual arts, reality, history, politics, cinema and a range of other influences. In so doing they take us back to Zola, the author who crafts his own originality by drawing on the voices, images and art works of others. When read in association, British and French adaptations of Zola offer a compelling vision of adaptation as a protean process whose breadth and wealth is damaged by too narrow a critical focus.

Zola's history in television in Britain and France is a nuanced one. His presence on the BBC is pronounced. As early as 1950, a television play of *Thérèse Raquin* aired on 2 March. It starred Nancy Price and Sonia Dresdel. Thirty years later, the corporation remade the same novel, this time as a three-part series dramatised by Philip Mackie and directed by Simon Langton in 1980. Other work by Zola was made and remade on BBC television in the intervening years. In 1968, the corporation offered a five-part version of *Nana* dramatised by Robert Muller and directed by John Davies. In 1970 it broadcast a five-part rendering of *Germinal*, again directed by John Davies. In 1996, David Suchet starred in a BBC adaptation of *La Bête humaine*, written and directed by Malcolm McKay. In 2012 the BBC broadcast a two-series adaptation of Zola's *Au Bonheur des dames* under the title of *The Paradise*. Zola's presence in French television is still more pronounced. The BBC's 1950 television version of *Thérèse Raquin* finds a cross-channel colleague in an adaptation of the same name aired in 1957 on the Première Chaine, directed by Lorenzi Stellio and accessible in the archives of the Inathèque of the Bibliothèque nationale de France. The catalogue of the Inathèque highlights the greater rate of adaptations of the works of Emile Zola in France. While a 1967 version of *L'Œuvre* directed by Pierre Cardinal is the sole work listed for the 1960s, four adaptations appear in the 1970s and seven in the 1980s.[29] In the 1970s, French viewers were offered *Le Bouton de rose* (Première Chaîne) in 1971, *Pot-Bouille* (Deuxième Chaîne) in 1972, *Germinal* (FR3) in 1976 and *Madame Sourdis* (Antenne 2) in 1979. In the 1980s, the following Zola adaptations were broadcast: *La Fortune des Rougon* (TF1) screened in 1980, as did *Une page d'amour* (FR3). *Nana* (Antenne 2) appeared in 1981, *Mirage dangereux* (TF1) in 1987 and *Une femme innocente* in the same year. *L'Argent* closed the decade's Zola adaptations, appearing in 1988 (Antenne 2). If the 1980s represents the heyday of Zola adaptations on French television, adaptations of the novelist remain a constant presence in each decade since. Two Zola adaptations appeared in the 1990s, *Une page d'amour* (France 3) in 1995 and *La Fortune des Rougon* in 1997, in addition to repeats of the 1981 *Nana* and the 1988 *L'Argent*. A further three adaptations have appeared since the new millennium: *Nadia Coupeau, dite Nana* (France 2) in 2001, *La Liberté de Marie* (an adaptation of *Thérèse Raquin*, France 3) in 2002 and *La Joie de vivre* (France 2) in 2011.

Zola is, as the adaptations detailed above suggest, adapted regularly for television in both Britain and France, yet the critical writing on these television adaptations is scant. Anna Gural-Migdal and Robert Singer's edited volume *Zola and Film: Essays in the Art of Adaptation* usefully lists some of the available television adaptations in its closing catalogue, but none of its chapters address them, focusing instead on cinema. My own monograph on cinematic adaptations of the novels of Emile Zola across eras makes reference to television adaptation in passing, yet there is real danger in addressing cinema and television together for the media cannot and should not be elided.[30] Television and cinema are distinct artistic media, with distinct aesthetics and modes of consumption, which ultimately produce very different cultural products and experiences. A few isolated articles exist specifically on Zola and television adaptations.[31] So too does the medium feature in isolated articles on the multimedia afterlives of Zola.[32] But the volume of work on Zola and television does not reflect the range and depth of the nineteenth-century novelist's presence in the medium. This critical silence on Zola and television speaks volumes about television in both physical and critical terms. It stems perhaps from the archival challenges which characterise the medium, challenges detailed below. But it also springs from the critical debate over the cultural value and artistry of television which has never fully gone away.

That television is an archivally challenging medium is clear on either side of the Channel. Zola is a tangible physical presence in British television, but he is an inaccessible one. Despite the reach, range and audience of Zola in British television, once broadcast, the television adaptations disappear as television. In its early years, television was live and went unrecorded. The BBC Genome archive thus lists the aforementioned 1950 adaptation of *Thérèse Raquin* starring Nancy Price and Sonia Dresdel, but it is a listing for an adaptation which no longer tangibly exists. Even when recording became a possibility, the process was expensive and tended to be used for reasons of practicality (i.e. to re-broadcast in different time zones across the British Empire) rather than for archiving purposes. Tapes, when used, were frequently reused subsequently. While archiving processes have developed over the decades within the BBC, space and very real financial constraints and cuts mean that they are not and cannot be universal. Neither are the outputs of the BBC, once they have been aired, publicly accessible in their entirety in any real sense. The corporation has put considerable time and energy into the release of key adaptations via BBC education initiatives, the re-airing of classic pieces in listen-in-the-dark sessions/cultural festivals and the modern use of watch-again facilities on platforms such as iPlayer (BBC) and the new platform BBC Sounds. They have also invested heavily in the Genome project, which, using the *Radio Times*, catalogues all BBC programming from 1927 to 2009. Genome makes visible the range and scope of production in the corporation, testifying for example to Zola's residual presence on various BBC channels. It allows the public to explore Zola's television presence without having to trawl through back copies of the *Radio Times* or having to apply for access to the diffuse system of regional BBC archives. Genome, though, often makes present the absence of the very television programmes it catalogues, labelling them as unavailable. It makes very visible, for example, Zola's fundamental absence in television since none of the television adaptations focused on in this book are amongst those made accessible on the Genome project. They have no click and watch function and thus the Genome entries serve, in relation to Zola, as markers of absence. They make visible a television presence which is no longer there.[33]

Zola's presence on French television initially feels more tangible, more readily accessible, as each of the French television adaptations studied in this book is provided by the Inathèque at the Bibliothèque nationale de France, often just at the click of a button in the INA work stations in Paris or potentially in the associated online shop. However, while Zola's works are easily, readily and plentifully available via the Inathèque and its computer screens, what they are not is television. Consumed in the Inathèque, abstracted from their televisual 'flow', to use Raymond Williams's term, from their viewing context, audience, channel, time and televisual platform, these Zola adaptations in some senses cease to be television.[34] Instead they become archive pieces, the matter for academic studies such as this. They may be paused, pored over, dissected in the academic isolation and silence of this public library constructed for the advancement of academic endeavour. The adaptation's value is not diminished by this process of archivisation, but it is recognisably different. What the Inathèque and the BBC archives hold is the matter from which one may try to reconstruct what television was. They underline the core spatial paradox of television, a medium vast in its reach, mass in its consumption and broad in its production; a medium whose outputs, once aired, in key periods of history, simply disappeared.[35] Broadcast in large part in eras when recording technology was either in its early days, or did not exist, once aired, the television pieces at the heart of this study often passed beyond public reach. The case study programmes at the heart of this monograph underscore the archival challenges of television as a medium.

The critical silence on Zola and television might, though, stem from more than said archival challenges. Writing in the *New York Times* in 2014, Armond White cuts to the heart of debates about whether television can ever merit the epithet 'art', debates which the medium has struggled to shake off. He writes: 'Film is a visual art form and television is merely a visual medium'.[36] Film, White suggests, is creative, television reproductive. For White, television is not and cannot be art because it has 'never proven to be a medium for artists — or auteurs — who express themselves personally and, primarily, visually'.[37] The medium does not fit the Romantic definition of art as the inspired and original product of an individual poetic genius, a definition which arguably continues to haunt our cultural judgements today. Television is a team-based product, fashioned via the intersecting influences of television commissioners, producers, critics, audiences, stars, writers and directors amongst a whole host of other commercial forces. Its outputs are rarely ascribable to the creative vision of a singular individual. Moreover, while, for White, cinema is an event, an artistic experience which you purchase and consume with concentration often in the culturally ratified venue of a cinema, television is endlessly on tap, consumed in the home or on the go via a proliferating range of possible devices and platforms. It is a medium which may have to fight harder for its audience's attention, running, White fears, the constant risk of being interrupted in its domestic or mobile setting by 'the latest text or viral video'.[38] It is entirely necessary to counter White's reading of television with divergent voices who make clear the medium's potential for artistry in its creative outputs, voices which will weave through the work of this book. Writing in 2009, Emily Nussbaum hails that decade precisely as the era in which television finally became art because it was able to demonstrate personal craftsmanship and clear aesthetic innovation:

> [F]or anyone who loves television, who adores it with the possessive and defensive eyes of a fan, this was most centrally and importantly the first decade when television became recognizable as art, great art: collectible and life-changing and transformative and lasting. As the sixties are to music and the seventies to movies, the aughts — which produced the best and worst shows in history — were to TV. It was a period of exhilarating craftsmanship and formal experimentation, accompanied by spurts of anxious grandiosity (for the first half of the decade, fans compared anything good to Dickens, Shakespeare, or Scorsese, because nothing so ambitious had existed in TV history).[39]

Television, though, has always had the potential to be art, as numerous critics underline. And this monograph, in which four out of the five television case studies precede Nussbaum's time frame, is intended to add grist to their mill.

Intriguingly, many television adaptations of Zola take the question of their own artistry head on by directly probing the boundary between television and fine art, amongst other art forms. Art in the form of painting features frequently in television re-workings of the novelist. But it refuses to be constrained by the intra-diegetic frames which would enclose it within the programmes' narratives, spilling beyond their confines to infiltrate the television adaptations themselves. Antenne 2's 1981 version of *Nana*, directed by Maurice Cazeneuve, is a case in point. The adaptation's credits and opening scene focus unwaveringly on an exhibited canvas of a copy of Manet's *Nana* (1876). In a static shot of the framed canvas on a red background, the television viewer, as if in an art gallery, is invited to contemplate the artistry of the painting. The camera then pans right, to a blank space on the red exhibition backdrop. In the space where a painting should be, the television adaptation places its own title, *Nana*, and creative staff, implicitly claiming for itself the status of art in this multimedia gallery of Zola adaptations. Serving as the viewer's museum guide, the character Fauchery introduces Manet's masterpiece as an interpretation of Zola's Nana ('Ce tableau, c'est le portrait imaginaire de Nana peint par Edouard Manet' [This painting is the portrait painted of Nana by Edouard Manet from his imagination]), before offering up the adaptation which follows as its own artistic version of Nana's life. Cropped and fragmented slivers of dialogue from the adaptation to come are played alongside this visual assertion of television artistry. They gesture, in aural terms, to the visual cropping which characterised the edges of so many Impressionist canvases in their attempt to underline their status as a mere slice of the life which spills beyond their confines. Spilling beyond the confines of Manet's *Nana,* this television adaptation situates itself as an artistic piece which is contiguous to that of Manet. The painting within this adaptation does more than just reference Zola's interest in the Impressionists and his famous defence of Manet. It also poses questions about the potential artistry of television as a medium. Pierre Cardinal's 1967 television adaptation of *L'Œuvre*, one of the case studies at the heart of Chapter Two, is even more direct in its claim for television artistry. Seeking to give visual form to the genius which marks him, the artist character Claude puts brush to canvas. The television adaptation, though, substitutes the camera lens for the canvas. The artist paints directly onto the lens. In a scene which italicises the camera screen, the character's brushstrokes mark television as art. The television adaptations of Zola's novels at the heart of this monograph engage precisely with the debates outlined by White above, asserting their potential status as art whilst probing the interstice between art forms in a manner which resonates with their inter-textual, inter-medial origins.

In a sense, this ongoing debate about whether television and its adaptations are or are not art aligns the medium in some ways with Zola as an author. The same debates dogged his writing. In May 1888, the British MP Samuel Smith, in a motion tabled on the 'spread of demoralising literature', labelled Zola's output 'inartistic garbage'.[40] If Zola's work is, in Smith's eyes, too smutty and sensationalist to be 'art', for the French critic Ferragus, Zola's work is too common, derivative and unconsidered a copy of reality to come close to meriting that epithet. Zola, he makes clear, has nothing of the individual genius about him. Ferragus writes: 'Les pourritures sont à la portée de tout le monde, et ne manquent jamais leur effet' [Filth is within everyone's reach and always has an impact]. True art works with better values, he suggests, 'ne se montrent pas sans vernis, coûtent plus de travail' [are never unvarnished and require far greater craftsmanship].[41] Ferragus's criticisms of Zola's core topics powerfully anticipate the terminology of White's attack on television, cited in part above. Ferragus attacked Zola for his unpolished, surgical, close focus on the filth and abnormalities of humanity in his damning assessment of the sensationalist subject matter of Zola's *Thérèse Raquin*. White writes of television: 'its content — what I perceive as all talk and a lot of grisly, forensic sensationalism — lacks an imaginative use of space or scale [...]. Television will always be a medium that is esthetically inferior'.[42] Zola's artistic credentials continued to be contested after his death. Henry James, in an extended essay on Zola's output, deemed it ultimately to have sacrificed art to the Naturalist system and philosophy behind it.[43] Zola himself, though, was clear that his creative mission was an artistic one. In what might be considered a side swipe at his arch-opponent Ferragus and those who objected to the adaptation of reality in literature, Zola appropriated the vocabulary of artistry while simultaneously blurring the boundary between art and life. He stated: 'Si vous me demandez ce que je viens faire en ce monde, moi artiste, je vous répondrai: "Je viens vivre tout haut"' [If you ask me what I come to do in this world, I, as an artist, will answer you: 'I am here to live out loud'].[44]

British and French television adaptations of Zola's novels not only trigger questions about what artistry might be in an adaptive context, they also make clear, like Lefevere, that both Zola and fidelity look very different in different national contexts. In Britain television adaptations have focused largely on the canonical core of Zola as an author, privileging the recognised classics of his corpus (*Germinal*, *Thérèse Raquin*, *Nana* and *La Bête humaine*). French television has proved both more willing and able to adapt the author's works in broader form. Thus, as early as 1971 it offered a production of Zola's 1878 play *Le Bouton de rose*. TF1's *Mirage dangereux* and *Une femme innocente* both work from minor works in the Zola canon: 'Pour une nuit d'amour' and 'Histoire d'un fou'. While Zola's classic novels do clearly feature in the output of French television, so too do his lesser-read works: *Pot-Bouille* (Deuxième Chaîne, 1972), 'Madame Sourdis' (Antenne 2, 1979), *La Fortune des Rougon* (TF1, 1980), *Une page d'amour* (FR3, 1980), *L'Argent* (Antenne 2, 1988), *La Joie de vivre* (France 2, 2011). The range of Zolas available for public consumption on French television is different from those broadcast by the BBC.

Not only are the Zola texts chosen for adaptation different in Britain and France, so too are there clear national divergences in the ways in which they are adapted. When considering how to translate texts from an earlier time and different culture, eighteenth-century translation scholar Friedrich Schleiermacher stated that there were two possible approaches: 'Either the translator leaves the writer in peace, as much as possible, and moves the reader toward him; or he leaves the reader in peace, as much as possible, and moves the writer toward him'.[45] Schleiermacher and his modern interlocutor Lawrence Venuti both argue that the translator has the choice either to immerse his/her reader in the foreignness of the source culture or, alternatively, to domesticate/accommodate that source culture for consumption in the reader's home context. Their ideas have key and unexplored purchase in Adaptation Studies when relocated to the sphere of time. Television, when reworking Zola's nineteenth-century era and narratives for a modern audience, has to choose a time for its action and audience. The BBC television versions of Zola all move the reader back as closely as they can to Zola's nineteenth-century era and context. They are all period pieces which offer not just an adaptation of the novelist's text as source but an adaptation of the history of his era. Robert Giddings, Keith Selby and Chris Wensley underline our complex nostalgia for this era. It is still recognisable to us. It is 'a major warehouse of historical commodities and evidence, and a period still almost within living memory in which culture we feel we have strong roots'.[46] The BBC adaptations, however, do not access this nineteenth-century past in any true form. They cannot. For adaptations are always, as Giddings, Selby and Wensley underline, something of a 'fake antique'.[47] They recreate a past era which is viewed from and consequently shaped by both the needs and the values of the contemporary era which both commissions and consumes it. Period television adaptations underline therefore that the poles of foreignisation and domestication as described by Venuti are not ultimately poles. The BBC may foreignise in temporal terms in the adaptations made, seeking to take the viewer back to Zola as past, but the adaptations offer a foreign which is always already domesticated, a past both legible in and indeed fashioned by the needs of the present from which we view it.

In the French output, while there are heritage adaptations of Zola, there is a greater willingness to modernise Zola, in Schleiermacher's terms, 'to move the author toward [the reader]', relocating the narrative to a contemporary era. In the 1980s in France such acts of adaptive relocation in temporal terms are the preserve of the two TF1 adaptations, *Mirage dangereux* (1987) and *Une femme innocente* (1987). *Mirage dangereux* jumps between time, text, places and characters in a shapeshifting adaptation which reworks both Zola's short story 'Pour une nuit d'amour' and Michel Tournier's 'L'Air du muguet' in one televisual offering. *Une femme innocente* pushes the borders, boundaries and time of adaptation still further. The television adaptation takes the form of a telefilm in five parts reworking five different sources/authors: Zola's 'Histoire d'un fou', Apollinaire's 'Le Matelot d'Amsterdam', François Coppée's 'Le Louis d'or', Théophile Gautier's 'Omphale' and Jean Cau's 'Un viol'. Anthology adaptations are not uncommon in contemporary French television, as the success of France 2's multi-nineteenth-century author series *Au siècle de Maupassant* (2009) shows. But while *Au siècle de Maupassant* makes no attempt to question or blur the borders and boundaries of its core authors, anthologising them in legible, separate, historic, adaptive form, *Une femme innocente* pushes against the borders and boundaries of adaptation, delighting in merging sources and source authors in disconcerting and challenging ways. The turn of the new millennium saw such acts of temporal relocation spread to works produced for the channels France 2 and France 3. Both *Nadia Coupeau, dite Nana* (France 2, 2001) and *La Liberté de Marie* (France 3, 2002) relocate Zola's source novels (*Nana* and *Thérèse Raquin*) to their contemporary era, moving them resolutely towards the audience. Nadia Coupeau, the victim of gang rape, goes on to star as fashion/advertising model before ultimately closing the adaptation, in a manner which perhaps tests the credulity of those who know the Zola ending, as a would-be childcare assistant conducting a children's Christmas concert.[48] Marie, France 3's modern incarnation of Thérèse Raquin, works in a shop in contemporary northern France, falling for motorbike-riding photographer Vincent (France 3's version of Laurent) who will ultimately shoot himself for love of her. In France core adaptations are faithful to Zola's belief that art should depict contemporary life. In Britain, the BBC is faithful to the nineteenth-century novelist's intention to show a slice of life in his historic era. Fidelity can look very different in different national contexts.

This is not to suggest that there is a uniform Zola on either side of the Channel. This monograph's case study adaptations, in their starkly different aesthetics and interpretations of Zola, blow such a notion out of the water. But it is to suggest, in keeping with Berman and Lefevere, that forces above and beyond the source text shape the adaptations in complex and intriguing ways. The BBC is key to my line of argument here. As the core body adapting Zola in Britain, one might expect a uniform BBC Zola to emerge. Yet not only do different eras and creative personnel in BBC history interpret Zola differently, but the author becomes subtly different on the BBC even with each repeat of the same adaptation, shaped as he is by the new viewing context (actor tribute series, director tribute series), altered channel, different era, changed paratextual material and new viewing platform (digital, on demand, VCR, museum archive) and technology (large-screen HD television, mobile phone, PC, laptop). The rescreening of Zola television adaptations between BBC channels and platforms places the author in a different context and audience and viewing time, shaping the meanings of his work. When adaptations of Zola's work air on BBC1, the author is usually the matter of mass entertainment. When his works air on BBC2, they are more clearly marked as works of literary adaptation. When BBC2 was set up in 1964, BBC1 had long had a Sunday evening teatime slot for adaptations aimed at a family audience which required them to be careful both with their choice and treatment of the adaptations they screened. Seeking to craft a distinct broadcast identity and audience for itself, BBC2, in 1967, created a new later Saturday evening slot dedicated to classical serial adaptations. As I. Kleinecke-Bates points out, 'This created a shift in the treatment of classic novels from early evening educational programming for the whole family to a stronger emphasis on drama and a sometimes more daring choice of material'.[49] When adaptations of Zola's works aired on the BBC under the aegis of the Open University (OU), Zola's work was clearly an educational artefact, a product designed to enable students to meet module learning outcomes.[50] The 1970 multi-part BBC television version of *Germinal* was complemented in 1984 by associated OU offerings on the BBC. Supporting programming aired around the adaptation as BBC2 screened a programme with John Berger visiting a mining community in Derbyshire to attempt to explain the imaginative power of Zola's novel. Immediately after this, a programme on the miners' wage claim in 1982 aired. Zola's presence on the BBC extends also to the short-lived BBC Knowledge, an early BBC digital channel providing documentary, cultural and educational content between 1999 and 2002.

Claude Berri's 1993 film for cinema, *Germinal*, aired on this channel in August and December 2001, preceded and followed by television programming (*Moments of Genius: The Pioneering Scientific Discoveries of John Snow* and *Allies at War: A Look at How Churchill and de Gaulle Began to Feud*) whose flow clearly marked Zola as history, culture and high-value content. Different BBC channels, as a result of their operating brief, flow and audience, offer very different Zolas. The well-documented nature of BBC broadcasting history and its cohesive status as a case study allows for detailed analysis of the formative function of the corporation's patronage and structures on the Zola adaptations it produces.

If this monograph pushes for a reading of fidelity as different in different national contexts and eras as per the translation theorists from whom it takes inspiration, so too does it, like said theorists, push for a reading of adaptation as an interpersonal process. Adding to the debates of Gutt, Nord and Venuti about the people shaping the process of adaptation, British and French television adaptations adapt Zola as a person as well as his novels. They rework his life as text. In 1991, BBC2 screened an episode based on Zola's actions in the Dreyfus affair as part of a drama series written by Jack Emery focusing on people who have passionately defended their beliefs or acts. The episode, part of the 'In My Defence' series, was entitled 'Can the Jew be Innocent?'. The biographical presence of Zola's life is not a new phenomenon on the BBC. The narrative synopsis for *Turn of the Century* on 1 August 1960, a programme narrated by Walter Cronkite, reads thus:

> Tsar Nicholas II of Russia relaxes with his family; Zola and Madame Dreyfus leave the prison where Captain Dreyfus is held, convicted of treason; Pavlova dances; Wilbur Wright demonstrates his flying machine. In this unique film scrapbook there are also glimpses of Edward VII, Rodin, Renoir, Bernhardt, Tolstoy, and many other historic figures who lived through the expansive era which ended for ever in August 1914.

Various French channels craft broadcast hours by reworking the personality and actions of Zola the man. France 2's 1995 telefilm *L'Affaire Dreyfus* is a case in point but it sits alongside myriad documentaries which adapt this historical case, its era and the author at its core. Zola's biography too features on BBC television in the frequent broadcasting of William Dieterle's 1937 biographical film, *The Life of Emile Zola*, a piece of cinema repeated on BBC television in 1971 and 1979. A comparably biographical film, *I Accuse*, aired on 9 December 1978, having originally been released for cinema in 1958. It featured a screenplay by Gore Vidal and direction from José Ferrer.[51] BBC television and its French counterparts adapt not just Zola's novels but also his person and its impact on history.

Dieterle's film and that from Vidal and Ferrer are important for they signal the frequent use of cinema versions of Zola in television: Roger Vadim's *La Curée* aired in 1974 as part of a BBC2 World Cinema Series; Jean Renoir's *La Bête humaine* was screened in 1975 and 1979; Fritz Lang's cinema remake of the same novel, *Human Desire*, appeared on the BBC in 1988 and 1989; Dorothy Arzner's *Nana* was shown on 10 November 1974 as part of a Goldwyn Greats Series on BBC1; Marcel Carné's *Thérèse Raquin* was broadcast in 1982 on BBC2, just two years after the BBC's own television adaptation on the same channel listed above. The broadcasting of such films usefully probes the boundary between television and cinema as the former rescreens the latter.[52] But these films also gesture to the complex play of people via whom adaptations are refracted, adding layers to the interpersonal visions outlined by Gutt, Nord and Venuti. The version of Raymond Leboursier's 1945 film *Naïs* rescreened on BBC 2 in 1971 is indicative here. *Naïs*, as a source text, belongs to Emile Zola. Yet its cinema script was written and partly directed by Marcel Pagnol, in conjunction with Raymond Leboursier. It screened on BBC television, however, as part of a three-part tribute to the canonical French actor Fernandel, an actor whose creative influence and formative persona are arguably more visible and at least as legible as the creative signatures of Pagnol and Leboursier. The BBC's billing of *Naïs* as a work in the canon of Fernandel the actor powerfully echoes Claude Gauteur and Ginette Vincendeau's work on how stars author in part the works in which they feature.[53] Other BBC television screenings of Zola adaptations privilege the director of the films they rescreen. The 1979 screening of *La Bête humaine* was part of a tribute series to its director Jean Renoir. The prevalence of the celebrated director's name in relation to the source author in the para-adaptive material underlines the negotiation of visible creative identities which is intrinsically part of the act of adaptation, a negotiation which television makes more visible in the televisual frames, be they series celebrating actors, directors or themes, via which it screens its adaptive offerings.

If adaptations are polyphonic creative artefacts in which multiple creative voices and different visions of fidelity are visible, so too is the theoretical framework of this book. Chapter One, 'Selling Zola to Twenty-First-Century Television Audiences: Zola, Gutt and *The Paradise*', explores and re-evaluates the relevance theory of Ernst-August Gutt in light of the BBC's recent reworking of Zola's *Au Bonheur des dames*, *The Paradise*. This controversial Functionalist translation theorist argues that for a translation to be successful it must meet first and foremost the needs of its audience, above and beyond the pull of its source text. Gutt's assertion that a translation must sell itself to the audience and their needs does not pull us away from Zola as source author, rather it leads us back to him. It maps powerfully onto both Zola's plot about the commercial construction of a personal empire as Mouret caters to his customer's every need and the way in which Zola himself carefully shaped and marketed his novel to meet the needs of his audience. So too does Gutt's model have clear traction with the BBC's 2012 adaptation of the novel, which had to gain sufficient creative purchase with its viewers to justify its existence within the corporation and merit a second season. The adaptation very clearly adapts the presumed needs of its target audience as well as Zola as authentic source, asking probing questions of the multiple imperatives of fidelity in historic adaptation.

Lawrence Venuti's translation theory drives Chapter Two, 'Bodies in Translation: Zola, Venuti, *L'Œuvre* and *Madame Sourdis*'. Venuti is perhaps most famous for his call for the translator to make him/herself visible both within society and within the translated products which enable that very society to exist and function. The invisibility to which translators are currently consigned both in their works and in society more broadly is, for Venuti, a dangerous thing for it hides the subjective processes and practices of translation, a process done by people for people. Venuti's theories have powerful purchase when applied to adaptations and this chapter reads Antenne 2's 1979 *Madame Sourdis*, an adaptation of Zola's short story of the same name, and the Deuxième Chaine's *L'Œuvre* of 1967 in their light. Both literary texts, in very different ways, are about the hidden identities which enable the production or reproduction of art. In Zola's short story 'Madame Sourdis', a wife paints in her progressively more incapable husband's stead, signing her works as him and translating his vision of the world in problematic canvases which impossibly belong to both and neither of them. In his novel *L'Œuvre* Zola explores the multiple sources and creative forebears which compete in the artist Claude's mind, giving him the potential to produce true art but depriving him of the ability to execute it fully. If Venuti's theory focuses on a singular creative identity, the translator, making possible the reproductive art of translation, this chapter, and indeed Zola's source works behind these adaptations, pluralise his vision. They focus on the multiple creative identities shaping, influencing and refracting these two adaptations and source texts, exploring the complex personal interplay of creative identities from which art is born.

Venuti's theory raises a broader point which spans this book's chapters. In the play of interpersonal transactions via which this book's adaptations are born, the role of the translator must not be forgotten. This book uses translation theory to read specific adaptations, but many of these adaptations are crafted not from Zola as source but from translations made of him, translations often not directly acknowledged or credited in the resulting television programmes. Chapter Two explores two French-language adaptations which do work directly from Zola, their creative personnel working in the same language as their source. But, just as these adaptations shape Zola to their context, culture, and creative team, so, Chapter Two argues, are translations shaped by similar forces. In an attempt to engage with these forces and with Venuti's call for translators to be visible, the majority of the English translations offered alongside French quotations throughout this monograph ostensibly stem from one translator: Ernest Alfred Vizetelly. Vizetelly (1853–1922), with his publisher father Henry, was integral to the dissemination of Zola in England. His translations, in their archaisms and silences when they do not translate things offensive to the mores and the cultural arbiters of the time, underscore the formative force of the era, identities and institutions of the translator's context. Vizetelly's translations make clear that there is always a gap between source text and translation. While Chapter Two explores the intricate interweaving of Vizetelly and Zola as personalities in close focus, this book as a whole allows that interweaving to permeate four of its five chapters, moving only to other translators for reasons of unavailability, accessibility or to underscore the ethnocentric omissions and alterations of Vizetelly's work. Vizetelly thus features as a visible identity in the majority of the book, shaping the version of Zola he offers. Vizetelly, though, forces us to problematise Venuti's vision of the translator as a singular, integral force. He, at times, reworks the translations of others, editing them and introducing them. At others, he creates his own translations. Both appear attributed to him. This book does not unpick the nature of his contribution, rather it embraces the plurality of voices which have come to be known as E. A. Vizetelly.

Chapter Three, 'Interpersonal Transactions: Zola, Nord and *L'Argent*', embraces and furthers the multiply interpersonal vision of reproductive art espoused by Chapter Two. Christiane Nord's theory of loyalty pushes in Translation Studies for a more plural vision of the creative interactions and personalities which collectively fashion a text. Instead of seeking the source in the re-creative work as the sole marker of quality, Nord instead leads us to contemplate the people, both hidden and visible, whose creative identities shape the artistic process in myriad ways. Her approach opens key dialogues with Zola's novel *L'Argent*, a novel both in and of translation. The novel translates contemporary politics, figures and narratives. It is reworked in translation by Vizetelly, who uses his preface both to reflect on how his translating body mediates the text and to contemplate the cultural bodies which shape his art. The novel is translated onto television in Antenne 2's 1988 version of *L'Argent*, a version which plays on the intersecting creative identities behind its images. Collectively, though, these versions of *L'Argent* not only explore and enact Nord's theory of translation as an interpersonal transaction, they also probe its fault-lines. Nord's approach, for all its plurality, charges the translator with a mediating role or duty, reconciling the needs and desires of the multiplicity of people in the re-creative process. Collectively these versions of *L'Argent* demonstrate the difficulty of said duty.

If the first three theorists and chapters of this book focus, in different ways, on the people in and of the translation process (the audience, the translator and the range of people influencing the production process), the translation theorists who form the critical frame of the final two chapters focus on people collectively and as a mass, in terms of nation and culture. In Chapter Four, 'The Art of Deformation: Zola, Berman and *Une page d'amour*', the work of translation theorist Antoine Berman is used to read Zola's *Une page d'amour* and Elie Chouraqui's 1980 reworking of it for FR3. Berman's use to Adaptation Studies stems from his insistence that, consciously or unconsciously, we re-work source texts ethnocentrically, deforming them to accommodate the time, tastes and look required by the target audience for which we work. Berman urges us both to identify and to move to counter our ethnocentric tendencies as we re-work texts for new contexts, cultures and climates. Zola and Chouraqui, in works which self-consciously situate themselves as adaptations, anticipate, evaluate and counter elements of Berman's model of ethnocentric deformation. They assess the changes they make to their source texts for their context and culture, integrating them into the images of their artefacts. Intriguingly, they resist their deformations of their source text by foregrounding them for their audience and forcing said audience to engage with them. Moreover, Zola's novel and Chouraqui's adaptation counter, to a degree, Berman's vision of ethnocentric deformation. They underscore both the complex fidelity which can be gleaned in relation to a source text in works which alter and shape that source text for a new time and audience as well as the power, artistry and beauty which can result from said deformations.

Chapter Five, '*Germinal* and the Politics of Patronage: Zola, Lefevere and the BBC', moves to apply André Lefevere's vision of translation as a process of cultural rewriting, mediated by the cultural bodies of patrons, national context and economics, to the BBC's *Germinal* (1970). As Lefevere explores the power of patronage in its many forms as it shapes and mediates translations and art forms, so this chapter explores the creative influence of the BBC, its mission, creative values and production, on this television adaptation. This BBC case study contrasts starkly in production values and ideals with the BBC adaptation explored in Chapter One. By opening and closing the monograph on temporally diverse BBC productions, the evolution of BBC approaches to the authenticity so often associated with their adaptations becomes clear. Both *The Paradise* (2012) in Chapter One and *Germinal* (1970) explicitly go in quest of authenticity, in keeping with the imperatives of the corporation producing them. But that authenticity visibly means very different things in the different stages of BBC history in which they are produced. Authenticity, like fidelity, is a shifting, adapting term in BBC history and its evolutions tell us much about the culture and context in which adaptations are produced and received.

This book thus draws specifically on key translation theorists of the Functionalist movement (Gutt, Nord) with its overarching intent to assess the needs and power of the audience in the translation process, as well as theorists more commonly associated with the Cultural Turn (Venuti, Berman and Lefevere) driven by their desire to underline the formative power of nation, culture and society over the creative product and how it is received. Collectively, the chapters of this monograph speak precisely to the cultural framework by means of which television adaptations are assessed and the term which dominates so many of those assessments: fidelity. They do not refute or reject fidelity as a concept, but they do seek to probe the borders and boundaries of the concept, underscoring its shifting, contextual nature as well as the need to read adaptations both interpersonally and intertextually. The book's case studies do not argue that all television adaptation is innately art or indeed even that all of the case studies in this monograph are necessarily art. What they move to suggest, though, using the fundamentally collaborative mechanisms behind translations and adaptations as artefacts, is that a reconsideration of how television artistry might be assessed is necessary. The plurality of creative personalities behind television adaptations does not disqualify them from being art. Rather it pushes for a different definition of what adaptive art might be.

Notes to the Introduction

1. See Ernst-August Gutt, *Translation and Relevance: Cognition and Context* (Manchester: St Jerome, 2000); Lawrence Venuti, *The Translator's Invisibility: A History of Translation* (London: Routledge, 2009) and *Translation Changes Everything: Theory and Practice* (London: Routledge, 2013); Christiane Nord, *Translating as a Purposeful Activity: Functionalist Approaches Explained* (Manchester: St Jerome, 1997); Antoine Berman, *L'Epreuve de l'étranger: culture et traduction dans l'Allemagne romantique* (Paris: Gallimard, 1984), and *La Traduction et la lettre ou L'Auberge du lointain* (Paris: Seuil, 1999); André Lefevere, *Translation, Rewriting and the Manipulation of Literary Fame* (London: Routledge, 1992).

2. Brian McFarlane, *Novel to Film: An Introduction to the Theory of Adaptation* (Oxford: Clarendon Press, 1996), p. 8.
3. Julie Sanders, *Adaptation and Appropriation* (London & New York: Routledge, 2006), p. 20.
4. David T. Johnson, working from James Naremore, unpicks the ways in which McFarlane's book circles back towards fidelity, having critiqued it: David T. Johnson, 'Adaptation and Fidelity', in *The Oxford Handbook of Adaptation Studies*, ed. by Thomas Leitch (Oxford: Oxford University Press, 2017), pp. 87–100 (p. 91).
5. *The Classic Novel: From Page to Screen*, ed. by Robert Giddings and Erica Sheen (Manchester: Manchester University Press, 2000), p. 2.
6. *In/Fidelity: Essays on Film Adaptation*, ed. by David L. Kranz and Nancy C. Mellerski (Newcastle upon Tyne: Cambridge Scholars Publishing, 2008).
7. *True to the Spirit: Film Adaptation and the Question of Fidelity*, ed. by Colin MacCabe, Kathleen Murray and Rick Warner (Oxford: Oxford University Press, 2011).
8. Johnson, 'Adaptation and Fidelity'.
9. Lawrence Venuti, 'Adaptation, Translation, Critique', *Journal of Visual Culture*, 6 (2007), 25–43.
10. Ibid., p. 25.
11. Krebs suggests, inter alia, the following thinkers in this context: Theo Hermans, *Conference of the Tongues* (Manchester: St Jerome, 2007), Linda Hutcheon, *A Theory of Adaptation* (London: Routledge, 2006), Ritta Oittinen, *Translating for Children* (London: Routledge, 2000) and Sanders, *Adaptation and Appropriation* (*Translation and Adaptation in Theatre and Film*, ed. by Katja Krebs (London: Routledge, 2013), p. 3).
12. In translation theory, the dichotomous debate over whether one should translate word-for-word or sense-for-sense became far more plural in the taxonomies of the seventeenth and eighteenth centuries. For an exploration of this, see Jeremy Munday, *Introducing Translation Studies: Theories and Applications* (London: Routledge, 2012), p. 41. In his preface to his own translation of Ovid's *Epistles* in 1680, John Dryden reduced all translation to three categories: Metaphrase: 'word by word and line by line' translation, which is akin to literal translation; Paraphrase: 'translation with latitude, where the author is kept in view by the translator, so as never to be lost, but his words are not so strictly followed as his sense'; this enables the alteration of phrases and largely corresponds to faithful or sense-for-sense translation; Imitation: 'forsaking' both words and sense; this enables very free translation. (John Dryden, 'Metaphrase, Paraphrase and Imitation', in Munday, *Introducing Translation Studies*, p. 42). Taxonomies of translation feature too in adaptation theory, but they are, as Thomas Leitch points out, more modern creations, products of the twentieth and twenty-first centuries (Thomas Leitch, 'Adaptation Studies at a Crossroads', *Adaptation*, 1 (2008), 63–77 (p. 64)).
13. George Bluestone, *Novels into Film* (Berkeley & London: University of California Press, 1957).
14. Laurence Raw, 'The Skopos of a Remake: Michael Winner's *The Big Sleep* (1978)', *Adaptation*, 4 (2011), 199–209.
15. Patrick Cattrysse, 'Film (Adaptation) as Translation: Some Methodological Proposals', *Target*, 4 (1992), 53–70.
16. Krebs writes, 'the ever-growing body of work investigating adaptation on screen tends to ignore translation issues and Translation Studies. This may partly reflect the monolingualism typical of Film Studies in its Anglo-American context as well as the dominant position North America holds with regards accepted film practice' (*Translation and Adaptation in Theatre and Film*, ed. by Krebs, p. 5). For further reading on the scholarship on transnational adaptation and the implications of moving works of art between languages, see Iain Robert Smith, *The Hollywood Meme: Transnational Adaptations in World Cinema* (Edinburgh: Edinburgh University Press, 2017).
17. Lefevere, *Translation, Rewriting and the Manipulation of Literary Fame*, p. 51.
18. Berman, *L'Epreuve de l'étranger*.
19. For explorations of Zola in translation, see, inter alia, P. Meseguer, 'Traducción y reescritura ideológica bajo el franquismo: *La Faute de l'abbé Mouret* de Emile Zola', *Cedille*, 11 (2015), 389–412; Brian Nelson, 'The Politics of Style', *Meanjin*, 64.4 (2005), 90–98; and A. Cummins, 'Emile Zola's Cheap English Dress: The Vizetelly Translations, Late-Victorian Print Culture and the Crisis of Literary Value', *The Review of English Studies*, 60 (2009), 108–32.

20. On the adaptation of Zola into theatre by others and by the author himself, see Lawson A. Carter, *Zola and the Theater* (New Haven, CT: Yale University Press, 1963).
21. On the afterlives of Zola's novels and persona in different media, see in particular Catherine Dousteyssier-Khoze, *Zola et la littérature naturaliste en parodies* (Paris: Eurédit, 2004).
22. See Anne Lecomte-Hilmy, 'L'Artiste de tempérament chez Zola et devant le public: essai d'analyse lexicologique et sémiologique', in *Emile Zola and the Arts*, ed. by Jean-Max Guieu and Alison Hilton (Washington, DC: University of Georgetown Press, 1988), pp. 85–89 (p. 87).
23. Cited by Henri Hertz, 'Emile Zola, témoin de la vérité', *Europe*, 30 (1952), 83–84. All translations are my own unless stated otherwise.
24. On Zola's translation and adaptation of key personalities in the Impressionist movement, see Patrick Brady, *L'Œuvre de Emile Zola: roman sur les arts, manifeste, autobiographie, roman à clef* (Geneva: Droz, 1967). On the well-explored interaction between Zola and the techniques of the Impressionists, see, among others, William J. Berg, *The Visual Novel: Emile Zola and the Art of his Times* (University Park: Pennsylvania State University Press, 1992), and Kate Griffiths, 'L'Œuvre and the Translation of Reality: Moving between Text and Image', in *Emile Zola and the Artistry of Adaptation* (Oxford: Legenda, 2009), pp. 37–59.
25. See Griffiths, *Emile Zola and the Artistry of Adaptation*.
26. Emile Zola, *Ecrits sur l'art*, ed. by Jean-Pierre Leduc-Adine (Paris: Gallimard, 1991), p. 313.
27. Cited in Anne Lecomte-Hilmy, 'L'Artiste de tempérament chez Zola et devant le public', p. 87.
28. An indicative index of the television adaptations of Zola novels around the world is to be found in *Zola and Film: Essays in the Art of Adaptation*, ed. by Anna Gural-Migdal and Robert Singer (Jefferson, NC: McFarland, 2005). The index includes adaptations for television and for cinema.
29. For a reading of Cardinal's adaptation, see Kate Griffiths, 'Visions and Revisions: Pierre Cardinal's *L'Œuvre*', in *The Art of Text*, ed. by Susan Harrow (Cardiff: University of Wales Press, 2013), pp. 171–85.
30. Griffiths, *Zola and the Artistry of Adaptation*, pp. 60–82.
31. See Gaël Bellalou, '*Nadia Coupeau, dite Nana*: A Modern Adaptation of Zola's Eponymous Work', *Bulletin de la Emile Zola Society*, 30 (2004), 16–22; Russell Cousins, 'Adapting Zola for TV: The Example of Jacques Rouffio's *L'Argent*', *Excavatio*, 12 (1999), 153–61; and Kate Griffiths, 'Mythical Returns: Televising *Thérèse Raquin*', *Nineteenth-Century French Studies*, 39 (2011), 285–95. See also A. M. Baron, 'Zola sur petit et grand écran, de la sagesse au délire', *Cahiers naturalistes*, 84 (2010), 391–92.
32. See Kate Griffiths, '*Thérèse Raquin* and the Anxieties of Adaptation', in *Adapting the Canon*, ed. by Ann Lewis and Silke Arnold-de Simine (Oxford: Legenda, forthcoming). The chapter focuses on Zola's novel in print, film, theatre, television and radio.
33. With the exception of the 1950 *Thérèse Raquin*, each of the five other adaptations listed is available within the BBC and can be called up by staff of the corporation's archives, subject to the application process.
34. Williams's term 'flow' to describe the way in which television programmes were shaped by their time slot, by the channel and sequence of programmes in which they were broadcast, no longer has the same purchase in a subsequent era in which television may be watched in very different ways, abstracted precisely out of televisual flow in technological platforms which allow television to be paused, consumed at will and out of context. However, it still applies to all of the case studies in this monograph which, with the exception of *The Paradise* (BBC, 2012), precede this new technological era and the questions it asks of Williams's telling vision of early television (Raymond Williams, *Television* (London: Routledge, 1975)).
35. See the Inathèque website for detailed readings of television as a mass medium both in France and in the United Kingdom. Pascal Rozat, 'Television History: The French Exception' (2011), <http://www.inaglobal.fr/en/television/article/television-history-french-exception> [accessed 31 May 2017]. The site also offers a useful overview of television history in France.
36. Armond White, 'Film is Art. Television is a Medium', *New York Times*, 3 April 2014 <https://www.nytimes.com/roomfordebate/2014/04/03/television-tests-tinseltown/film-is-art-television-is-a-medium> [accessed 1 May 2017].
37. Ibid.

38. Ibid.
39. Emily Nussbaum, 'When TV Became Art', *New York Entertainment*, 4 December 2009, <http://nymag.com/arts/all/aughts/62513/> [accessed 15 May 2017]. Others make the case that television became art in the 1990s as the medium gained new artistic respect having attracted directors like David Lynch (*Twin Peaks*), launched franchises like the *X-Files* and *ER* and seen the debut of HBO, a cable channel which freed itself of specific industry restrictions in order to offer edgy programming such as *The Sopranos*. See Joshua Rothman and Erin Overbey, 'How TV Became Art', *New Yorker*, 28 August 2017, <https://www.newyorker.com/culture/culture-desk/how-tv-became-art> [accessed 18 October 2018].
40. For details of Smith's speech and an overview of the reception of Zola's work in different eras, see Robin Buss, *J'accuse*, *Guardian*, 28 September 2002, <https://www.theguardian.com/books/2002/sep/28/classics.emilezola> [accessed 29 April 2017]. For evaluations of the reception of Zola's texts in temporal terms, see: Robert Lethbridge, 'L'Accueil critique des premières œuvres de Zola (1864–1869): vers une bibliographie intégrale', *Cahiers naturalistes*, 53 (1979), 124–31, and 'L'Accueil critique à l'œuvre de Zola avant *L'Assommoir*', *Cahiers naturalistes*, 54 (1980), 214–23; Alma W. Byrd, *The First Generation Reception of the Novels of Emile Zola in Britain and America: An Annotated Bibliography of English Language Responses to his Work, 1877–1902*, (Lampeter: Edwin Mellen Press, 2007); and G. Sigaux, 'Les Rougon-Macquart en 1962', *Cahiers naturalistes*, 22 (1962), 241–48. For evaluations of the reception of Zola's work in geographical terms, see: David Baguley, 'Zola devant la critique de langue anglaise (1877–1970)', *Cahiers naturalistes*, 43 (1972), 105–23; Chantal Morel, 'La Fortune de Zola en Angleterre: les œuvres illustrées', *Cahiers naturalistes*, 66 (1992), 195–208; M. J. Kulczycka-Saloni, 'Zola en Pologne', *Cahiers naturalistes*, 25 (1963), 24–25; and V. Matviichyne, 'Emile Zola en Ukraine', *Cahiers naturalistes*, 33 (1967), 68–72.
41. Ferragus, 'La Littérature putride', *Le Figaro*, 23 January 1868.
42. White, 'Film is Art. Television is a Medium'.
43. Jeanne Delbaere-Garant, *Henry James* (Liège: Presse universitaire de Liège, 1970), pp. 173–83.
44. Emile Zola, *Œuvres critiques I*, in *Œuvres complètes*, ed. by Henri Mitterand, 15 vols (Paris: Cercle du Livre Précieux, 1966–69), X, 39.
45. Friedrich Schleiermacher, 'On the Different Methods of Translating', in Lawrence Venuti (ed.), *The Translation Studies Reader* (London: Routledge, 2000), pp. 43–63 (p. 49).
46. Robert Giddings, Keith Selby and Chris Wensley, *Screening the Novel: The Theory and Practice of Literary Dramatization* (London: Palgrave, 1990), p. 31.
47. Ibid.
48. For futher readings of this adaptation, see Griffiths, *Emile Zola and the Artistry of Adaptation*, and Bellalou, 'Nadia Coupeau dite Nana', pp. 16–24.
49. I. Kleinecke-Bates, *Victorians on Screen: The Nineteenth Century on British Television 1994–2005* (London: Palgrave, 2014), p. 24.
50. OU television broadcasts began on 3 January 1971 on the BBC. Over 300 programmes were initially made with the BBC to cover four foundation courses for the new UK university. BBC television was seen as a key higher education tool. The last OU course-related television programme was broadcast on 16 December 2006 at 5.30 am. Changes in technology have meant that the OU now delivers its distance learning via podcast, DVD and virtual learning environments. For further details on the relationship between the OU and BBC television in programming terms, see Open University, 'End of a Cultural Era — But OU on TV Evolution Continues', 11 December 2006, <https://www3.open.ac.uk/media/fullstory.aspx?id=9898> [accessed 27 May 2017].
51. The boundary between television and film is a much debated one. Initially it was felt that television would eclipse film, damaging cinema box-office takings. In the early years of the medium there were intense but ultimately blocked negotiations to secure cinema's output for the small screen on the BBC largely due to the resistance of the film industry. The BBC has, throughout its history, reused cinematic incarnations of the author's novels, screening large-screen cinema adaptations in the smaller-screen televisual format several years or more after their cinema release. Thus, in cultural products whose screening probes the very ontologies and boundaries of television and film, Zola appears repeatedly on the BBC.

52. A comparable probing of what counts as adaptation takes place in French television. Zola's presence on French channels is more expansive than on its British counterparts and a key element of it takes the form of on-air readings. The author, for example, features prominently and expansively in the *Voyage au bout de la nuit* series on D8 where texts in the novelist's corpus are read by well-known faces, stars, key figures in the world of the arts. Comparably, in 1985, Antenne 2 broadcast *Arbres de vie*, a one-off programme in which Claude Girard sang or spoke poems or extracts of texts celebrating trees. An extract of Zola's *La Faute de l'abbé Mouret* featured in his dramatised reading. Readers, as studies of fan fiction underline, are often passionate adapters of the sources they love, producing literal, often dialogic adaptations in the form of continuations, prequels and sequels in online fora. Reading itself, though, might be seen always to produce metaphorical adaptations of the source from which it works, as each of us internally embodies our vision or version, interpreting the text we hold in our hands. The readers in the *Voyage au bout de la nuit* series voice, enact, embody, abridge, add emphasis to and shape the words they speak. They voice their version of it for the audience even as they hold Zola in their hands as visible source text, making manifest the presence of his works. Their acts of reading fetishise the physical presence of the book as source text, even as they read and re-channel it in their own voice.
53. Claude Gauteur and Ginette Vincendeau, *Jean Gabin: anatomie d'un mythe* (Paris: Nouveau Monde, 2006).

CHAPTER 1

❖

Selling Zola to Twenty-First-Century Television Audiences: Zola, Gutt and *The Paradise*

Art does not sit at the forefront of the translation theories of Ernst-August Gutt, the controversial functionalist thinker who maintains that translation, a commercially driven endeavour, is only successful if the artefact produced meets the needs and desires of those consuming it. Gutt's relevance theory depicts translation as an interpersonal, communicative process initiated and re-initiated by people, for people in different ways in different eras, contexts and nations. Gutt's theories have clear currency when applied to the adaptive transactions of Zola's 1883 novel *Au Bonheur des dames*, a novel which formed the basis of a two-season series on BBC1 entitled *The Paradise* (2012–13). Zola's novel about cash, desire and the circulation of goods to a consuming audience itself circulated in highly altered commodified form as *The Paradise*, to meet the desires of both the BBC and its twenty-first-century viewers. *The Paradise* triggered very little academic comment, perhaps as a result of the liberties and licence it takes with Zola's novel as artistic product. Yet, the adaptation serves as a useful case study for those who would theorise the potential artistry of television adaptations. It does so because, in keeping with Gutt's theories, it underlines the commerce which drives the artistry of this adaptation. It places in the foreground the way in which success, in novel and adaptation alike, is predicated on meeting and satisfying the audience's needs and desires. Gutt's theories, when applied to *The Paradise*, underline the innate accommodation that this avowedly heritage piece makes for its twenty-first-century viewers. The series may promise to take us back to a nineteenth-century culture and time, but what it sells us is a twenty-first-century vision of them. Zola's novel and its BBC adaptation not only engage with Gutt's notion of the formative function of the audience as they sell their wares to the reader/viewer, they also evaluate Gutt's theory. Success, for Gutt, lies in the approbation of the audience. Both Zola's *Au Bonheur des dames* and the BBC's *The Paradise* concur. But both work in their fictions to underline the multiple, shifting, ungraspable nature of said audience and the ceaseless need to re-engage with that audience in quest of its approbation.

Gutt, a peripheral member of the Functionalist group of translation theory, has little to no presence in the sphere of Adaptation Studies.[1] While Functionalist readings of adaptations do exist, such readings remain rare.[2] Gutt, though, has much to offer Adaptation Studies. His value lies in the way in which his work breaks the text-to-text focus of core elements of Adaptation Studies and Translation Studies, recasting both processes as interpersonal, subjective exchanges undertaken by people for people. Fidelity approaches, in Adaptation Studies, focus on the relationship between texts as their adherents seek the presence of the source text in the target text. Fidelity has a long and comparably text-to-text focus in Translation Studies prior to the twentieth century and finds off-shoots in the twentieth-century focus on 'equivalence'. Gutt defines equivalence in the following terms: 'the quality of the translated text is assessed in terms of its equivalence to the original text'.[3] For Gutt, though, equivalence is an empty concept. He cites Koller:

> The concept of equivalence postulates a *relationship* between source-language text [...] and target-language text [...]. The concept of equivalence does not yet say anything about the *nature of the relationship*. [....] The mere demand that a translation be equivalent to a certain original is void of content.[4]

Translation, Gutt suggests, cannot be approached as a straightforward transaction between texts for meaning is necessarily refracted by, through and for multiple people. The people who, according to Gutt, dominate this translation process are those for whom the target text is designed: the audience. For a translation to succeed, to Gutt's mind, it must be relevant to its receiver, communicating with him or her. Gutt works to the concept of 'relevance theory', a philosophy which he defines thus:

> The central claim of relevance theory is that human communication crucially creates an expectation of *optimal relevance*, that is, an expectation on the part of the hearer that his attempt at interpretation will yield *adequate contextual effects at minimal processing cost*.[5]

The communicator/translator must give the audience communicative clues that allow the inference to be made. The translator evaluates the contextual environment of the receiver and addresses his work to it. Success, Gutt argues, is found by translations which meet their audience's expectations. Gutt, citing Robert A. Dooley, writes about a failed translation of the New Testament in the Guaraní language of Brazil completed in 1982. After a year's testing, the translation was entirely redone because it did not meet its readers' expectations/requirements for a biblical translation that more closely corresponded to the form of the high-prestige Portuguese.[6] Gutt's relevance theory is not without its critics or its shortcomings. For some, it moves Translation Studies too far from the sanctity of the original, empowering the translator with too great a creative licence, focusing too strongly on the power of the audience. But Gutt's theory has radical and intriguing implications for the study of adaptation. Gutt's theory breaks the focus on how one text may be found in another. Instead, it envisions adaptation in interpersonal terms as a commercial, communicative process done by people for people in a range of national, cultural, commercial and temporal contexts.

Gutt's suggestion that a translated text must sell itself to and meet the needs of its target audience speaks to the core narrative of Zola's *Au Bonheur des dames*. The novel, one of Zola's rare outputs with a happy ending, focuses on the commercial ambition of Octave Mouret, a man who seeks to sell himself and his wares to Paris and its consumers. Breaking away from existing sales models and crushing the small businesses on which such models rest, Mouret builds a department store, a superstructure designed precisely to harness and sustain itself from the needs and desires of its target consumer audience. Having fallen in love with lowly sales-girl Denise, a woman who resists his charm, Mouret's self-worth demands that she love him back, ratifying his existence just as his female customers do. The novel closes, after a tangled love story, with Mouret winning the love of both Denise and the consumers of Paris. For both Gutt and Zola's novel, success is to be found in the ratifying gaze or purchase of the customer or audience.

If Gutt's theory opens up key lines of investigation in Zola's source novel, so too is it borne out by the BBC's *The Paradise*. The series, as per Gutt's relevance theory, clearly sells Zola's French nineteenth-century novel *Au Bonheur des dames* to a twenty-first-century British audience. The adaptation works to make accommodations for its audience in two respects: place and time. Its geographical alterations are perhaps the most visible. Zola's novel depicts the birth of the department store in nineteenth-century Paris; the BBC adaptation relocates his narrative to the site of key early British department stores: Newcastle upon Tyne.[7] The past that Zola represents is 'geographically domesticated', to use Lawrence Venuti's term. Parisian streets are exchanged for the north of England, French accents and vocabulary for their Geordie counterparts. Nowhere is the attempt to bring Zola's novel closer to the culture of its audience more visible than in *The Paradise*'s translation of Zola's character names. Names in *The Paradise* bear witness to the composite nature of the cultural product in which they exist. They frequently bear the fleeting phonetic trace of their French source text in names which have become resolutely British. Denise Baudu, from Valognes, retains her transferable first name and becomes Denise Lovett of Peebles in the rural Scottish borders. Her surname, though now recognisably British, like the adaptation in which she features, is French in origin. It stems from *lo(u)vet* and means 'young wolf'. Octave Mouret becomes John Moray. His adapted name allows the phonetics of the French source to be conveyed while clearly situating the character in a British context: Moray is a council area in the north east of Scotland. Noticeable in *The Paradise* is a tendency to give characters names which are geographical, names which place both the characters and the adaptation in a British spatial context. Mouret's side-kick Bourdoncle becomes Mr Dudley. In its invention of the characters Tom Weston (the love interest of Katherine Glendenning, *The Paradise*'s version of Madame Desforges) and Joseph Fenton (the man who seeks to wrest The Paradise from Moray), the adaptation references the multitude of towns in Britain which share their surname. France does not disappear entirely as a geographical space in *The Paradise*, for the adaptation invents a Parisian character, Clémence, a supplier of fireworks to The Paradise and a colleague from when Moray trained in Paris. Aside from a subsequent visit to Paris by Moray, Clémence offers the only reference to Moray's Parisian back story, a back story which gestures to the content of Zola's novel even while foreclosing it. Moray's time in Paris is not depicted. *The Paradise* references the Frenchness of its source and the text which is no longer there in an adaptation which has become British.[8]

The Paradise not only makes the geographical space of Zola's novel more relevant to the British channel on which it is screened, it also works to make the era of the novel more relevant to its contemporary audience, in keeping with Gutt's theory. The adaptation is a period piece. It situates itself in the nineteenth-century era Zola depicted. The conventions of the BBC slot in which it aired required it to do so. Writing in the *Guardian*, Mark Lawson underlines that *The Paradise* adapts the conventions of the adaptation slot and the period drama it screens, as much, if not more so, than Zola's source text. Lawson writes: 'Bill Gallagher's drama [dramatist of *The Paradise*] uses the book as a spring board for the sort of winter-evening heart-warmer he previously created in *Lark Rise to Candleford*'.[9] *The Paradise* clearly seeks to sell its viewer 'heritage' or the past as a product. In his work on 1980s and 1990s film adaptation, Andrew Higson defines 'heritage' works as pieces which display 'a museum aesthetic: the particular visual style of the films is designed to showcase these various heritage attractions, to display them in all their supposed authenticity'.[10] *The Paradise* sells us the past as artefact in a variety of ways. It showcases period properties such as Katherine Glendenning's mansion in lingering, highly aestheticised shots. Such shots do not further the narrative or build a discourse. Rather, they offer the past for public consumption, infusing, to use Sarah Cardwell's words on period television adaptation in general, 'the audience with a sense of appreciation of and pleasure in these articles and a longing for the days for which they are referents'.[11] These aestheticised long shots stand out in their sheer space as a result of the contrast they pose to the spatially restrained approach of this adaptation.[12] *The Paradise* uses such shots to mark itself as a heritage product. It also epitomises what Higson characterises as the obsession with period detail in the heritage genre.[13] Its production designer Melanie Allen researched the architecture of the time at the Royal Institute of British Architects, working from contemporary visuals of Regent Street as the production renovated a period street in order to film.[14] Costume designer Joanne Eatwell worked from paintings by James Tissot, a nineteenth-century French painter who, like Zola's novel in its adapted form, moved from France to England to ply his trade.[15] Zola's original novel offers its reader lingering descriptions of products in the department store, products which represent modernity and progress for their desiring, purchasing audience in the shop. The BBC's *The Paradise* offers comparably lingering images of the shop's merchandise in shots which often feel like point-of-view shots, placing us as desirous consumer in the department store itself. But if Zola's lingering product descriptions offered their consumers modernity and progress, *The Paradise* offers the contemporary viewer 'heritage'.

This past, though, is highly adapted so as to be relevant to the contemporary viewer and his/her era. It is a past very much of our present. While the production team researched in detail the era they sought to depict, the aesthetic they develop is both conditioned by current BBC production values and budgets and by current tastes and fashions. The make-up team, led by Marella Shearer, scanned hundreds of *cartes de visite* from the years around 1870.[16] But they deliberately altered the contemporary fashion for mutton-chop side burns and facial hair for men, as well as the unattractive short curly fringes for women, in order that the characters' look be attractive, relevant and engaging for the younger audience the corporation sought. Whilst, Higson argues, our thirst for heritage works stems from a nostalgia to escape to the wholesome values of the past, the values of *The Paradise* are clearly largely relocated to the present.[17] Far from enshrining a rigid class structure, *The Paradise* challenges it. Denise and Moray circulate between classes as a result of their hard work and endeavour. Denise, before stealing her man from her social superior, states: 'My father always told me I was a child of God and that makes me the equal of any person'. Moray, while speaking of besting the aristocratic Katherine Glendenning and her father, suggests: 'we must practise the art of letting them believe they are masters of every situation. Let's call them our betters while we seek more subtle ways to win the day'.[18] Gender stereotypes are comparatively pronounced in Zola's *Au Bonheur des dames* as Mouret seeks to exploit the innate financial stupidity of women in a shop he conceptualises as 'cette mécanique à manger les femmes'/'this machine for devouring the women' (p. 767/76). Such gender stereotypes disappear in the BBC's adaptation. Denise states to her colleague Clara, 'I don't want to marry Moray, I want to be him'. Series Two sees her delaying her marriage to Moray precisely to set up a business to rival his success. Comparably, the ideas of capitalism which surface in the adaptation are visibly of our era. Gone is Zola's vision of capitalism as a necessary but essentially destructive process in which the class members consume each other in their quest for advancement and material gain. In its place in the television adaptation stands a vision of an entirely more benevolent capitalism. Moray, now transformed into a class warrior, cherishes, protects and nurtures, as extensions of himself, the work force who live in harmony and mutual self-protection. Moray refuses a place at an upper-class hunt with the words 'I'm a draper who's done rather well'. He defends his employee Sam from false accusations of molestation of his social better in the very terms he applied to himself: 'All I'm asking is that a draper [Sam] be given the same opportunity to defend himself [as his social superior]'. The idyllic vision hinted at in the novel — the shop is, even at its most mercenary and destructive, described in terms of the *phalanstère* utopian structures towards which Denise will push it — is realised in the BBC's twenty-first-century adaptation of it.[19] *The Paradise* clearly sells Zola's novel to the twenty-first century, offering a heritage product which is both aesthetically and morally of our present.

The BBC's quest to meet the desires of its audience takes us to the very heart of Zola's novel. Mouret's success stems precisely from his ability to harness his audiences'/customers' needs. In a model which is in some ways highly Lacanian, Zola's Mouret is driven by a need for plenitude, by a desire to make something of himself. To realise this desire, he circulates his own image in the collective female gaze of his customers, a gaze which is repeatedly described in water-like, reflective ways. Contemplating the mass of female shoppers, the novel states: 'Et cette mer, ces chapeaux bariolés, ces cheveux nus, blonds ou noirs, roulaient d'un bout de la galerie à l'autre'/'And this sea of faces, these many-coloured hats, these bare heads, both dark and light, rolled from one end of the gallery to the other' (p. 901/253). Mouret's shop is something of a hall of mirrors: 'partout les glaces reculaient les magasins, reflétaient des étalages avec des coins de public'/'on all sides the mirrors carried the departments back into infinite space' (p. 901/253). And the image which circulates in this hall of mirrors is that of Mouret. He stands in a position of prominence and dominance watching the shoppers below him as they desire the products which make him and purchase the objects which reinforce both him and his mission. He seeks insistently both to harness and to trap the female gaze. Significantly, Denise, the female gaze which Mouret thinks he cannot harness or tame, threatens him with a poignant sense of Lacanian lack. Having spurned Mouret, Denise leaves the shop for the evening:

> Et elle aperçut Mouret. Il était toujours en haut de l'escalier, sur le grand palier central, dominant la galerie. Mais il avait oublié l'inventaire, il ne voyait pas son empire, ces magasins crevant de richesses. Tout avait disparu, les victoires bruyantes d'hier, la fortune colossale de demain. D'un regard désespéré, il suivait Denise et quand elle eut passé la porte, il n'y eut plus rien, la maison devint noire.
>
> [And she perceived Mouret, who was still at the top of the stairs, on the great central landing, dominating the gallery. But he had forgotten the stock-taking, he did not see his empire, this building bursting with riches. Everything had disappeared, his former glorious victories, his future colossal fortune. With a desponding look he was watching Denise's departure, and when she had passed the door everything disappeared, a darkness came over the house.] (p. 942/306).

Denise's rejection of Mouret, though, proves temporary. Ultimately, she too comes to gaze with love at the store owner and to boost the sales which reinforce and ratify him. Success, plenitude and satisfaction are, the novel suggests, to be found in the gaze of the audience.

Giddings, Selby and Wensley, writing on costume drama adaptation, suggest that it stems, as a genre, from the failings of the present, from a desire to escape to a past perceived as superior, from a contemporary moment found lacking.[20] Zola's sales model in *Au Bonheur des dames* resonates with their findings. Mouret markets to women who feel a sense of lack and he offers products which promise plenitude. *Au Bonheur des dames* posits the female experience as one of insistent lack. Women in Zola's shop are described as 'une poussière humaine'/'human dust', as a substance which in its very presence encodes absence (p. 901/253). The shop is littered with fragmented visions of the female body:

> Des bas de soie, pendus à des triangles, montraient des profils arrondis de mollets [...] les chair dont le grain satiné avait la douceur d'une peau de blonde; enfin, sur le drap de l'étagère, des gants étaient jetés symétriquement, avec leurs doigts allongés, leur paume étroite de vierge byzantine, cette grâce raidie et comme adolescente des chiffons de femme.
>
> [A quantity of silk stockings, hung on rods, showed the roundness of the calves [...], the silky grain of which made them look as soft as a fair woman's skin; and

at the bottom of all, a symmetrical array of gloves, with their taper fingers and narrow palms, and that rigid virgin grace which characterizes such feminine articles before they are worn.] (p. 710/3)

Zola's window displays fragment women, offering mutilated metaphorical bodies: 'La gorge ronde des mannequins gonflait l'étoffe, les hanches fortes exagéraient la finesse de la taille, la tête absente était remplacée par une grande étiquette'/'The well-rounded neck and graceful figures of the dummies exaggerated the slimness of the waist, the absent head being replaced by a large price-ticket pinned on the neck' (p. 711/4). The clothing the shop sells offers the promise of plenitude and being in the play of desires that is shopping. Rachel Bowlby writes in *Just Looking*: 'nineteenth-century consumer culture transforms the narcissistic mirror into a shop window, the *glass* which reflects an idealized image of the woman (or man) who stands before it, in the form of the model she could buy or become'.[21] Zola's novel might be seen to anticipate her findings. Women seek their own identity in the clothes they purchase from Mouret, as the narcissistic, reflective imagery of the following quotation makes clear:

> Des satins clairs et des soies tendres jaillissaient d'abord: les satins à la reine, les satins renaissance aux tons nacrés d'eau de source; les soies légères aux transparences de cristal, vert Nil, ciel indien, rose de mai, bleu Danube. Puis, venaient des tissus plus forts, les satins merveilleux, les soies duchesse, teintes chaudes, roulant à flots grossis [...]. Des femmes, pâles de désirs, se penchaient comme pour se voir.
>
> [At first stood out the light satins and tender silks, the satins *à la Reine* and Renaissance, with the pearly tones of spring water; light silks, transparent as crystals — Nile-green, Indian-azure, May-rose and Danube-blue. Then came the stronger fabrics: marvellous satins, duchess silks, warm tints, rolling in great waves [...]. The women, pale with desire, bent over as if to look at themselves.] (p. 788/103)

The Paradise echoes this reading of clothing. When dismissed by Moray as a mere clothes horse, Katherine reveals the lack and absence she felt as an identity on her mother's death. Clothes allowed her to find and present a fuller version of herself. She states: 'And then they put the dress on me, and I knew exactly who I was. Ever since then I have used clothes to declare who I am and if, on a particular day, I am not who I am of a mind to be, why then I use clothes to transform myself'. Within their narratives, both Zola's novel and the BBC's adaptation of it, show how the gaze of the audience may be harnessed as a means to counteract any sense of lack.

As Mouret seeks to sell clothes to the masses, the BBC seeks to sell *The Paradise* to its audience. It does so in the belief that Zola remains relevant enough/may be made relevant enough to capture the viewing figures necessary to sustain/justify the BBC's funding model.

The need for adaptations to be profitable amongst a mass audience is partly responsible for the critical suspicion with which such adaptations are regarded. Art and money are not happy bed fellows. Charlotte Brunsdon writes thus of television adaptations of classic texts: 'Formally unchallenging, while nevertheless replete with visual strategies that signify "art", their only specifically televisual demand is that the viewer switch on at the right time and watch'.²² Yet it should not be forgotten that Zola's *Au Bonheur des dames* is a novel about money, written for money and circulated in as many altered forms as possible by the author to elicit more money (serial form, novel form, illustrated novel and theatrical adaptation). Mouret's shop is decorated with the gold which it seeks to elicit from its customers. In Mouret's 'salon oriental', 'l'or fauve dominait'/'A barbarous gold tone prevailed' (p. 775/87). Gold is the very soundtrack to the shop's existence as we hear 'de l'or sonnant sur le cuivre des caisses'/'gold jingling on the brass of the pay desks' (p. 792/108). Customers walk 'au milieu d'une prodigalité d'or, des flots d'or, des moissons d'or, jusqu'aux vitrages dont les verres étaient émaillés et niellés d'or'/'amidst a prodigality of gold, floods of gold, heaps of gold, even to the glazed-work, the glass of which was enamelled and inlaid with gold' (p. 901/252). But gold's value, Mouret makes clear, is only achieved through its circulation: 'L'argent est bête, si on ne le dépense pas'/'Money is so stupid, if it isn't spent' (p. 952/319). Mouret himself is described in terms of gold and the cloth he sells to try to elicit it: 'il avait des yeux couleur de vieil or, d'une douceur de velours'/'he had eyes the colour of old gold, of a velvety softness' (p. 731/30). Mouret's value though, is not innate, it is generated by means of circulation in three key respects. His success is built on the rapid circulation of goods as he buys cheaply in bulk, seeking the fast turnover of items even at a loss. To safeguard the circulation of goods he requires women to circulate in his shop, frequently changing the location of departments and goods in order that they perambulate and that the money static in their purses moves to his cashiers. To oversee this circulation of money, Mouret himself circulates in the shop and in society beyond, his money allowing him, to an extent, to traverse the class and social boundaries which would constrain him. He does so in order that he may seek yet more of the substance which powers his very movement. Gold, significantly, all but disappears in the BBC adaptation, which is nevertheless driven by mercantile impulses, by the need to win enough viewers to justify the licence fee. Coins, notes and specific prices and figures are largely absent in this adaptation precisely about commerce. Gold features only in the brown and gold waistcoats which Moray wears in sharp contrast to the stark black or grey outfits of his male counterparts. Moray, like his novelistic counterpart, incarnates money and currency, circulating in different social contexts, driven by the money which gives him movement and motion and enables him to glean still more.

Television adaptations, in keeping with the models of Moray and Gutt, need to find creative purchase or currency in their audience's gaze, to be relevant to their viewers, in order to continue to exist. *The Paradise* achieved good launch figures of 6.6 million viewers and consequently a second series was commissioned. These figures, though, slipped to just over 5 million in Series Two. In the face of competition from its commercial rival ITV's period adaptation set in the world of commerce, *Mr Selfridge*, which achieved viewing figures of 9.4 million, the BBC decided to axe *The Paradise* at the close of the second series. The BBC, like Gutt's relevance theory, makes the audience, as a mass, the ultimate arbiters of an adaptation's success or failure. However, collectively, *The Paradise* and the Zola source novel behind it not only explore Gutt's relevance theory, they evaluate it, underlining that the audiences by which Gutt sets such stock are themselves shifting, mobile entities which are, in so many ways, ultimately ungraspable. Zola's novel depicts the seismic shift in shopping habits and the revolution in patterns of consumption in retail. It is adapted in a medium whose patterns of audience consumption have themselves transformed so radically in the last fifteen years as to have a profound impact on the nature of television itself. With the development of online media such as iPlayer (BBC) and a host of personal, remote and automatic recording devices, television audiences and their ways of watching have diversified and become far more personalised. Audiences are no longer necessarily tied to scheduling or faithful to channels. They can watch in their own time and space and impose their own order on television products. New media allow them both to watch and consume television in a variety of ways. They are capable of bingeing, watching in scraps and even watching without ever tuning directly into broadcast television at all. As television audiences continue to shift and evolve, so too does the product they watch. *The Paradise* is not the static, singular artefact around which this chapter is built, but a product which is subtly different for each consumer, varying according to the means, time and mode of its consumption. Watched on terrestrial television, its ontology is conditioned by the shape of the BBC adaptation slot, by the programmes which precede and follow it in the shaping flow of television, by the shared viewing experience of the millions watching collectively in space, time and perhaps sharing their experience via social media. Watched in any of the recorded technological forms currently available, *The Paradise* becomes an artefact out of time and space, moulded to the viewer's will as they pause, fast-forward and replay in their own time and space. Karen Lury writes: 'television images are *promiscuous* images — in that they are rarely destined to appear in just one context, for just one time — [...] many television images will remain, or become, compromised images — shrunk, blown up and cut about — both at the point of transmission and, increasingly, at the point of reception, as viewers at home use their remote controls to manipulate the images they see'.[23] Watched on DVD, *The Paradise* becomes a collectable item, a collected experience far more meta-textual than either terrestrial or recorded television as a result both of its interviews with cast members and production team and its documentation of the genesis of its television product. Having been a static, domestic phenomenon as individuals, in the medium's early years, came together around the family set to watch collectively, the processes and practices of television consumption have been radically transformed with the increased mobility and choice of its users. The audience and the way they consume television products is neither singular nor easily graspable.

The audiences in Zola's department store are no less mobile, no less shifting. Essential to Mouret's very survival, the shop's consumers are constantly framed in liquid, evanescent descriptions which, in their elemental nature, make clear the power of this seemingly ungraspable force. Zola writes of the crowd circulating with 'son bruit sourd de marée montante'/'its dull noise like the rising tide', depicting 'un océan de têtes vues en raccourci'/'a sea of heads foreshortened' (p. 904/257). The crowd is at once essentialised as one figure — Mouret claims of his clientele, 'J'ai la femme, je me fiche du reste'/'I have the women, I don't care a hang for the rest' — and endlessly diluted into difference, be it difference of class, age, wealth or style (p. 766/75). Madame Desforges watches the crowds around her, unable to grasp them with her eyes or categorise them fully in her mind:

> En bas, autour d'elle, continuait le remous de la foule, dont le double courant d'entrée et de sortie se faisait sentir jusqu'au rayon de la soie: foule encore très mêlée, où pourtant l'après-midi amenait davantage de dames, parmi les petites bourgeoises et les ménagères; beaucoup de femmes en deuil, avec leurs grands voiles; toujours des nourrices fourvoyées, protégeant leurs poupons de leurs coudes élargis. Et cette mer, ces chapeaux bariolés, ces cheveux nus, blonds ou noirs, roulaient d'un bout de la galerie à l'autre.
>
> [Below, around her, continued the eddying of the crowd, of which the double current of those entering and those going out made itself felt as far as the silk department; a crowd still very mixed in its elements, though the afternoon was bringing a greater number of ladies amongst the shopkeepers and house-wives; a great many women in mourning, with their flowing veils, and the inevitable wet nurses straying about, protecting their babies with their outstretched arms. And this sea of faces, these many-coloured hats, these bare heads, both dark and light, rolled from one end of the gallery to the other.] (p. 901/253)

Just as television audiences consume televisual products differently, *Au Bonheur des dames*'s clientele shop differently, even while within the same commercial setting. Madame Bourdelais shops practically, with guile, buying only that which she seeks at the lowest price possible. Madame Marty buys compulsively, indiscriminately and sensually, carried away by the thrill of purchase and matter. Madame de Boves buys nothing, raging inside at what she cannot afford, stealing all she can (p. 769/78–79). The audiences so necessary to the existence of *The Paradise*, the store Au Bonheur des dames and Gutt's relevance theory are shifting, evolving, endlessly diverse entities whose gaze needs to be courted and re-courted in a range of different ways.

Intriguingly, social media platforms offer a snapshot of the ungraspable diversity of the audience. They give voice to some of the different ways we view television, recording diverse reactions and, most importantly, underscoring that social media are modifying the televisual viewing experience. Twitter is key to my line of argument here. The platform's hashtags allow readers to construct, share, participate in and record/archive a real-time community of shared reactions to a television adaptation. Twitter allows people to watch communally and to engage in a community of viewing. A search of #Theparadise reveals an online archive of personal voices, documenting their response to the BBC programme in both English and French. Threading the fabric of her own life through that of the BBC adaptation both in her words and in her attached dressmaking project photo, @cherryredpixie tweets her review of the adaptation to those strangers watching with her:

> I do love live tweeting (read mocking) guilty pleasure television, but I'm really enjoying **#TheParadise**. It is making me want to start a Edwardian/Victorian era dress when I'm done with my Jacobean/Georgian era dress. @EmunElliott is a particular delight; so much expression! (pic.twitter.com/os8Z26tXcF)

Her attached photograph of a period dress on a dress-making mannequin gives physical form to the viewing body which her words represent. Her words signal the communal viewing experience which Twitter allows its users to share as they tweet their thoughts and reactions to an adaptation in a medium which serves as something of an unofficial archive of their otherwise unheard and unrecorded voices. Twitter not only allows elements of the audience to record the presence and hermeneutic interpretations of their viewing bodies, it also allows them to engage interpersonally with many of the creative bodies shaping the adaptation. @cherryredpixie copies the adaptation's leading man, Emun Elliott, on her tweet, feeding her praise for his performance directly to him. Archiving her own response to the adaptation, @kipps writes 'I am late to the #**TheParadise** game but it's so good. I started out hating Katherine but now I feel sorry for her Bc she's had so much heartbreak and now she's in a loveless marriage' [*sic*]. Twitter has in many ways changed the way in which television, among other art forms, may be consumed. It creates virtual viewing communities who review the adaptation collectively, watching communally, exchanging their endlessly diverse responses to the adaptation at hand often as they watch it. It underscores that the way we view adaptations changes in different eras, shaped by different technological possibilities. It also offers valuable insight into elements of the viewing public by archiving personal audience responses to a medium in which they have so often gone largely unrecorded. It gives a place, albeit a limited one, to the physical bodies of elements of the viewing audience. It does not allow us to capture that audience or represent it in its entirety; rather it gestures, like Zola's *Au Bonheur des dames*, to their shifting diversity.

As Mouret's machine seeks to sell and make itself endlessly relevant to its customers, so too does *The Paradise* seek to harness our gaze to it, seeking creative purchase in the audience whose decision to view or not to view will decide the continued existence of the series. While direct address shots are frequent in television as newsreaders and presenters address us directly, they are comparatively rare in television drama, which, like cinema, largely chooses to abide by André Antoine's belief that actors should perform as if a fourth wall separated them from their audience.[24] *The Paradise*, however, has the camera acknowledge its viewer, inviting him or her into the televisual process. The camera enters the shop in full trade and the liveried doorman acknowledges it in a shot attributable to no specific character in the cast. *The Paradise* addresses us as its viewer, seeking to sell us its wares. The camera subsequently browses the empty shop at night, pausing to lay out the spectacular wares and setting of the commerce which seeks to seduce all who survey it. The network of hidden viewers around which *The Paradise* constructs its plot in some senses references the extra-textual viewers who, although unseen, are no less important to this BBC adaptation. While the security guard Jouve functions as the core all-seeing eye in Zola's novel, hidden, powerful viewers proliferate in *The Paradise*. Moray berates Denise for subterfuge, claiming 'I see everything'. His alter ego, the shop boy Arthur, opens the whole series claiming similar omniscience: 'I know every face in this place and every name an'all'. Jonas, *The Paradise*'s version of Jouve, is as omniscient as his textual predecessor. *The Paradise*'s Jonas sees and describes the scented invitation from a flighty French woman which Mr Dudley (*The Paradise*'s version of Bourdoncle) keeps hidden in his pocket. Jonas not only sees all, but he writes all in the mysterious book of truth which the audience sees but is barred from accessing. In an act of multi-layered spying, Denise hides behind partially closed shop curtains to eavesdrop on Jonas's admission to Moray that he was not close enough to hear Dudley's conversation with his suppliers in the inn. Subsequently, the adaptation frequently films through partially closed curtains in shots which are attributable to no one but the audience. We, as viewers, invade the most intimate of spaces in this adaptation. We hear and see what no one else can/does, penetrating the bedrooms, private spaces and even the heads of characters. Moray, having staked his store on the success of the extravagant sale of goods for which he has not yet paid, strides through the shop. A voiceover, striking precisely because of its rarity in this adaptation, reiterates the challenges which drive him in words which do not leave the confines of his skull. In an echo of Zola's liquefaction of the female crowd whose purchases offer Mouret ontology, *The Paradise*'s Moray gazes at the crowd streaming past him to ensure the success of his sale. In a shot all the more unusual in the functional, largely non-distracting *mise en scène* which this television adaptation adopts, the crowd blurs and becomes hazy before the camera's gaze in a slow-motion shot which allows us access to the joy Moray feels but does not vocally express. *The Paradise* allows us access to the private and personal spaces of its characters, in a manner entirely in keeping with the adaptation of a Naturalist novelist. But so too does it come into our private viewing space. Consumed in the home or on personal electronic devices, television can be a particularly intimate medium even in its mass, multiple reach. As the adaptation works insistently to take us into the private spaces of its world, so too does it enter our private spaces both physically as it airs and metaphorically in its quest to be relevant to our contemporary values, ethics and desires.

The Paradise's paradoxical play on the shifting borders and boundaries of private and public spaces echoes that found in Zola's novel. Mouret works hard to make the department store a private, intimate, seductive space, all the better to work his wiles on his captive female audience. Pointing to his shop, he insists of the female clientele, 'elles sont chez elles'/'you see they are quite at home' (p. 900/252). His creator concurs, as Zola describes the shoppers on sale day thus: 'Toutes, la tête haute, les gestes brusques, étaient chez elles, sans politesse les unes pour les autres, usant de la maison tant qu'elles pouvaient, jusqu'à emporter la poussière des murs'/'They were all there, with heads high and abrupt gestures, quite at home, without the slightest politeness one for the other, using the house as much as they could, even carrying away the dust from the walls' (p. 914/269). The massive and ever-increasing space of the department store is metaphorically mapped onto the confines of a female bedroom. Zola repeatedly has recourse to the vocabulary of the 'alcôve'. Contemplating the shopping experience in general, he writes: 'On eût dit que toutes les séductions des magasins aboutissaient à cette tentation suprême, que c'était là l'alcôve reculée de la chute, le coin de perdition où les plus fortes succombaient'/'It seemed as if all the seductions of the shop had converged into this supreme temptation, that it was the secluded alcove where the customers were doomed to fall, the corner of perdition where the strongest must succumb' (pp. 912–13/267). He observes the shop 'qui tenait du tabernacle et de l'alcôve'/'partook of the tabernacle and of the alcove' (p. 1016/403). Commenting on the seductive intimacy of the shopping experience, Hannah Thompson writes:

> Although shops like the 'Bonheur des Dames' were public places, the very nature of their merchandise, which included female underwear as well as dresses and coats, and the clientele, that is women whose realm was usually the private, domestic sphere, gave an air of intimacy and privacy to the department store which was lacking in other spaces of nineteenth-century public leisure, such as the *café-concert* or the *boulevard*.[25]

But for many nineteenth-century women, public spaces such as the café-concert and the boulevard were socially and therefore physically inaccessible. While such women were unable to access such spaces in literal terms, Zola offers them both the café-concert and the freedom to be a *flâneuse* in metaphorical terms in his fictional shop as boulevard. The shop becomes a metaphorical café-concert. It not only offers refreshment, but Mouret also constantly emphasises the need for spectacle in a narrative whose musical motifs are pronounced. Zola writes:

> Dans l'apparent désordre des tissus, tombés comme au hasard des cases éventrées, il y avait une phrase harmonique, le blanc suivi et développé dans tous ses tons, qui naissait, grandissait, s'épanouissait, avec l'orchestration compliquée d'une fugue de maître dont le développement continu emporte les âmes d'un vol sans cesse élargi.

> [In the apparent disorder of the tissues, fallen as if by chance from the open drawers, there was a harmonious phrase, the white followed up and developed in all its tones, springing into existence, growing, and blossoming forth with the complicated orchestration of a master's fugue, the continual development of which carries away the mind in an ever-increasing flight.] (p. 1016/403–04)

Similarly, in the white sale Zola explores 'cette chanson du blanc, que chantaient les étoffes'/'this song in praise of white that the goods of the entire establishment were singing' (p. 1016/403). If Zola's novel offers its female shoppers the café-concert, so too does it offer them the space and time to be a boulevard *flâneuse*. Brian Nelson suggests that, for the small number of women who had the time, the new department stores offered the pleasures of looking, talking or simply walking. In the department store women could become 'flâneuses'.[26] Mouret, in his shop, brings both the world and outside space within female grasp. Thus, the inside of the shop becomes a metaphorical outside. The Goncourts famously felt fundamentally lost in the newly constructed and nearly unrecognisable space of Haussmann's Paris, writing in their diary on 18 November 1860: 'I am a stranger to what is coming, to what is, as I am to these new boulevards'.[27] Madame de Boves voices the same emotion in relation to the newly reconfigured space of the department store: 'C'est un monde [...] on ne sait plus où l'on est'/'There's quite a world here! [...] You hardly know where you are' (p. 895/245). The shop gives its female clientele not just the street lights and boulevards of Paris, it also gives them the right to roam the world in metaphorical form. The white sale is revealing in this respect. Of the shoppers, Zola writes: 'on eût dit les patineurs d'un lac de Pologne'/'And the crowd seemed to be [...] like skaters on a Polish lake' (p. 1016/404). In the shop he describes:

> Tout un peuple voyageait au milieu de ces espaces couverts de neige [...]. Le bourdonnement des voix faisait un bruit énorme de fleuve qui charrie. Au plafond, les ors prodigués, les vitrines niellées d'or et les rosaces d'or semblaient un coup de soleil, luisant sur les Alpes de la grande exposition de blanc.
>
> [An endless procession of small figures, as if lost amidst the snowy peaks of a mountain. [...] The buzz of voices made a great noise like a rushing stream. Up above, the profusion of gildings, the glazed work picked out with gold, and the golden roses seemed like a ray of the sun shining on the Alps of the grand exhibition of white goods.] (pp. 1016–17/404)

Private yet public, exploitative yet liberating, the space of the shop is a shifting, moving one which seeks above all to make itself relevant to its audience in order to sell.

Gutt's relevance theory of translation is itself relevant to Zola's novel because the Naturalist writer depicts his text precisely as a translation of reality, as a translation whose contemporaneity made it particularly pertinent to readers of the era. Good art, for Zola, adapts reality. He writes: 'Jamais le public ne sera juste envers les véritables artistes créateurs, s'il ne se contente pas de chercher uniquement dans une œuvre une libre traduction de la nature en un langage particulier et nouveau' [The public will only ever be truly be fair to true creative artists when that public seeks in a work of art a free translation of reality in a personal and new language].[28] The ability to offer such a translation is, for Zola, the precondition of artistic greatness: 'Chaque grand artiste est venu nous donner une traduction nouvelle et personnelle de la nature' [Each great artist offers us a new, personal translation of reality].[29] That Zola adapts reality in *Au Bonheur des dames* is clear. Much has been written on the historical veracity of the novel. Zola's novel translates his contemporary commercial landscape. Vaheed Ramazani unpicks a letter Zola wrote in 1882 detailing his research on department stores such as the Bon Marché and their revolutionary impact on commerce in France.[30] Zola not only translated the locales and philosophies of real department stores, he also interviewed their staff.[31] And Zola's novel translates not just commercial history but the broader history of the era. The reconstruction of Paris under Haussmann is crucial both to Mouret's construction of his edifice and Zola's construction of the novel. Haussmann himself features in the novel's fictions in barely disguised terms as Baron Hartmann. But the translation Zola's novel offers of his near contemporary reality is clearly tailored to his reader's needs and desires. He sells it to us as a product just as Mouret sells satins, silks and lace to the desiring public of the department store. Hence, it is far from insignificant that reality in the novel is couched in textile terms. Denise goes with Pauline and Baugé to the country. Though they have left the shop, its textile vocabulary seeps into the descriptive landscape which Zola seeks to sell his reader as product. They contemplate the shadows as 'dentelles'/'lace' (p. 823/149). Comparably, descriptions of the architecture of the shop itself are invaded by the products the edifice offers. The narrative deems the stone, metal and mirrors of the building to be 'une dentelle compliquée'/'a complicated lacework' (p. 901/252). While the materials in the shop take on, as this chapter has underlined, the characteristics of nature, underlining the space and freedom they offer women, the outside world in Zola's novel is repeatedly described in the material terms of the shop's contents. Zola seeks to sell us his novel as product. Zola is not alone in his conceptualisation of the text as textile. Roland Barthes writes: 'Le texte, pendant qu'il se fait, est semblable à une dentelle de Valenciennes qui naîtrait devant nous sous les doigts de la dentellière: chaque séquence engagée pend comme le fuseau provisoirement inactif qui attend pendant que son voisin travaille'/'The text, while it is being produced, is like a piece of Valenciennes lace created before us under the lacemaker's fingers: each sequence undertaken hangs like the temporarily inactive bobbin waiting while its neighbour works'.[32] Zola weaves the era, events and environment of his time into a material artefact, but he does so with the reader's textual desires firmly in view.

Zola's novel, though, is not a translation of a singular source — reality — rather it adapts multiply across sources. It ekphrastically recreates specific paintings and movements in his creative offering. Henri Mitterand persuasively situates Zola's Rougon-Macquart series as a 'musée textuel' [textual museum].[33] Mouret's aesthetic sensibilities are such that he is hailed as a *chef d'école*:

> Il avait pris les pièces, ils les jetait, les froissait, en tirait des gammes éclatantes. Tous en convenaient, le patron était le premier étalagiste de Paris, un étalagiste révolutionnaire à la vérité, qui avait fondé l'école du brutal et du colossal dans la science de l'étalage.
>
> [He had taken the pieces, throwing them together, crushing them, producing an excessively fast effect. Everyone allowed the governor to be the best displayer in Paris, of a regular revolutionary stamp, who had founded the brutal and colossal school in the science of displaying.] (p. 745/47)

But his artistry is matched, if not surpassed, by the word paintings of his creator. Zola metamorphoses Mouret's oriental display into a textual painting which resembles Delacroix's *La Mort de Sardanapale* [The Death of Sardanapalus] (1827). Delacroix's Assyrian leader peruses from on high the massacre taking place beneath him, a massacre of bodies in movement and in fragments, a scene driven by images of battle and lust against a flowing red background which metaphorically represents the blood implicitly spilt. Mouret, lord of all he surveys from on high, contemplates his shop built on seduction and commercial warfare, a shop peopled by the fragmented bodies of its female shopping clientele. His eyes fall on the oriental display, as vibrant, tumultuous and overpacked as Delacroix's painting, threatening, like its painterly predecessor, in its mass, detail and movement to spill beyond the confines of its frame. Zola's word painting depicts 'Cette tente de pacha somptueux'/'This sumptuous pacha's tent', dominated by 'l'or fauve'/'a barbarous gold tone' (p. 775/87) and red touches — the counters in view have 'un fond rouge sang de flanelle'/'a blood-red ground of flannel breaking out' (pp. 786–87/101). Characters make explicit the ekphrastic word painting which Zola leaves implicit.

They contemplate the carpets and exclaim: 'voyez donc! un Delacroix'/'Just look, a Delacroix' (p. 798/116). Zola's words conjure 'un fondu de fournaise éteinte, d'une belle couleur cuite de vieux maître. Et des visions d'Orient flottaient sous le luxe de cet art barbare'/'a beautiful burnt hue suggestive of the old masters. Visions of the East floated beneath the luxury of this barbarous art' (p. 775/87). But if Zola's novel clearly exhibits Romantic masterpieces, they are outnumbered by their Impressionist counterparts. Zola famously claimed, as this book's Introduction underlined, to translate Impressionist techniques into his fiction.[34] *Au Bonheur des dames* bears out his claim, offering the reader visions of the shop in which light and the sun liquefy objects, playing with their outlines, characteristics and colours in word paintings which are Impressionist studies in movement and motion:

> Et, sous la fine poussière, tout arrivait à se confondre, on ne reconnaissait pas la division des rayons: là-bàs, la mercerie paraissait noyée; plus loin, au blanc, un angle de soleil, entré par la vitrine de la rue Neuve-Saint-Augustin, était comme une flèche d'or dans la neige; ici, à la ganterie et aux lainages, une masse épaisse de chapeaux et de chignons barraient les lointains du magasin. On ne voyait même plus les toilettes, les coiffures seules surnageaient, bariolées de plumes et de rubans; quelques chapeaux d'hommes mettaient des taches noires, tandis que le teint pâle des femmes, dans la fatigue et la chaleur, prenait des transparences de camélia.

> [And amidst the fine dust, everything finished by getting mixed up, it became impossible to recognize the divisions of the different departments; the haberdashery department over there seemed drowned; further on in the linen department, a ray of sunshine, entering by the window in the Rue Neuve-Saint-Augustin, was like a golden dart in a heap of snow; close by, in the glove and woollen departments, a dense mass of bonnets and chignons hid the background of the shop from view. The toilettes were no longer visible, the head-dresses alone appeared, decked with feathers and ribbons. A few men's hats introduced here and there a black spot, whilst the women's pale complexions assumed in the fatigue and heat the transparencies of the camellia.] (p. 792/108–09)

The Paradise's adaptation of Zola's *Au Bonheur des dames* via a series of paintings by Tissot and others itself adapts Zola's originary urge to adapt visual art into fiction.

Zola's novel, though, is an adaptation not just of visual arts but also of fairy tale. The department store is an intentionally magical space where the onlooker witnesses 'tout un peuple en l'air, voyageant dans les découpures de l'énorme charpente métallique'/'an entire population in the air, travelling in the cuttings of the enormous ironwork construction' (p. 902/253). The oriental rugs hang suspended from the ceiling like flying carpets. The shop workers have the power to bring all they touch to life. The narrative contemplates a display: 'toute l'écharpe de l'arc-en-ciel, des pièces retroussées en coques, plissées comme autour d'une taille qui se cambre, devenues vivantes sous les doigts savants des commis'/'all of the colours of the rainbow, pieces set up in the form of shells, others folded as if round a pretty figure, [brought to life] by the clever fingers of the window dressers' (p. 711/3). Both the shop and its owner are depicted in ogre-like terms. The shop is described thus: 'il s'était engraissé, pareil à l'ogre des contes, dont les épaules menacent de faire craquer les nuages'/'it had grown bigger and bigger, like the ogre of the legend, whose shoulders threatened to pierce the clouds' (p. 1010/397). Mouret too, for all his charm, has touches of the ogre as Denise looks at him: 'Toutes les histoires contées par son oncle, revenaient à sa mémoire, grandissant Mouret, l'entourant d'une légende, faisant de lui le maître de la terrible machine qui depuis le matin la tenait dans les dents de fer de ses engrenages'/'All the stories related by her uncle came back to her, increasing Mouret's importance, [...] making him the master of the terrible machine by whose wheels she had felt herself being seized all the morning' (p. 751/56). The shop also, Dominique Jullien suggests, has its Cinderella in Denise, the girl who rises from rags to riches, marrying her prince as a result of her honesty and purity.[35] At the heart of Zola's realism lies the fantasy of fairy tale. While this fairy tale seems at odds with the realist urges driving the novelist, it serves, in a sense, as an allegory for the adaptive, intertextual endeavour that is authorship in Zola's case. Fairy tales are, Julie Sanders suggests, a metaphor for the adaptive process. They are tales constantly told and retold in new contexts, eras and nations, tales which circulate and are made relevant by new authors for successive and overlapping generations of audiences.[36]

Fairy tale largely disappears from Zola's novel when it is translated in the BBC's *The Paradise*. While Denise's Cinderella-like ascension remains at the heart of the adaptation, she never experiences the abject poverty of her novelistic forebear, nor the queen-like triumph of the latter's ascent. *The Paradise* though echoes Zola's engagement with other creative spirits in other ways, retelling biblical tales in forms, in keeping with Gutt, made relevant for a modern audience. Jouve, the novel's security guard, responsible for policing the morals of both the shop workers and those they serve, is metamorphosed in *The Paradise* into Jonas, the dour Scot who functions as a television adaptation of the biblical Jonah. As Jonah was swallowed by a whale and regurgitated three days later to start a new life of purity and righteousness, so Jonas in *The Paradise* is swallowed in a mine collapse and consequently propelled to a new life of judgements as strict as those desired by his biblical ancestor. As Jonah went to prophesy against the great weaknesses of Nineveh in a quest to bring repentance, so Jonas militates against sin amongst the shop workers, policing their moral rectitude. With a biblical prescience, he sees all, knows all, and writes all in the book of truth he religiously carries with him. In a manner highly resonant for a work of adaptation, Jonas plays with precisely the borders, boundaries and very possibility of origin. A man of mystery throughout the adaptation, in a drunken moment, the teetotal Jonas reveals to Dudley how he came to lose his arm, to become a partial body. However, when subsequently asked about his personal origins, he refuses to confirm them, questioning the very nature of what truth is. Comparably, the book of truth he carries remains endlessly inaccessible to us. The adaptation offers the viewer the closed book in point-of-view shots which suggest we may get access to it, but ultimately has Jonas throw into the river. The book is swallowed by the waters which swallowed Jonas's biblical forebear in this adaptation which plays with and ultimately denies us access to a founding book of truth.

If Zola borrows from the Bible, so too does he adapt from his own corpus within *Au Bonheur des dames*. Steven Wilson reads Zola's *Nana* as a text buried in the buildings and structures of *Au Bonheur des dames*, commenting on the ingestive, sexual, war-like metaphors driving the commerce of bodies in both novels.[37] Dominique Jullien casts *Au Bonheur des dames* and *Le Rêve* as intertexts, unpicking the shared idealism, predictive value of clothes and triumphal marriage in both.[38] But Zola's novel does not engage singularly or in a binary form with specific Rougon-Macquart texts; rather, it might be seen to engage with them multiply and simultaneously. As the 'serre' [hothouse], the unnatural landscape which makes things grow out of season, serves as the illicit space of incest and infraction between stepmother and stepson in Zola's *La Curée*, so the shop in *Au Bonheur des dames* becomes a place of financial transgression and infidelity in terms of household budgets. A landscape as sensual and sexual as the hothouse in *La Curée*, the shop in *Au Bonheur des dames* is dominated by 'une chaleur de serre, suffocante'/'a hot-house heat, moist and close' (p. 895/245). This heat metaphorically metamorphoses the materials and objects offered for sale into plants and flowers whose names and characteristics Zola itemises as carefully as the vegetation in *La Curée*: 'une moisson de foulards mettait le rouge vif des géraniums, le blanc laiteux des pétunias, le jaune d'or des chrysanthèmes, le bleu céleste des verveines'/'a quantity of silk handkerchiefs displayed the bright scarlet of the geranium, the creamy white of the petunia, the golden yellow of the chrysanthemum, the sky-blue of the verbena' (p. 896/247). Zola in *Au Bonheur des dames* not only textually sends us back to *La Curée*, so too does he reach forward to his later novel *Germinal*. The personified, animated shop gluttonously consumes produce and customers with a voracity paralleled by that of the mine in Zola's coalfield novel. Traversing the shop at night, Denise looks at it in fear, envisioning it precisely as a coal field: 'et ces clartés éparses, pareilles à des taches jaunes et dont la nuit mangeait les rayons, ressemblaient aux lanternes perdues dans les mines'/'these scattered lights, like yellow patches, their rays lost in the gloom, resembled the lanterns hung up in a mine' (p. 825/151). As if to reinforce the link, Baron Hartmann speaks thus to Mouret of his enterprise: 'Tirez donc tout de la femme, exploitez-la comme une mine de houille'/'Bleed the women, work them as you would a coal mine' (p. 952/319). Some, all or indeed none of these Zola self-references may resonate in the mind of the reader as he or she consumes Zola's text. The novelist constructs a work which both reflects and predicts his textual identity/personality.

The textual identities and personalities which influence *The Paradise* extend beyond that of Zola himself. The formative function of a competitor adaptation is clearly visible in the BBC's adaptation of Zola: the ITV period drama also on the world of commerce, *Mr Selfridge*. While both were initially planned to launch at the same time (January), the BBC brought forward the release of *The Paradise* by four months, claiming to have commissioned the series first. Airing on competing channels, the two series adapt and react as much to each other as *The Paradise* does to Zola. There are striking overlaps between the rival series. Both fetishise period properties and items in their quest to sell us heritage. The movement and motion of characters and camera in *The Paradise*, an adaptation about the turnover and turnaround of products, takes place at an even faster rate in *Mr Selfridge*, as the breathlessness of the opening credits makes clear. The ITV adaptation moves the viewer between scenes with a dynamism akin to its lead character. In this rush between scenes *Mr Selfridge* offers hooks or mini cliffhangers to keep the viewer watching through advert breaks and between episodes. It offers a compulsively linked narrative-based form to capture its viewer, echoing Zola's publication in serial form. The narrative structures of *The Paradise* and *Mr Selfridge* in some ways overlap more than the BBC adaptation does with its Zolian source novel. Both television series structure themselves around the same premise: a man from lowly origins gambles all to make it big and be happy. In both he is torn between diametrically opposed women. Both series feature French characters with un-subtitled dialogue, *Mr Selfridge* offering teasing comment on the French source text which has nothing and yet, via *The Paradise*, everything to do with its own existence.[39] Both are structured around the progress of an ambitious shop girl in a hugely successful enterprise. *The Paradise*'s Denise repeatedly states she wants to be Moray while *Mr Selfridge*'s eponymous character looks at shop girl Agnes Towler and states: 'You remind me of myself when I started out'. And the overlap between the two series is not restricted to narrative. Aesthetic overlap features too. As previously discussed, *The Paradise* liquefies the audience streaming past Moray in his first successful sale day, speaking his joy in the money, ratification and currency they bring him. *Mr Selfridge*, an adaptation whose visual special effects are even more pared down and rare than those of *The Paradise*, nevertheless echoes and adapts the shot as the crowds streaming past Mr Selfridge blur into a slow-motion haze to visualise for the audience the euphoria the master salesman feels. *The Paradise* cannot be approached in a binary intertextual exploration in relation to Zola's *Au Bonheur des dames* because it is simultaneously an adaptation of, or reaction to, both the content and style of its ITV competitor *Mr Selfridge*.[40]

Gutt's value to Adaptation Studies lies precisely in the way in which he undoes the binary of source text and subsequent translation, proposing a model whereby there are as many possible translations are there are audiences for a text. Zola's novel *Au Bonheur des dames* initially appears to structure itself around and reinforce binary terms. The Vieil Elbeuf and Mouret's shop stand opposite each other, representing opposing eras and societies, the modern department store drawing life force from its outclassed competitor. In Denise's mind, 'la pensée de la boutique du *Vieil Elbeuf*, noire et étroite, agrandissait encore pour elle le vaste magasin'/'the thought of The Old Elbeuf, black and narrow, increased the immensity of this vast establishment' (p. 745/48). Denise has a male double when she seeks work in the department store. Deloche mirrors both her silence and her shyness in an encounter whose aftermath witnesses her inexorable positive thinking and success and his parallel pessimism and stagnation. Mouret has his own double in the aristocratic Paul, the boy who was top of the class when Mouret was always bottom, the man who witnesses Mouret's inexorable ascent and action as he himself struggles and falters. On closer inspection, though, Zola's novel works like Gutt's theory to undercut and pluralise binary structures. Hannah Thompson underscores the way in which Zola undoes gender binaries.[41] Mouret is hyper-masculine and endlessly seductive to women. He is feminised even in his seductive masculinity: 'Il était femme, elles se sentaient pénétrées et possédées par ce sens délicat qu'il avait de leur être secret, et elles s'abandonnaient, séduites'/'He seemed to be a woman himself, they felt themselves penetrated and overcome by this delicate sense of their secret that he possessed and they abandoned themselves, captivated' (p. 772/83). But the binaries which Zola's novel undoes extend beyond gender and things sexual. Zola animates the inanimate and mechanises the living. Hence, his shop and its wares live:

> Et les étoffes vivaient, dans cette passion du trottoir: les dentelles avaient un frisson, [...] les pièces de drap elles-mêmes [...] respiraient, soufflaient une haleine tentatrice; tandis que les paletots se cambraient davantage sur les mannequins qui prenaient une âme, et que le grand manteau de velours se gonflait, souple et tiède, comme sur des épaules de chair, avec les battements de la gorge et le frémissement des reins.

> [And the materials came alive]: the laces [shivered] [...] even the lengths of cloth [...] exhaled [...] while the cloaks threw out their folds over the dummies which assumed a soul, and the great velvet mantle particularly, expanded, supple and warm, as if on real fleshy shoulders, with a heaving bosom and a trembling of the hips. (p. 720/14)

Conversely, the animate beings who serve and desire this living material themselves become mechanical. Denise and her brothers walk 'machinalement'/'mechanically' to the shop. The cursory description, shared verbs and actions appearing in stark contrast to the pervasive life force of the department store on which they gaze (p. 710/3).

The Paradise, like *Au Bonheur des dames*, also works to overwhelm the binary structures it ostensibly sets up. Binary links serve a key narrative purpose in *The Paradise*. The adaptation cannot show us Moray's childhood and background as *Pot-Bouille* did Mouret's, but it can hint at them by making the shop boy, Arthur, Moray's reflective double. Arthur, clearly in awe of his boss and patron, mimics and echoes both his words and his stances. He is as young and inexperienced as his boss is successful and world-wise. Their relationship is a reflective one as Moray envies Arthur being born in the shop whose structures construct Moray's own identity. The adaptation itself is driven by Moray's relationship with two women who offer the clearest binaries of the series: Denise and Katherine. The two are polar opposites in class, honesty and colour palette. Katherine is as wealthy as Denise is working-class, as scheming and duplicitous as Denise is forthright and as clothed in sensuous ornate palettes suited to her brunette colouring as Denise is simply dressed and blonde. Scene transitions serve only to underline the binary relationship between the two. *The Paradise* cuts from the steamy stages of Katherine's initial seduction of Moray to a shot of the chaste Denise asleep in white in her shared bedroom. *The Paradise*, though, undoes binaries by multiplying them in so many ways that they are overwhelmed. Moray, for example, is doubled at once by Katherine and Denise, the two women who remain polar opposites. Both Moray and Katherine are berated by those close to them for their haste — Katherine for her rush to get Moray to propose and Moray for the incessant speed of his commercial expansion. Moray and Denise unwittingly set themselves up as doubles when they both gamble their livelihood on the success of a sale. Denise offers to resign if Katherine does not take to the dress she is proposing and Moray offers his shop to his suppliers if he cannot pay for the goods he buys for his massive sale.

The Paradise multiplies comparisons in a way that is always more than binary. The episode where caged birds of paradise are sold is important in this respect. The episode opens with an extended contemplation of the animals in captivity. The shot recurs at regular intervals, each time applied as comment to the entrapment of a different character. It is the scene transition when Katherine's father plans to buy the street lease, implicitly underlining that he will trap Moray into marriage. It is the scene transition following Denise's declaration of love to Moray, a declaration which at once frees her and forces her to leave for the stifling confines of her uncle's shop. The bird cage is also the scene transition after Jonas's attempt to silence Arthur's knowledge of the crime he has committed, a symbol of the encroaching forces which threaten to reveal him. Binaries are multiplied to such an extent that they cease to function in *The Paradise*. Jonas himself is a case in point. Biblical in his address, upright and moral in the behaviour he requires of others, Jonas kills the usurping interloper Bradley (the barber Moray makes a partner in order to buy his premises) in the name of love, loyalty and duty to The Paradise. An adaptation which chooses infrequently to experiment with shot and special effects, *The Paradise* chooses at this point to superimpose repeatedly a shadowy image of Jonas's face on the floating body of Bradley in the water. This special effect implies the identity behind this crime, affixing Jonas's identity to the murder. But it simultaneously dissolves Jonas as identity. It links this moral, upright man with the morally questionable Bradley, the man who initially seemed his polar opposite, and with his murder. Jonas's biblical forebear was swallowed by the sea only to be spat out three days later to go and spread the word of truth, yet this version of Jonah instead throws a man into the waters, only to have him resurface days later to bring the truth to light. Binaries, in *The Paradise*, are played with and ultimately overwhelmed.

The Paradise, too, plays with and, to an extent, undoes the possibility of a binary equivalence between source text and adaptive copy, in keeping with Gutt's interpersonal vision of translation. A subtly self-reflexive piece, *The Paradise* enacts and depicts its fragmentation of Zola as a source author in its adaptive endeavour. It underlines that it cannot and does not capture all of its source. The opening credits are key to my line of argument here. They offer us various fragments of beings whose identity the audience can only surmise. We are offered quick, partial shots of Katherine's neck, Moray's wrists, Denise's eyes in a point-of-view shot in a compact mirror as well as veiled images of Denise and Moray behind a curtain. The adaptation makes art out of fragmentation. These fractured images appear against a decorative graphic background reminiscent of lace, a background weaving and reaching out to cover the whole of the opening credits. Lace stands as something of a metaphor for the present absence of Zola in this adaptation of the novel so fascinated by that material. It is, as Rae Beth Gordon points out, a fabric of 'empty spaces — holes — in its composition and texture'.[42] The fabric of *The Paradise*'s fictions in its adaptation of Zola as source promises not plenitude and equivalence but fundamental absence. It is an adaptation which playfully refuses access to a series of key original texts. The book of truth which Jonas writes about the realities of the shop and its workers circulates very visibly and yet, as has already been discussed, is never accessed by the audience. Origins, its author Jonas suggests, shift and mutate according to the desires of the listener/reader/audience. He discusses the tales which circulate about how his arm came to be lost, suggesting that 'there is a story for every day of the year. None of them even close to the truth'. When asked why he does not correct them and reveal the original story behind his loss of limb, he responds in a line whose resonance is magnified because it appears precisely in a work of adaptation: 'Because the story can change all it likes'. Stories, *The Paradise*, makes clear, are not always reflective of their source.

The fragmentation which *The Paradise* situates at its very core as it assesses its own equivalence to Zola the novelist as source echoes the fragmentation innate to Zola's novel. The novelist makes clear in *Au Bonheur des dames* that his attempt to translate reality, amongst other sources, can never truly be equivalent. The contemporary landscape which Zola's novel works to copy and adapt into fiction disintegrates before the narrative's gaze:

> Paris s'étendait, mais un Paris rapetissé, mangé par le monstre; les maisons [...] s'éparpillaient ensuite en une poussière de cheminées indistinctes, les monuments semblaient fondre, à gauche deux traits pour Notre-Dame, à droite un accent circonflexe pour les Invalides, au fond le Panthéon, honteux et perdu, moins gros qu'une lentille.
>
> [Beyond, stretched forth Paris, but Paris diminished, eaten up by the monster [...] dying away in a cloud of indistinct chimneys; the monuments seemed to melt into nothing, to the left two dashes for Notre-Dame, to the right a circumflex accent for the Invalides, in the background the Pantheon, ashamed and lost, no larger than a lentil.] (p. 1010/397)

Zola's insertion of orthographic symbols into the visual landscape of Paris offers not the city itself as source, but a description that is meta-textually clear about its status as a textual copy, adaptation or mediation. The novelist's two main weapons — sight and words — are both, *Au Bonheur des dames* makes clear, approximate things. Zola's novel cannot fully see and make seen the landscape it seeks to convey. Speech, too, falters. Baudu stammers and repeats the same vitriolic tirades in his quest to vanquish the new department store in speeches which ultimately will amount to nothing. He recants his words to Denise inviting her to stay after her father's death as having no relation to real meaning (p. 716/9). Madame Aurélie uses speech to hide the truth of her son's indiscretions: 'Elle ne criait si fort que pour embrouiller les choses, car elle n'avait aucune illusion sur son fils'/'Her only object in making such a noise was to complicate the business, for she knew what her son was' (p. 814/138). The female customers stand and contemplate the commercial performances that Mouret puts on for them, their words endlessly couched in terms of inadequacy: 'Mme Marty cherchait une phrase pour dire son ravissement, et elle ne trouva que cette exclamation "C'est féerique"'/'Madame Marty endeavored to find a phrase to express her rapture, but could only exclaim "It's like a fairyland!"' (p. 895/245). Enacting language's inability to be equivalent to the desire behind it, Zola, like *The Paradise*, leaves gaps in the fabric of his fiction. Characters' speech, all too often, is paraphrased rather than given, their words an absence in their very presence. Denise's conversations with her aunt and cousin are a case in point: 'Alors, jusqu'au déjeuner, toutes trois parlèrent des enfants, du ménage, de la vie à Paris et en province, par phrases courtes et vagues'/'Until lunch time the three women sat and talked about children, housekeeping, life in Paris and life in the country, in short, vague sentences' (p. 717/10). Comparably, when Mouret tells his life story to Hartmann in an attempt to win financial and planning support, we receive only the paraphrased approximation of his words and life:

> Il se confessa en effet, il raconta ses débuts, il ne cacha même pas la crise financière qu'il traversait, au milieu de son triomphe. Tout défila, les agrandissements successifs, [...] les sommes apportées par ses employés, la maison risquant son existence à chaque mise en vente nouvelle, où le capital entier était joué comme sur un coup de cartes.
>
> [He did make his confession, he related his start, not even concealing the financial crisis through which he was passing in the midst of his triumph. Everything was brought up, the successive enlargements, [...] the sums bought up by his employees, the house risking its existence at every fresh sale in which the entire capital was staked, as it were, on a single throw of the dice.] (p. 763/71)

And Zola introduces other gaps which deliberately perforate his fiction. A nameless, class-less client, 'la jolie dame', appears on three occasions in the novel (p. 782/97). Each time the salesmen speculate about her personal, geographical and social origins, inventing and re-inventing stories about her. While such stories circulate and re-circulate in increasingly altered form, the truth of 'la jolie dame' is never revealed. Stories, in Zola's *Au Bonheur des dames*, do not always reveal the truth.

As an adaptation, though, *The Paradise* offers a means to evaluate the terms of Gutt's assertion that for a translation to be successful, it must meet the needs of its audience. The audience is, *The Paradise* makes clear in the fabric of its fictions, a necessary but ultimately ungraspable, elusive entity. Moray's dead first wife, Hélène, is a case in point. Her gaze, in portrait form, watches over The Paradise, driving many of the actions of those in it. In this adaptation of relentless movement and locomotion, numerous characters sit and contemplate her painted, static image. This image drives Jonas to murder to protect her. It spurs Moray to push himself to new heights. It pushes Katherine to scheme to replace the dead woman. Ever present in the adaptation, Hélène functions as an audience which is ever beyond reach. Characters are forbidden to talk of her and this figure who drives all remains endlessly beyond our reach. Hélène may offer an image of a static, clear viewer, but *The Paradise* as a whole gestures towards the fluid, shifting nature of the human mass in which Gutt suggests approbation for creative works may be found. Words, texts and identities shift between individuals, slipping beyond absolute ownership. Miss Audrey, the head of ladies' wear, passes off Denise's words and ideas as her own, reinforcing her position at work via them. Denise, though, will later write a speech for her uncle, mouthing the words as he utters her ventriloquised ideas to a cooperative of the trade people threatened by Moray. Moray is driven by a desire to own Talbot Street in order to expand the shop which represents and validates him. Katherine's father buys the freehold of the street, usurping him with the phrase 'what does it matter whose name is on the lease?' In the penultimate episode of the second series, the store hosts a dramatic party to sell the final instalment of the imaginary serial novel, *The House on the Hill*, which, like *The Paradise*, is about to end. This episode implicitly references Zola as a person. It features not only a photographer who photographs the entire cast, replicating Zola's famous interest in the new medium, but it also echoes his Naturalist philosophy. The photographer states that his images have 'the power to hold a mirror to your subject, to glimpse uncompromising truths'. The episode references not just Zola as a person, but also the means by which he chose to publish himself. *Au Bonheur des dames* was released in serial form and, like the invented *House on the Hill*, was devoured by the city's readers. *The Paradise* both proffers and refuses access to the fictional feuilleton *The House on the Hill*, making it visible to us while denying us access to its core story. What it chooses to focus on instead is the mass audience that consumes it. These masses may drive its production, fight over its pages and ensure its success, but they are unnamed, uncounted and unquantifiable in number as they consume the serial whose success depends upon them. They spill beyond the confines of the camera shots, eluding the very artefact they construct. Success, Gutt underlines, may lie in the gaze of the audience, but that audience, both Zola and *The Paradise* make clear, is no easy thing to know, conquer or define.

When considered in association, Zola's *Au Bonheur des dames*, the BBC's *The Paradise* and Gutt's functionalist relevance theory offer intriguing insights into the adaptive process. Collectively they underline the interpersonal nature of the adaptive endeavour as works are remade by people for people in a shifting range of situations, eras and target audience contexts. In their interactions, they push away from a binary text-to-text analysis of source and adaptation, underlining the formative role of the consuming audience in the production and success of the creative work. They make visible, with varying degrees of explicitness, the range and source of personal influences from which they are created. But Zola's *Au Bonheur des dames* and the BBC's *The Paradise* do not just engage with and illustrate elements of Gutt's relevance theory, they also offer a means to assess its limitations. For Gutt the audience is king and in its gaze success is to be found. Zola's *Au Bonheur des dames* and the BBC's *The Paradise*, however, underline how difficult that success is to glean and maintain. The audience is, they make clear, a mercurial, elusive and diverse entity whose approbation must be sought and re-sought in a continual process of shifting cultural transactions.

Notes to Chapter 1

1. For an introduction to the Functionalist approach, see Munday, *Introducing Translation Studies*, p. 110. Munday writes: 'The 1970s and 1980s saw a move away from the static linguistic typologies of translation shifts and the emergence and flourishing in Germany of a functionalist and communicative approach to the analysis of translation' (p. 111). Broadly speaking, the members of this group sought, to varying degrees, to identify the function or purpose of the text and to translate that in an attempt to elicit the desired effect on the target audience.
2. See, for example, Laurence Raw's aforementioned article, 'The Skopos of a Re-Make'. Raw uses the skopos theory of another Functionalist translation theorist, Hans J. Vermeer, to approach Adaptation Studies.
3. Gutt, *Translation and Relevance*, p. 10.
4. Werner Koller, *Einführung in die Übersetzungswissenschaft* (Heidelberg: Quelle &Meyer, 1983), p. 186, cited in English in Gutt, *Translation and Relevance*, p. 10.
5. Gutt, *Translation and Relevance*, pp. 31–32.
6. Robert A. Dooley, 'Style and Acceptability: The Guraní New Testament', *Notes on Translation*, 3.1 (1989), 49–57 (p. 49). Cited in Gutt, *Translation and Relevance*, p. 193.
7. The site of Britain's first department store is the subject of contention but two key early stores were in Newcastle: Bainbridge (1838) and Fenwick (1882). John James Fenwick founded Fenwick's but his son Fred travelled to Paris to train in retail and was both impressed by and sought to emulate what he saw at Le Bon Marché. Le Bon Marché is generally regarded as the first department store and also served as the basis for much of Zola's research in preparation for the writing of *Au Bonheur des dames*.
8. Moray's training in Paris not only references Zola as source, it also adapts its British context as it replicates, in historical terms, the creation of the Fenwick department store described above and specifically the apprenticeship which Fred Fenwick did in the French capital as he took inspiration from Le Bon Marché (Fenwick, 'Our Story. Our Heritage', <https://www.fenwick.co.uk/our-story.html> [accessed 3 September 2018]).
9. Mark Lawson, '*The Paradise*: Do Viewers Really Need More Period Drama?', *Guardian*, 25 September 2012, <https://www.theguardian.com/tv-and-radio/tvandradioblog/2012/sep/25/the-paradise-another-period-drama> [accessed 9 August 2017].
10. Andrew Higson, 'The Heritage Film and British Cinema', in *Dissolving Views: Key Writings on British Cinema*, ed. by Andrew Higson (London: Cassell, 1996), pp. 232–49 (p. 233).
11. Sarah Cardwell, *Adaptation Revisited: Television and the Classic Novel* (Manchester: Manchester University Press, 2002), p. 119.
12. BBC period drama prior to and in the 1980s traditionally relied on a boxy 3:4 ratio with a preponderance of mid-shots in dialogue-heavy interior studio scenes. See for example the BBC's 1972 adaptation of Jane Austen's *Emma*, starring Doran Godwin.
13. Higson, 'The Heritage Film and British Cinema', p. 233.
14. *The Paradise*, created by Bill Gallagher (BBC, 2012), DVD audio commentary.
15. Ibid.
16. Ibid. *Cartes de visite* were a type of small photograph patented in Paris by photographer André Disdéri in 1854.
17. Higson, 'The Heritage Film and British Cinema', p. 233.
18. Zola's novel does suggest that commerce subtly challenges contemporary class structures by creating shop girls as a new class apart: 'Presque toutes les vendeuses, dans leur frottement quotidien avec la clientèle riche, prenaient des grâces, finissaient par être d'une classe vague, flottant entre l'ouvrière et la bourgeoise'/'Nearly all the saleswomen, by their daily contact with the rich customers, assumed certain graces, and finished by forming a vague nameless class, something between a work-girl and a middle-class lady' (Emile Zola, *Au Bonheur des dames*, in *Œuvres complètes*, ed. by Henri Mitterand, 15 vols (Paris: Cercle du Livre Précieux, 1966–69), IV, 699–1053 (p. 828); *The Paradise*, trans. by Ernest Alfred Vizetelly (London: Penguin, 2013), pp. 156–57 (all further quotations and translations will be drawn from these two editions, with references indicated in the main text). But in his novel where a shop girl marries a successful shop boy, class structures emerge largely unscathed.

19. Zola's novel explicitly likens the shop to a *phalanstère*, the building designed for a self-contained utopian community working together for communal benefit, as envisioned by the philosophy of Charles Fourier. Zola writes, in *Au Bonheur des dames*, of the dining hall: 'Toute une queue de commis grossissait, il y avait des rires, des poussées. Et, maintenant, les deux jeunes gens, la tête au guichet, se communiquaient leurs réflexions, devant cette cuisine de phalanstère/'Quite a string of shopmen had now arrived; there was a good deal of laughing and pushing. The two young men, their heads at the wicket, exchanged their remarks before this phalansterian kitchen' (p. 930/292).
20. Giddings, Selby and Wensley, *Screening the Novel*, p. 31.
21. Rachel Bowlby, *Just Looking: Consumer Culture in Dreiser, Gissing and Zola* (London: Methuen, 1989), p. 32. On this point, see also Hannah Thompson, *Naturalism Re-dressed: Identity and Clothing in the Novels of Emile Zola* (Oxford: Legenda, 2004), pp. 72–76.
22. Charlotte Brunsdon, *Screen Tastes: Soap Opera to Satellite Dishes* (London: Routledge, 1997), p. 144.
23. Lury writes: 'The DVR has the potential to impact on the relationship of time to television in two ways. First, by apparently "pausing" live television, the DVR can effectively detach the viewer's individual experience of "live" television from the actual transmission of the "live" broadcast. Second, it allows viewers to ignore the vast range of scheduled programming by the individual channels and develop their own personalized schedule, tailored to their own particular tastes and routines of viewing' (Karen Lury, *Interpreting Television* (London: Bloomsbury, 2005), pp. 25 & 110).
24. André Antoine, *Mes souvenirs sur le Théâtre-libre* (Paris: Arthème Fayard, 1921).
25. Thompson, *Naturalism Redressed*, p. 86.
26. Brian Nelson, 'Désir et consummation dans au Bonheur des dames', *Cahiers naturalistes*, 70 (1996), 19–34 (p. 27).
27. Translation cited in David Baguley, *Napoleon III and his Regime: An Extravaganza* (Baton Rouge: Louisiana State University Press, 2000), p. 200.
28. Emile Zola, *Ecrits sur l'art*, p. 167.
29. Cited in Anne Lecomte-Hilmy, 'L'Artiste de temperament chez Zola et devant le public', p. 87.
30. Vaheed Ramazani, 'Gender, War and the Department Store: Zola's *Au Bonheur des dames*', *SubStance*, 36.2 (2007), 126–46. Brian Nelson situates Aristide and Marguerite Boucicaut, the founders of the Bon Marché department store, as the foremost model for Zola's fictional novel, analysing their innovative sales concepts. Nelson argues that the Boucicauts, like Zola's fictional Mouret, made their shop the stage of a new commercial world order, a locale geared up to the seduction of the shopper (Nelson, 'Désir et consummation dans *Au Bonheur des dames*', p. 20).
31. For further details of Zola's interviews with *chef du rayon*, Mademoiselle Dulit, and his interaction with information from Karcher, the *secrétaire général* at the Bon Marché, see the introduction to the novel written by Jean Mistler in Zola, *Au Bonheur des dames*, pp. 701–06.
32. Roland Barthes, *S/Z* (Paris: Seuil, 1970), pp. 165–66; *S/Z*, trans. by Richard Miller (New York: Noonday Press, 1993), p. 160.
33. Henri Mitterand, 'Le Musée dans le texte', *Cahiers naturalistes*, 66 (1992), 13–22.
34. Cited by Hertz, 'Emile Zola, témoin de la vérité'.
35. Dominique Jullien, 'Cendrillon au grand magasin: *Au Bonheur des dames* et *Le Rêve*', *Cahiers naturalistes*, 67 (1993), 97–105.
36. Sanders, *Adaptation and Appropriation*, pp. 82–93.
37. Steven Wilson, '*Nana*, Prostitution and the Textual Foundations of Zola's *Au Bonheur des dames*', *Nineteenth-Century French Studies*, 41 (2012), 91–104.
38. Jullien, 'Cendrillon au grand magasin'.
39. *Mr Selfridge* is actually an adaptation of a biography of the historical figure: Lindy Woodhead, *Shopping, Seduction and Mr Selfridge* (London: Profile, 2012).
40. Influence, in this television context however, is neither singular nor one way. Both *The Paradise* and *Mr Selfridge* engage and adapt aspects of other milestone adaptations, notably, as Katherine Byrne suggests, *Downton Abbey*. See Katherine Byrne, 'From Downton to the Department Stores: Sex, Shopping and Heritage in *Mr Selfridge* (2013–)', in *Edwardians on Screen* (London: Palgrave, 2015), pp. 90–111.

41. Thompson, *Naturalism Redressed*, p. 72.
42. Rae Beth Gordon, *Ornament, Fantasy and Desire in Nineteenth-century French Literature* (Princeton: Princeton University Press, 1992), p. 57.

CHAPTER 2

❖

Bodies in Translation: Zola, Venuti, *L'Œuvre* and *Madame Sourdis*

Ernst-August Gutt, the theorist featured in Chapter One, suggested that the translator's focus should be the audience as a body, that his or her core concern should be the provision of 'adequate' contextual clues to ensure comprehension and engagement. Chapter Two's theorist, Lawrence Venuti, places a different body in the foreground of Translation and Adaptation Studies: the body of the translator him- or herself. For Venuti, this body is a key but overlooked space in the sphere of cultural production. The historic predominance of transparency and fidelity discourses in both Translation and Adaptation Studies have, Venuti's theory argues, required the translator's body to be invisible in the texts and words which it creates or mediates. Such invisibility is, for Venuti, a dangerous thing for it hides the subjective processes and practices of translation, a process done by people for people. Translation is, Venuti underlines, a hermeneutic endeavour in which a translator mediates the words and images of the source text via the prism of his/her own identity. Venuti's vision of translation as a personal interpretation of a source text meshes with Zola's vision of authorship. The nineteenth-century novelist famously characterised a great artist as having the ability to translate reality via his or her personal perspective or temperament.[1] Venuti's writing urges the translator to step out of his or her invisibility and make visible his or her role in the mediation of texts. This chapter's case study texts by Zola, the novel *L'Œuvre* and the short story 'Madame Sourdis', read in association with their French television adaptations, *Madame Sourdis* (1979) and *L'Œuvre* (1967), take up Venuti's call.[2] They explore precisely the impact of the body of the creative artist/translator as he or she mediates a text or source for a new audience. However, these case study literary works and television adaptations do not just foreshadow and enact elements of Venuti's theory, they also raise interesting questions about it. Venuti calls for the translator to reveal his/her bodily presence in the fictions which he or she mediates. What *L'Œuvre* and 'Madame Sourdis' make clear, though, is that Venuti's call to arms is far from easily achieved. The body of the translator can never be entirely visible in the text he or she translates. It is always a negotiated, partial space, a composite identity where source author and translator meet and overlap. And while Venuti talks of the body of the translator in the singular, *L'Œuvre* and 'Madame Sourdis' reframe it in insistently plural ways, underscoring the range of bodies via which the text is mediated and the complex, composite bodily presence which those bodies glean from their acts of adaptive mediation.

Venuti functions as a key theorist for those who would align translation theory and Adaptation Studies. His physical presence is essential in a book such as this. His is one of the strongest and most persuasive voices pushing for a closer relationship between the theorists in both disciplines. Though Venuti does not elide translation and adaptation, he does align them in his hermeneutic vision:

> Every second-order creation, I argue, in any medium regardless of its material basis, is an interpretation enacted during the production process and subject to further interpretation by the gamut of receptors who use it, whether the work in question is a translation or an imitation, a textual edition or an anthology, a dramatic or film adaptation, even a museum exhibition.[3]

Pointing out that the distinction between translation and adaptation is historically variable, Venuti repeatedly allies the two creative processes:

> In advancing this hermeneutic model, I am not suggesting that no formal or semantic correspondences can exist between the source text, on the one hand, and the translation or adaptation, on the other, but rather that any such correspondences are shaped by the exigencies of an interpretative act.[4]

Translation and adaptation, moreover, share a common history in relation to Venuti's notion of the invisibility of the translator/person adapting a text. Both have been dominated by transparency discourses, by a quest to find in translation the body of the source text. In his book entitled precisely *The Translator's Invisibility*, Venuti underlines the way in which fidelity, transparency and equivalence discourses in translation have erased the translator's body from the text in which he or she is so corporeally imbricated. Venuti writes:

> A translated text, whether prose or poetry, fiction or non-fiction, is judged acceptable by most publishers, reviewers and readers when it reads fluently, when the absence of any linguistic or stylistic peculiarities makes it seem transparent, giving the appearance that it reflects the foreign writer's personality or intention or the essential meaning of the foreign text — the appearance, in other words, that the translation is not in fact a translation, but the 'original'.[5]

The body most readers seek in the translation is not, Venuti suggests, that of the translator, but rather that of the source text itself. Translation is thus, according to Venuti, 'a weird self-annihilation', for the translator and his or her own creative identity.[6] The readers' expectations of finding the body of the source text in absolute form in the translation are, Venuti makes clear, problematic. Citing Derrida, Venuti argues that the body of the source text is dematerialised as it passes into a new language and cultural context.[7] But, according to Venuti, this bodily loss is followed, albeit unequally, by a corporeal gain as the text, via a translator, gains a new body, a new personal materiality in its translated interpretation. Absent in its very presence, and present in its very absence, the body of the translator constitutes a complex space in Venuti's theory.[8]

Venuti's theories on the bodily presence and visibility of the translating artist have clear purchase in relation to the Zola texts at the heart of this chapter.

Zola's *L'Œuvre* recounts the construction and destruction of an artist, Claude, in bodily terms, as he struggles to capture reality on a canvas, mediating it via his consciousness and his painterly hands. Pushed towards madness as reality and the ability to complete his canvases escape him, ultimately he commits suicide, his body vanquished by the source it sought to conquer. Zola's 'Madame Sourdis' contemplates translating, adapting bodies in a different context. Ferdinand, a handsome, talented but ultimately work-shy artist, marries Adèle, a would-be artist with less talent but the ability to copy and continue the work of great masters. Adèle increasingly paints in Ferdinand's place, creating the works which Ferdinand signs as artistic body in a complex creative transaction which raises probing questions about source artists and the bodies reworking them.

At first glance, Deuxième Chaine's 1967 television adaptation of *L'Œuvre* appears to enact Venuti's theory of the invisibility of the translator. The telefilm's opening credits may proclaim it to be 'une émission de Pierre Cardinal' [a programme by Pierre Cardinal] but it then seemingly consigns Cardinal to creative invisibility by focusing, in the subsequent shot, on Zola's identity in its integrity. While numerous adaptations use words of approximation — 'd'après le roman de' [based on the novel], 'inspiré du roman' [inspired by the novel] — this adaptation proclaims itself not as derivation but, in the following words which span and mark the entirety of the establishing screen shot, '*L'Œuvre* d'Emile Zola' [Emile Zola's *L'Œuvre*]. The piece is not, its para-textual material suggests, adapted from Zola's novel. It is Zola's novel. And the adaptation works hard to make the body of Zola present in two key respects. First, the body of Zola's dialogue is materially very present in this adaptation which broadcasts, aurally at least, almost like an abridged reading of Zola's text. The words of the nineteenth-century novelist pass all but unchanged to the mouths of the twentieth-century bodies which perform them on television. Second, while the television adaptation cuts almost all of the band of artist friends so key to Claude's life, it retains Sandoz, the author figure who has so readily been identified by readers as Zola himself. Vizetelly, the translator and friend of Emile Zola, whose English translation this chapter uses, characterises Sandoz thus in his preface:

> Pierre Sandoz, clerk, journalist, and novelist; [...] Sandoz, it may be frankly admitted, is simply M. Zola himself. Personal appearance, life, habits, opinions, all are those of the novelist at a certain period of his career; and for this reason, no doubt, many readers of *His Masterpiece* will find Sandoz the most interesting personage in the book.[9]

The television Sandoz is played by Jean-Paul Cisife, an older, stocky, dark, full-bearded actor whose appearance perhaps owes more to the iconic image of Zola the novelist rather than his intradiegetic writerly cypher. Sandoz, in the novel, is sketched in the most fleeting of terms: 'Pierre Sandoz [...] était un garçon de vingt-deux ans, très brun, à la tête ronde et volontaire, au nez carré, aux yeux doux, dans un masque énergique encadré d'un collier de barbe naissante'/'Pierre Sandoz, a friend of his boyhood, was about twenty-two, very dark, with a round and determined head, a square nose, and gentle eyes, set in energetic features, girt round with a sprouting beard'.[10] Sandoz, despite his key presence in the adaptation, is significantly not introduced by name to the audience until midway through the adaptation. Such is his appearance and so identifiable is the Naturalist project he enunciates that the telefilm presumes and plays with the audience's recognition of Sandoz as Zola. It is far from insignificant that the audience's first sight of Sandoz is a reflective one. Sandoz stands, his back to us, as the adaptation teasingly asks us to identify his identity and his body, contemplating Claude's new painting, *Plein air*. The painting he considers already contains him as a painted artefact as he sits as a model for it. In a shot with striking reflective symmetries, Sandoz contemplates the painting in almost the exact stance that the painted version of him in the work assumes. Cisife, the actor whose body interprets Sandoz, stares at the painterly double of his own identity which also reflects the identity of Zola himself. In this play of creative bodies and identities in this adaptation, Cardinal seems entirely absent.

Yet, intriguingly, traces of Cardinal's presence are visible in the midst of his foregrounding of Zola and his avatars. His adaptation is constructed around a series of highly visible frontal face shots of both Sandoz and Zola's artist character Claude. These two characters speak, in isolation, to the camera. They are pulled out, in these shots, from the fictive universe that encloses them. The creative identity of Cardinal as director and writer of this adaptation is visible precisely via this core series of close-up face shots of Zola's alter ego Sandoz. Such face shots are a signature feature of Cardinal's own television aesthetic, an aesthetic recognisable from his well-known work on the series *Gros plan*. Tamara Chaplin writes:

> The brainchild of director Pierre Cardinal, *Gros plan* was structured as a half-hour show in which an important celebrity (usually an actor or playwright) spoke alone to a camera. Interpolated into the resultant monologue were excerpts from films that shed light on the character and personality of the guest. Technically, the focus on an individual, and particularly the face shot in close-up, reflected an aesthetic that fascinated French television directors throughout the 1950s and early 60s. The close-up was implicitly invoked not as something to interpret but rather as a lucid access to truth. Thus, Cardinal insisted, 'What is most important is the face, for the simple reason that it is the only thing that appears as large as life on television'.[11]

Cardinal's face shots in close-up of Sandoz underline the director's presence even as he places Zola's identity and its cyphers in the foreground of his adaptive translations. They encode his metaphorical presence in the adaptation, underscoring the complex visibility of the adapting director.

Cardinal's *L'Œuvre* may seek to offer the body of Zola's text in its integrity, but what it dramatises in its images is its inability to do so. Venuti, as I suggested above, argues that the body of the source text is dematerialised as it is translated.[12] Cardinal's television adaptation enacts that process of dematerialisation, dramatising the fractures to the source text that result from the process of adaptation. The adaptation clearly crops aspects of its source text. Scenes frequently start *in medias res*, their dialogues only partial fragments of a clearly larger and missing whole. The adaptation's opening scene is a case in point. Christine reluctantly takes shelter from the storm in Claude's studio. Her identity, their conversation to date and her journey to get there are severed from the adaptation. The adaptation's scene transitions add to this sense of fragmentation and fracture. Fades to black and dissolves — smooth, seamless ways to move the viewer between scenes — are comparatively rare in this adaptation, which instead favours more abrupt jump cuts to new scenes, cuts which often entail considerable leaps in time, space and plot. Such cuts, in their very visibility, emphasise the matter, plot, time and space which are taken out of the plot. Physical bodies, like the body of Zola's text itself, appear in cropped, abbreviated form in this adaptation. Christine's body, which dominates proceedings in painted form, is repeatedly hidden from view in the adaptation. Her nakedness obsesses Claude, fills his paintings, but is not allowed to occupy the camera's gaze in any direct form. Claude, at the adaptation's close, gazes at her body on canvas, lovingly touching its reproduced form. The source of that painted body, Christine herself, appears only as a fragment at the edge of the shot, her feet cropped as severed objects at the bottom right hand of the screen.[13] Such acts of cropping have much to do with the shaping forces of contemporary television practice in relation to nudity and the time constraints of viewing slots. Zola's several hundred-page novel is condensed into a telefilm of 122 minutes. These cuts, though, stem also from the technical possibilities of the medium at the time. Television drama of this era was largely studio based, with channels offering works which were dialogue heavy, constructed around interior scenes filmed in boxy 3:4 ratio. Television's technical and aesthetic constraints meant that the sheer expanse of Zola's panoramas in this novel, with its endless outside spaces, had to be cropped into a very different material artefact in spatial terms. Hence, in televisual form, Claude may paint the expanses of Paris, but the adaptation does not fully venture out into them. Instead, as the painter describes the vast landscape he seeks to paint, the film cuts in fleeting, abbreviated shots of the landscape neither it nor Claude will ever fully be able to master. When Claude and Christine do venture outside, the shots they occupy are close-ups or mid-shots which occlude the landscape they purport partially to show. Outside shots are frequently barred or blocked, their foreground obfuscated by barriers which deny the very space they seem to proffer. Such outside scenes, significantly, are habitually filmed without dialogue. The adaptation is as unable to put this outdoor space into words as it is to offer it in visual terms. The time, technology and aesthetic of 1960s television perforates the body of Zola's text and, via its cropped dialogues, abrupt scene transitions, cropped bodies and cropped spaces, this adaptation works to italicise the dematerialisation of the source body which Venuti describes. Such fractures to the body of the source text, Venuti argues, are innate to translation as a fundamentally transformative process: 'Translators [...] can never entirely avoid the loss that the translation process enforces on the source text, on its meanings and structures, figures and traditions'.[14] Cardinal's adaptation promises the body of Zola's text but reflects meta-adaptively on its own ability only to offer it in partial form.

While the 1967 adaptation of *L'Œuvre* contemplates and emphasises the material losses that Zola's textual body experiences at its hands, so too does it revel in the televisual body which it creates for itself. Venuti famously argues that the translator should combat his or her cultural and textual invisibility by making visible the machinery, moment and means of his or her own translations. He pushes him or her to signal the processes and practices of his or her translative acts in prefaces, notes, interviews and book covers. The 1967 television adaptation of *L'Œuvre* anticipates and takes up Venuti's challenge, choosing, as it adapts, to italicise the means and machinery of its medium of adaptation: television. Thus, while it is comparatively unadventurous in terms of its dialogue as it seeks linguistic parity with its source, aesthetically the adaptation is innovative and experimental, drawing attention, as the Nouvelle Vague did in film of the same era, to the machinery of its own production. In a startling shot, the adaptation has Claude paint directly on the camera screen. The thick materiality and trace of the paint not only probes the borders between art forms (here television and painting), it also draws the viewer's attention to the lens of the camera and to the medium in which Zola's textual body is adapted for a new audience. The 1967 adaptation of *L'Œuvre* has extensive recourse to highly visible point-of-view shots which gently push the viewer to contemplate, self-reflexively, their place in the construction of these televisual fictions. The generative function of our vision in this adaptation is underscored. Claude and Christine share an exuberant and loving meal in the inn at the start of their idyll at Bennecourt. Christine consumes her food with sensual abandon, flirting lovingly with the camera screen and audience who have taken the place of Claude. Comparably, in the amorous boat scene which follows, Christine acts to the camera, smiling and seducing it as her lover. Like the nude lover in Manet's *Olympia* (1865), who gazes directly at the onlooker in the art gallery, Christine looks at us in these shots, highlighting our place in the machinery of the art work, in the televisual transaction in which we are complicit. Cardinal's adaptation requires us to consider our desiring and enabling gaze in the fictions proffered to us. And the adaptation's technical experimentation is not restricted to these visible, desiring point-of-view shots. Again probing the boundaries between painting and television, the adaptation experiments with colour washes. Celebrating the onset of colour in French television drama, Cardinal experiments with colour in highly visible ways. The opening storm scene in Claude's *atelier* is first flooded violently in red like a hellscape and then jarringly purple. While the pseudo-Impressionist painters in Zola's novel experimented with natural light's ability to alter the colour of objects, the adaptation's use of colour, in keeping with the canvases Claude increasingly paints, is more Expressionist than Impressionist. The adaptation's colour washes, in their lurid clash, express Christine's subjective perspective, radically distorting the colours of nature to emotional effect. Comparably, the mocking multitude of spectators who view Claude's *Plein air* painting at the Salon, spectators filmed from the personified perspective of the canvas itself, each have their faces flooded a different violent shade of green, yellow or orange. The colours have no Impressionist link to a light source or moment. Rather, in their jarring dissonance, the clashing colours underscore both the ugliness of the words pouring from the mouths of the spectators and Claude's emotional distress upon hearing them. Via a series of experimental shots and techniques, the 1967 adaptation of *L'Œuvre* draws attention to the means and machinery of its own adapted televisual body. It makes visible elements of its acts of adaptation.

L'Œuvre, thus, in both its source and adapted form, anticipates core elements of Venuti's theory. This resonance is perhaps unsurprising given the commonalities between Zola's view of translative creativity and Venuti's approach to translation. For Zola, great art, whatever its medium, translates the world around it. His writing on Manet is revealing in this respect. What Zola admires above all in Manet is his ability to translate reality and he repeatedly praises him using the vocabulary of translation:

> Désormais, Edouard Manet avait trouvé sa voix, ou, pour mieux dire, il s'était trouvé lui-même: il voyait de ses yeux, il devait nous donner dans chacune de ses toiles une traduction de la nature en cette langue originale qu'il venait de découvrir au fond de lui.[15]
>
> [Edouard Manet had found his voice, or, rather, he had found himself. He saw things from his own perspective, and worked in each canvas to give us a translation of nature in the original language which he had discovered within his own being.]

The vocabulary of translation abounds in Zola's definitions of great art. But Zola, like Venuti, conceives of translation in fundamentally hermeneutic, physical, corporeal terms. The great artists do not and cannot transfer reality as an object direct to the page, stage or canvas. Rather, they translate it, interpreting and adapting it via the prism of their personality, mediating it via the very materiality of their body. Zola's view of artistry as 'un coin de la création vu à travers un tempérament' [a corner of creation seen through a personality] anticipates and complements Venuti's reading of translation as innately personal and interpretative.[16] Venuti writes:

> In the hermeneutic model, any correspondence is partial and contingent: partial because it is incomplete in re-creating the source text and slanted toward the receiving culture; contingent because it is fixed by one among other possible interpretations, each of which established a criterion of accuracy that varies among receiving cultural constituencies, social situations and historical moments.[17]

For Venuti, translation is a personal act as the source text is mediated through the consciousness, personal moment and materiality of the translating artist him- or herself. Zola concurs and expresses his admiration for the Impressionists in terms which echo Venuti's hermeneutic approach: 'Chacun d'eux, d'ailleurs, a heureusement pour lui sa note originale, sa façon de voir et de traduire la réalité à travers son tempérament' [Each one of them, moreover, has, happily for them, his/her own originality, his/her own way of seeing and translating reality through the prism of his/her own personality].[18] Zola continues: 'Chaque grand artiste est venu nous donner une traduction nouvelle et personnelle de la nature. La réalité est ici l'élément fixe, et les divers tempéraments sont les éléments créateurs qui ont donné aux œuvres des caractères différents' [Each great artist gives us a new and personal translation of nature. Reality is the fixed point. The different personality of each artist is the creative element which ensures that works of art are different in character].[19] Zola's vision of art as personal translation feeds into the creation of his characters. He writes thus of Claude in *L'Œuvre*:

> Brusquement, il se leva, se rassit avec une feuille de papier et un crayon, se mit à jeter des traits rapides, sous la clarté ronde et vive qui tombait de l'abat-jour. Et ce croquis, fait de souvenir, dans le besoin qu'il avait de traduire au-dehors le tumulte d'idées battant son crâne, ne suffit même bientôt plus à le soulager.
>
> [Suddenly he rose, sat down again with a sheet of paper and a pencil, and began sketching rapidly, in the vivid circle of light that fell from under the lampshade. And such was his longing to give outward expression to the tumultuous ideas beating in his skull, that soon this sketch did not suffice for his relief.] (p. 612)

Claude's acts of translation, the narrative makes clear, are innately corporeal as the artist's source, reality, is mediated both by his consciousness and his digits. Sandoz too characterises his literary translations of reality in an extended series of novels in fundamentally bodily terms. He enunciates his plan to capture reality as follows: 'étudier l'homme tel qu'il est, non plus leur pantin métaphysique, mais l'homme physiologique, déterminé par le milieu, agissant sous le jeu de tous ses organes'/'To study man as he is, not man the metaphysical puppet but physiological man, whose nature is determined by his surroundings, and to show all his organism in full play' (p. 566). Their corporeal conceptions of art as translation echo those of Zola. For Zola and Venuti, bodies lie at the heart of this creative process.

Zola conceptualises his writing in *L'Œuvre* as an act of translation, one which is clearly corporeal and manifests his own body. Susan Harrow underlines the prevalence of the body in Zola's work:

> Zola is a chronicler of corporeality: he documents and analyses his own bodily symptoms in his correspondence; in his theoretical writings, he scrutinizes the body in the wake of contemporaneous critical thought (Taine, Dr Toulouse, Darwin) and his novels inscribe the bodily fate — ordinary and extraordinary — of his fictional characters.[20]

Zola conceives of Claude's body as a genetic adaptation of the tainted blood he inherits from Tante Dide, blood which manifests itself in him as a destructive incapacity to capture and complete the visions of reality which he seeks to translate onto canvas. Bodies, those of his models and those of his tainted forebears, drive Claude's reality. But if the novel's narrative focuses on Claude, Zola's paratextual material on *L'Œuvre* makes clear that the body specifically at play in the novel's reworking of reality is that of Zola himself. Zola writes in his plan for the novel:

> Avec Claude Lantier, je veux peindre la lutte de l'artiste contre la nature, l'effort de la création dans l'œuvre d'art, effort de sang et de larmes pour donner sa chair, faire de la vie [...]. En un mot, j'y raconterai ma vie intime de production, ce perpétuel accouchement si douloureux, mais je grandirai le projet par le drame, par Claude.
>
> [With Claude Lantier, my aim is to depict the struggle of the artist against nature, the creative effort invested in the work of art; that is an effort of blood and tears in order to flesh, to create life [...]. In a word, I will relate my intimate

experience of creating art, the unceasing agony of giving birth; but I will enlarge the project dramatically, through Claude.]²¹

Significantly, the corporeal terms which Zola uses to enunciate his personal acts of fictional reworking — 'sang', 'larmes', 'chair' — feature prominently in the fictional reworkings of the Parisian landscape which the novel produces. Blood runs through and stains the body of the word paintings Zola offers of the capital's skyline. Christine sees the cityscape in the storm 'dans un éclaboussement de sang'/'spattered with blood' (p. 437). Claude and Sandoz remember the landscape of their youth and specifically the 'Jas de Bouffan, d'une blancheur de mosquée, au centre de ses vastes terres, pareilles à des mares de sang'/'sheep walk of Bouffan, showing white, like a mosque, amidst a far-stretching blood-red plain' (p. 462). The lovers contemplate a series of sunsets on Christine's walk home: 'le soleil, pareil à une boule de feu, descendait majestueusement dans un lac de saphir [...] puis, la boule se violaçait, se noyait au fond du lac devenu sanglant'/'the sun, like a fiery ball, descended majestically in an unruffled sapphire lake [...] then the globe assumed a violet tinge and at last became submerged in the lake, which had turned blood-red' (p. 517). Claude works to infuse his art with his very life-blood and paints, in particular, 'un ventre de femme [...], une chair de satin, frissonnante, vivante du sang qui coulait sous la peau'/'a woman's trunk with quivering satin-like skin [alive thanks to the blood in its veins]' (p. 465).²² If Zola's word paintings bleed, so too are they associated with the bodily fluid of tears. Not only does Mahoudeau's abandoned statue appear to cry as water leaks onto it, 'le visage creusé par les grandes larmes noires de la pluie'/'[its face] riddled by the rain's big, grimy tears', so too does the landscape in Claude's childhood memories (p. 616). The painter remembers, and his creator paints in words, 'le bois des Trois-Bons-Dieux, dont les pins, d'un vert dur et verni, pleuraient leur résine sous le grand soleil'/'the wood of Le Trois-Bons-Dieux, with hard, green, varnished pines shedding pitchy tears beneath the burning sun' (p. 462). Zola repeatedly corporealises the novel's landscape, offering his flesh to the city he seeks to rework in fiction. Thus, whilst the bodies Claude paints take on the characteristics of the landscape — Claude hails Christine's stomach as 'un vrai soleil de chair' — the landscapes Zola describes in his word paintings repeatedly take on the characteristics of people and their flesh (p. 634/the Vizetelly translation cuts this bodily description of Christine nude).²³ Claude obsessively paints and repaints a female figure, painting through her 'la chair même de Paris, la ville nue et passionnée'/'the city bare and impassioned' (p. 628). Zola writes in his art criticism in relation to the artist: 'ce que je demande à l'artiste [...] c'est de se livrer lui-même, cœur et chair' [what I ask of the artist is that he gives himself entirely, in flesh and blood, to his work].²⁴ The personification of the landscape in Zola's word paintings in *L'Œuvre* underlines the formative power of milieu as a shaping force in Zola's reading of human life as borrowed from Hippolyte Taine. However, this personification might also be seen in part, in a manner which speaks to Venuti's thought, to make visible the invisible body of the adapting author in the novelistic fictions so dependent on his corporeal organs, existence and moment.

Claude may seek to make his body visible as he adapts reality in paint, but his body is always a mediated one, refracted through the landscape and through the painted figure of his wife. He paints Christine, a figure who becomes his reflective double, to find a complex presence for himself on canvas. Claude's body as a painter who seeks to capture reality as source drives the narrative. He gleans bodily health and being from his painted versions of reality. They feed and sustain him physically in the money they earn him and provide him sustenance in more metaphorical terms (p. 463). And the relationship between body and canvas is reciprocal, for what Claude metaphorically paints is his own body over and over again. Ostensibly he paints images of Christine and her body. But, as the narrative repeatedly underlines in ways which echo the gendered processes of production which this chapter will explore in 'Madame Sourdis', Christine's body is a reflective cypher for that of Claude. Her body, when put into paint, reflects Claude as creator. It is not for nothing that Christine's face is likened to a mirror for she comes to reflect Claude in his entirety: 'elle épousait ses passions, identifiée à ses goûts, défendant sa peinture qui était devenue comme une dépendance d'elle-même'/'she entered into his feelings and passions, identified herself with his tastes, defended his painting which had become, as it were, part of herself' (p. 605). When Claude embraces Christine, 'il la serrait d'une étreinte à la faire sienne, à l'entrer au fond de sa propre chair' [He held her so tightly to make her his own, to amalgamate her flesh into his own] (p. 555; the Vizetelly translation does not translate this sex scene).[25] His love for her is about integration and absorption. Thus, the television adaptation works to depict Christine as Claude's reflective double. It does so via a series of inverted match shots which underline their corporeal symmetry, establishing Christine as Claude's reflective other. In their initial meeting, the two not-yet-lovers are pictured in their separate beds. Their poses mirror each other — Claude facing left and Christine facing right — as the camera cuts between the two shots to have them impossibly face each other, seemingly sharing the same televisual space and bed. The shot not only predicts their liaison which will follow, it is also reinforced by the subsequent symmetrical shots of the characters sleeping, Christine's pose reflecting entirely that of Claude which has already been featured.[26] Christine ratifies Claude, functioning as his reflective double even as he seeks to capture her on canvas.

But if Claude seeks to make himself visible in his translations of reality and Christine in paint, Zola's novel makes clear that the presence which the character gleans for himself is ultimately an impossible one in bodily terms. Zola, very deliberately and visibly, uses the artist's body to translate the creative identities of a whole host of very famous, very recognisable real artists whose bodies in some senses reinforce and materialise Claude as artistic body. They mark him as authentic body. Zola's private statements to friends and colleagues underline the idea that he wished his readers to seek the original bodies behind the fictional translations of real artists he inserted into his novel. In a letter to Jacques Van Santen Kolff on 6 July 1885 he wrote: 'Je me suis mis à mon prochain roman [...]. J'ai repris mon Claude Lantier du *Ventre de Paris*. C'est toute ma jeunesse que je raconte, j'ai mis là tous mes amis, je m'y suis mis moi-même' [I wrote myself into my next novel [...] I used the character Claude from *The Belly of Paris*. I told the complete story of my childhood, I wrote about all my friends, I wrote about myself].²⁷ Zola's preparatory work for the novel reinforces this suggestion. Making notes on the character who will become Claude, he suggests: 'Un Manet, un Cézanne dramatisé; plus près de Cézanne' [A Manet, a Cézanne; closer to Cézanne].²⁸ The part of Fagerolles is envisaged as a fictional translation of the contemporary painter Gervex. Zola anticipates that he will be 'un autre peintre, le Gervex de la chose' [another painter, the Gervex of the piece].²⁹ Zola's paratextual material on the novel links almost all of the characters with a pre-existing and real artistic body. Such translations of real bodies, according to Henri Mitterand, reinforce the realist effect of Zola's novel in general and the body of Claude in particular. He writes that although Claude borrows some traits from Cézanne, Manet, Gill and Monet, 'ce sont des traits destinés à lui donner une vraisemblance extérieure, à charger sa carrière d'épisodes typiques de la vie des peintres' [they are traits designed to make him seem believable, to imbue his life story with events emblematic of the life of a painter].³⁰

However, while the real bodies behind Claude as fictional translation serve to afford him a certain corporeal presence, so too do they diffuse and dilute the very body they fashion for him in their very multiplicity. So numerous are the painterly originals repeatedly cited as the original source behind Claude as translation, that his body as artist becomes inaccessible in its multiple refraction and possibility. Claude is simultaneously all of these bodies and none of them. He becomes a body in and of translation. But the process of translation, Zola makes clear, is refracted via the personality and history of multiple real individuals. Zola's preparatory work for the novel may identify specific characters with existing artistic bodies, but Zola shifts between originals, overlaps names, merges a number of creative bodies to create one fictional translation. Fagerolles, the character he linked with Gervex, subsequently moves to borrow from Maupassant's public persona and body: 'le Gervex devient le Maupassant, très malin, tournant contre la bande, se mettant à part, cajolant les critiques' [The Gervex character becomes more of a Maupassant, turning his back on the group, striking out on his own, courting the critics].³¹ The novelist conceives of the character who would become Bongrand as 'Un Manet très chic, un Flaubert plutôt' [a very chic Manet, more of a Flaubert].³² The attempt to access the materiality of the human sources behind *L'Œuvre* leaves critic and reader alike not with a fixed source materiality but rather a series of overlapping, plural, partial and shifting translated bodies. According to Mitterand, 'il convient [...] d'être prudent dans la recherche des modèles. Car toutes sortes de souvenirs, d'idées, d'inventions, se superposent et se mêlent ici' [we should be wary in our search for source models. Because multiple memories, ideas, created characteristics mix and merge in this process].³³ Niess concurs: 'When he [Zola] did borrow events or details or even personal characteristics from his friends and acquaintances, he so combined, transposed, and modified them that it is almost impossible to recognize any of them surely'.³⁴ Zola's multiplication of the physical, real artistic bodies which Claude partially translates may be interpreted in a variety of ways. It was perhaps an attempt to safeguard himself and his work from reprisals. Monet, to an extent, sees it in this light:

> Vous avez pris soin, avec intention, que pas un seul de vos personnages ne ressemble à l'un de nous, mais malgré cela, j'ai peur que dans la presse et le public, nos ennemis ne prononcent les noms de Manet ou tout au moins les nôtres.[35]
>
> [You have clearly and carefully made sure that none of your characters equates with one of us, but despite this care, I fear that our critics in the press and amongst the public will seek to label your characters as Manet or one of our number.]

It was also, perhaps, as Adolfo Fernandez-Zoïla suggests, a marketing tactic to encourage people to buy and decode his work.[36] Whatever Zola's motivations, his insistent pluralisation of Claude both as a translator and a translation resonates with Venuti's theory, probing the boundary between source text and translator, italicising the plurality of identities at play in the translational act.

Such pluralities are arguably visible in this chapter itself. This monograph makes Zola visible via the process of citation, quoting his text to afford the nineteenth-century writer a physical presence in the body of his text. Yet, Zola's body is not the only one visible in this chapter's citations, which appear both in French and English. Visible in the body of the English citations of *L'Œuvre* in this chapter is the physical presence of translator, Ernest Alfred Vizetelly. Though Vizetelly's *His Masterpiece* is a composite translation (Vizetelly edited and prefaced an earlier translation in a work which is now ascribed to him), it is stamped with the identity of Vizetelly himself. Vizetelly is a key translator of Zola's work as a whole — he covered much of Zola's textual corpus. But he is particularly noteworthy for his physical presence in the translations he published (he charted his actions as a translator in published books and prefaces) and, above all, for his anticipation of and engagement with elements of Venuti's translation theory. Vizetelly, in keeping with Venuti's model, works in some ways to be invisible, driven as he is to make Zola visible in both textual and personal terms in an English context. Vizetelly's preface to *His Masterpiece* frequently focuses on Zola the man. It places Zola's biography in the foreground, engaging the reader to seek the novelist in the translated text which follows:

> The reader may take it from me that everything attributed in the following pages to Pierre Sandoz was done, experienced, felt or said by Emile Zola. In this respect, then *His Masterpiece* is virtually M. Zola's *David Copperfield* — the book into which he has put most of his real life. I may also mention, perhaps, that the long walks on the quays of Paris which in the narrative are attributed to Claude Lantier are really M. Zola's walks; for, in his youth, when he vainly sought employment after failing in his examinations, he was wont, at times of great discouragement, to roam the Paris quays, studying their busy life and their picturesque vistas, whenever he was not poring over the second-hand books set out for sale upon their parapets. From a purely literary standpoint, the pictures of the quays and the Seine to be found in *L'Œuvre* are perhaps the best bits of the book, though it is all of interest, because it is essentially a *livre vécu*, a work really 'lived' by its author.

Vizetelly not only claims to protect the core of Zola's textual body in the numerous English-language translations he produced, he also protected Zola's physical body in literal terms when the novelist fled France and the ramifications of the Dreyfus affair. Vizetelly offered shelter, counsel, aid and sustenance of both the physical and moral variety, writing up his role in Zola's English exile in a publication entitled *With Zola in England*, a publication which he presented precisely as a proxy for Zola's own version of events, a version he felt might soon be in print:

> In a third volume will he be able to deal with his English experiences. The last work can scarcely be ready before the end of 1900, and possibly it may not appear until the following year. And this is one of the reasons which have induced me to offer to all who are interested in the great French writer this present narrative of mine. Should the master's promised record duly appear, my own will sink into oblivion; but if, for one or another reason, M. Zola is prevented from carrying out his plans, here, then, will at least be found some account of one of the most curious passages in his life. And then, perchance, my narrative may attain to the rank of *mémoire pour servir*.[37]

Like Venuti, Vizetelly makes clear that he cannot, in his translation, offer Zola's textual body in its integrity. His translations are, he underlines, adaptations, texts mediated for the target culture whose mores will not allow an integral translation of Zola. This chapter enacts the cultural constraints on Vizetelly's translation by highlighting the gaps in his texts and introducing another translating body — that of Roger Pearson — into the palimpsest of translating voices. The body of Pearson's text offers the sexual descriptions of the female body which Vizetelly was unable to publish.[38] Vizetelly's body is constrained in its translation not just by its era but also, he makes clear, by the subjective frailties and oversights characteristic of any individual translating body.[39] Vizetelly's recognition of his own frailties as a translator are important for they underline his reading of his own acts of translation as hermeneutic exercises. Anticipating Venuti's call, Vizetelly does make himself visible as a translator. His translations are always accompanied by prefaces which detail his translation strategies and his monographs on Zola visibly entwine Vizetelly's biography with that of Zola. If Zola's novels focus on the family tree of the Rougon-Macquart family, Vizetelly's family tree is itself entwined with Zola. His father, Henry Vizetelly, published a range of Zola's novels and was famously imprisoned having been prosecuted for obscene libel after releasing a translation of Zola's *La Terre*. Vizetelly not only reworks some of the translations his father commissioned, he also translates new works. He writes, in his prefaces, of how he came to be Zola's agreed English translator, visibly interlocking Zola's biography with his own.[40] And when Vizetelly translates Zola, he does so because translating Zola allows him to translate himself. Vizetelly's preface to Zola's *Le Ventre de Paris* is revealing in this respect:

> And bred as I was in Paris, a partaker as I have been of her exultations and her woes they have always had for me a strong attraction. My memory goes back to the earlier years of their existence, and I can well remember many of the old surroundings which have now disappeared. I can recollect the last vestiges of the antique *piliers*, built by Francis I, facing the Rue de la Tonnellerie. Paul Niquet's, with its 'bowel-twisting brandy' and its crew of drunken ragpickers, was certainly before my time; but I can readily recall Baratte's and Bordier's

and all the folly and prodigality which raged there; I knew, too, several of the noted thieves' haunts which took the place of Niquet's, and which one was careful never to enter without due precaution. And then, when the German armies were beleaguering Paris, and two millions of people were shut off from the world, I often strolled to the Halles to view their strangely altered aspect. The fish pavilion, of which M. Zola has so much to say, was bare and deserted. The railway drays, laden with the comestible treasures of the ocean, no longer thundered through the covered ways. At the most one found an auction going on in one or another corner, and a few Seine eels or gudgeons fetching wellnigh their weight in gold. Then, in the butter and cheese pavilions, one could only procure some nauseous melted fat, while in the meat department horse and mule and donkey took the place of beef and veal and mutton. Mule and donkey were very scarce, and commanded high prices, but both were of better flavour than horse; mule, indeed, being quite a delicacy. I also well remember a stall at which dog was sold, and, hunger knowing no law, I once purchased, cooked, and ate a couple of canine cutlets which cost me two francs apiece. The flesh was pinky and very tender, yet I would not willingly make such a repast again. However, peace and plenty at last came round once more, the Halles regained their old-time aspect, and in the years which followed I more than once saw the dawn rise slowly over the mounds of cabbages, carrots, leeks, and pumpkins, even as M. Zola describes in the following pages. He has, I think, depicted with remarkable accuracy and artistic skill the many varying effects of colour that are produced as the climbing sun casts its early beams on the giant larder and its masses of food — effects of colour which, to quote a famous saying of the first Napoleon, show that 'the markets of Paris are the Louvre of the people' in more senses than one.[41]

Vizetelly ratifies Zola's translation of contemporary Paris, echoing his tendency to accumulate detail against a broad landscape of historical, political events. But he also translates his own experiences of that Paris, mediating Zola's fictions through his experience and memories. In a prefatory passage notable for the time and space which it devotes to the translator's personal interaction with the subject matter behind Zola's novel's fictional translations, Vizetelly makes himself biographically visible, entwining his creative identity with that of Zola in what are complex, composite bodily translations.

The body of the source author appears, at first glance, more fixed in Zola's short story, 'Madame Sourdis'. The would-be painter, Ferdinand, achieves stellar success precisely because he has a body which is visibly and legibly marked as that of the artist. His body seeks in the art it produces to capture the reality around him. The short story revolves around Ferdinand's body as creative artist, a body which not only drives the narrative but is an object of universal admiration. Adèle and her father cultivate him as a successful painter before so much as seeing one of his canvases, recognising his ilk. When offered Morand's powerful patronage in the adaptation, Ferdinand, bemused, asks 'Mais comment savez-vous que j'ai du talent, je ne vous ai rien montré'/'But how do you know if I have any talent? You haven't seen any of my works'. Morand replies confidently 'mon instinct'/'my instinct'. He gestures, as he speaks, to the painterly body which ensures that Ferdinand stands apart from the rest of the masters at the school: 'on dirait que vous appartenez à un autre monde'/'you look like you belong to a different world'. What Adèle comes to love is not Ferdinand the man, but rather Ferdinand the artistic body. Zola writes: 'Elle aimait Ferdinand pour la couleur d'or de sa barbe, pour sa peau rose, pour le charme et la grâce de toute sa personne'/'She worshipped Ferdinand's golden beard, his pink flesh, the grace and charm of his whole person'.[42] Ferdinand's 'barbe d'or' metaphorises the currency of his painterly body, currency on which he trades and lives. Even when age and excess have ravaged him physically, the currency of his painterly body and golden beard remain:

> Il était très ravagé, le teint jauni, le visage creusé de rides profondes, mais il avait gardé sa barbe d'or, qui pâlissait sans blanchir, et qui le faisait ressembler à quelque dieu vieilli, doré encore du charme de sa jeunesse.
>
> [His sallow face was now fearfully ravaged and deeply lined; but he still had his golden beard, paler but with no trace of grey, so that he looked like some venerable god still possessing the golden charm of youth.] (p. 1151/338)

Adèle, Ferdinand's wife, circulates Ferdinand's artistic body as currency, as the repeated narrative insistence on the gold of his beard underlines. A portrait of Ferdinand as artist is circulated as widely as possible to validate Ferdinand's body as a creative entity: 'on publiait le portrait de Ferdinand, on reproduisait son tableau par tous les procédés et dans tous les formats'/'Ferdinand was being photographed and his painting was being reproduced by every possible process and in every possible format' (p. 1135/321). What matters is not so much Ferdinand's work itself as the body presumed to produce it. Ferdinand's body visibly fits public stereotypes or expectations of what an artist is in Zola's short story: 'Lui, courait les rues, allait Dieu savait où, s'attardait dans les endroits louches, revenait brisé de fatigue et les yeux rougis'/'He was gallivanting about all over the town, God alone knew where, visiting all sorts of shady haunts and coming home dog-tired, with bloodshot eyes' (p.1136/323). Adèle, 'en bourgeoise pleine de légendes sur les désordres nécessaires du génie, [...] finissait par accepter l'inconduite de Ferdinand ainsi que le fumier fatal des grandes œuvres'/'with her conventional middle-class notion of the typical man of genius fated to live a wild bohemian life [...], ended by accepting Ferdinand's conduct as being the dunghill on which alone great works of art could flourish' (p. 1139/325). Ferdinand's body as artist, and the myth that he and his wife unconsciously and consciously weave around it, sell the canvases associated with it.

But the body of Ferdinand as artist, Zola's 'Madame Sourdis' underlines, is a complex, composite thing. Ferdinand has the look of an artist, but no work ethic. So his wife, a would-be painter herself, comes initially to finish the works which he cannot, before subsequently translating his ideas and concepts into canvases entirely of her own making. She paints, anonymously, canvases which bear his signature and are affixed to his highly visible body as artist. Raising questions of gender, questions which are not part of Venuti's focus but loom large in the history of translation, Adèle, despite being an artist in her own right at the start of the short story, is depicted in derivative, reproductive terms. The story's first vision of her painting is a case in point: 'Elle dessinait sous la lampe, s'appliquant à reproduire avec une exactitude mathématique une photographie d'après un Raphaël'/'She had been busy drawing under the lamp, trying to reproduce, with mathematical accuracy, a photograph of a Raphael' (p. 1127/313). She develops her artistry by translating the work of great masters onto new canvases. When asked why she does not send her watercolours to the Salon, her body language and words speak volumes: 'Mais elle eut un haussement d'épaules et dit avec une modestie sincère, gâtée pourtant par une pointe d'amertume: "Oh! De la peinture de femme, ça ne vaut pas la peine"'/'She gave a shrug and said without false modesty, though not without a touch of bitterness: "Oh, it's woman's painting.... It's not worth the trouble you know!"' (p. 1126/312). In her world, female bodies copy art, but they do not create art in and of themselves. When Adèle first looks in the mirror, what she experiences is a material sense of lack: 'Lorsqu'elle se regardait dans une glace, elle avait bien conscience de son infériorité, de sa taille épaisse et de son visage déjà plombé'/'When she looked at herself in the mirror, she was acutely conscious of her inferiority, her dumpy figure and her already fading complexion' (p. 1134/320). Painting for Ferdinand, painting as Ferdinand, she finds a material presence for herself: 'elle se mettait de moitié dans son talent, dans ses victoires, dans cette célébrité qui allait la hausser elle-même au milieu d'une apothéose'/'she was an equal partner in his talent, his success, his celebrity and [...] she would be able to rise to dazzling heights of fame at his side' (p. 1134/320). Rennequin notes to Adèle of Ferdinand's initial painting: 'ça te ressemble [...] C'est toi, avec de la puissance'/'It's a bit like your work [...] Your work, but with more force' (p. 1129/315). Ferdinand's painting allows Adèle to become herself, in a material body which simultaneously is and is not her own: 'Tout ce qu'elle avait rêvé se réalisait, non plus par elle-même, mais par un autre elle-même, qu'elle aimait à la fois en disciple, en mère et en épouse'/'All her dreams were coming true, not now through herself but through another self whom she loved as a disciple, as a mother and as a wife' (p. 1134/320). The measure of materiality which Adèle wrests for herself as she paints under Ferdinand's name, translating his beliefs and persona, does not materially diminish him. Ferdinand's artistic body is initially associated with lack, but Adèle augments and reinforces it. The origins of Ferdinand's physical body are uncertain. The young man 'arrivait de Lille, disait-on'/'was rumoured to have come from Lille' (p. 1124/310). The output of this creative body is also shrouded in mystery as, in his youth and prior to his first success, Ferdinand 's'occupait de peinture avec passion, s'enfermant, donnant toutes ses heures libres à des études qu'il ne montrait pas'/'was an enthusiastic painter and spent all his spare time shut away in his room pursuing his hobby, although he never revealed the results of his work' (p. 1124/310). Ferdinand's body gains materiality and a stronger identity even as Adèle in part supplants it, painting in its place. Zola writes, at the close of Adèle's endeavours, 'le nom de Ferdinand Sourdis ne pouvait plus grandir'/'By now the name of Sourdis could hardly have been more famous' (p. 1149/336). She gives his body power, animation and ratification: 'Ce qu'elle voulait, c'était qu'il signât le tableau de sa personnalité. Et, par des miracles de patience et de volonté, elle lui en donna l'énergie'/'What she wanted was for him to give the picture his own personal touch and, by dint of patience and willpower, she managed to perform the miracle of infusing him with sufficient energy to do it'

(p. 1142/329). The bodily relationship between husband and wife shifts constantly throughout the story. Their bodies simultaneously erase and complete each other in a complex translational relationship in which both find a paradoxical body for themselves. Zola underlines this point in an extended play of textual reflections. Ferdinand starts the short story as a *pion* (someone paid to supervise school children) and Adèle will become his pupil, copying and learning from him like a child. Yet, as she becomes supervisor of his morals and lifestyle, 'Ferdinand se sentit redevenir un enfant. Adèle le dominait de toute sa volonté'/'Ferdinand felt himself reduced to the level of a little boy; he had fallen completely under Adèle's thumb' (p. 1139/325). However, 'quand il travaillait, Adèle [...] redevenait petite à son tour'/'when he was working, Adèle would [...] bring herself down to his level' (p. 1139/326). Husband and wife exchange and swap bodily materiality. At the story's close, Ferdinand paints the watercolours, the 'œuvres de pensionnaire'/'of schoolgirlish subject' which used to occupy Adèle at the story's opening, sitting at the same small table (p. 1155/343). Symmetrically, Adèle paints and sends in Ferdinand's name a pendant work to his earlier *Promenade* [The Walk]. The same students and reading *pion* feature in a canvas entitled *L'Etude* [The Preparation Room]. Adèle paints Ferdinand as *pion* in the painting which simultaneously allows her to paint herself. What Adèle and Ferdinand create are art works which complete them both in different ways. Between them, they create painterly life: 'Et ce fut ainsi qu'il retravailla la toile, qu'il revint sur le travail d'Adèle, en lui donnant les vigueurs de touche et les notes originales qui manquaient. C'était peu de chose et ce fut tout. L'œuvre vivait maintenant'/'In this way he reworked the whole picture, going back over what Adèle had done and adding the vigorous individual touch which it lacked. It might not have seemed much but in fact it was everything: the entire painting had come to life' (p. 1142/329). Zola makes clear in the following use of the grammatically ambiguous construction of possession, 'son' (a word which means 'his' or 'her' in French), that assertions of textual possession in relation to these shared artefacts simply are not possible. Ferdinand enters his studio: 'il éprouva un saisissement, à trouver ainsi Rennequin installé derrière Adèle et la regardant faire son tableau'/'At first he seemed shocked to see Rennequin sitting behind Adèle and watching her at work on his [her] picture' (p. 1147/334). The painting is both Ferdinand's and Adèle's, as is the painterly body both behind and created from it.

Venuti's call for the translator to make him- or herself visible focuses on the translator as a singular, integral, given entity. Zola's 'Madame Sourdis', as has been argued above, probes this notion of singularity and asks questions of where the body of the source author stops and that of the reworking artist begins. It depicts both bodies in mercurial, shifting, multiple terms. The play of source identities and bodies and their translations is, if anything, even more pronounced in the 1979 television adaptation of 'Madame Sourdis'. The television initially asserts the importance of Ferdinand as artistic body and creative source. Dark on screen, his gold beard replaced, the adaptation nevertheless maintains the currency value of Ferdinand as painterly body by insisting: 'tout ce qui porte votre signature vaut de l'or désormais' [anything signed by you is now worth its weight in gold]. His painterly body functions as the guarantor of success. As the canvases purportedly signed by him proliferate, Ferdinand is linked with increasing plenitude. He is surrounded by a range of reflective doubles who, in many ways, reinforce him. The adaptation opens with Rennequin boasting of the success of his canvases as he sells them overseas, predicting the success Ferdinand will enjoy at the adaptation's close as Adèle seals a crate of paintings signed by him before they depart for comparable destinations. Adèle, in stark contrast, finds nothing but absence in the reflective surfaces which she contemplates. This work, which reflects in televisual form Zola's source story, significantly starts with a circular tracking shot, one of many in this adaptation, moving from Adèle's reflection in a mirror to the source of that reflection, Adèle's body painting at a canvas. As it moves, the circular shot takes in a series of copies and originals, a range of paintings and the sources from which they are derived. What this circular tracking shot promises is a return to a point of origin, an ontological and material source. But the body at the source of its reflections, that of Adèle, is, as per Zola's short story, insistently associated with absence and lack. When finally the camera reaches Adèle's body, it is depicted copying the work of Raphael, replicating the identity of a painter Adèle clearly is not. As if to reinforce this point, Adèle's paintings, in the initial stages of the adaptation, are repeatedly obfuscated and blocked from the viewer's gaze. We see her paint but are gifted only morsels of those paintings. Ferdinand paints his first masterpiece from nature, deliberately absenting Adèle from it. It is a scene in which he sits with his pupils, a scene through which Adèle walks. Yet when he reproduces the moment in paint, Adèle is corporeally excised from it. Ferdinand inserts instead the local woman reconfigured as a classical nude in an otherwise realist scene. When point-of-view shots are offered from Adèle's perspective, they are consistently barred and blocked. She speaks through the slats and bars of the window to Rennequin, the painter who lives in the art world she can never truly access under her own aegis. Once she has entered that world, via her marriage to Ferdinand, it still remains blocked to her personally and creatively. Barred shots again speak her experience. She watches Ferdinand leave their home through the bars of the conservatory, pointing out that it does nothing for painters to be seen in public with their wife.

In this television adaptation, Adèle negotiates a complex creative body and currency for herself by translating the concepts and signature of her husband. Her love for her husband Ferdinand is predicated precisely on the painterly body she fashions for herself via him. She tells the sleeping, incapacitated painter: 'Je t'aime Ferdinand. Je t'aime parce que tu es beau, parce que tu es célèbre. Tu as tout ce que je n'ai pas et c'est pour cela que je t'aime' [I love you Ferdinand. I love you because you are handsome and because you are famous. You have everything which I do not and it is for that reason that I love you]. Ferdinand, for the adaptation, is a blank canvas upon whom Adèle may paint something of herself. It is far from insignificant that in one of his first interactions with the Morand family, the adaptation offers a point-of-view shot from Ferdinand's perspective of a blank canvas, framed by his hands, in a shot in which he does not otherwise feature, his identity cropped. Having contemplated Ferdinand's *Promenade*, Adèle rubs her finger on the red paint of her palette, smoothing it on to her lips in a manner symbolic of her desire for Ferdinand and of the shape and colour she can give herself as painterly body from him. When Adèle copies Ferdinand's painting, the painting in which he deliberately omits her, she dissects and learns from it. Significantly, though, she reinserts herself into the canvas, painting a female figure, clothed this time, who resembles her. She wrests a physical space for herself on the canvas. In Zola's story the marital, painterly relationship is collaborative and largely conducive. Adèle does not seek to supplant Ferdinand: 'elle disait toujours "Ferdinand a fait ceci, Ferdinand va faire cela" lors même que Ferdinand n'avait pas donné et ne devait pas donner un seul coup de pinceau'/'She would always say "Ferdinand did this, Ferdinand's going to do that", even when he had not provided nor would be providing a single brushstroke' (p. 1150/337). And Ferdinand feels no sense of painterly loss to his artistic body: 'Il ne souffrait pas de sa déchéance. Il disait également "mon tableau, mon œuvre" sans songer combien peu il travaillait aux toiles qu'il signait'/'His moral decay did not cause him to suffer excessively; he, too, would speak of "my picture", "my work", without thinking how little of his work had gone into the pictures he was signing with his name' (p. 1150/337). However, in stark contrast to Zola's story, questions of creative bodies are significantly more charged in the television adaptation. Ferdinand's anxiety at his wife's supplanting of him is manifest. He cannot go to the exhibition to hear critics acclaim the work signed by him which he has not created, works which, in the privacy of their own home, his wife acknowledges as her own. She describes one painting to him thus: 'C'est quand je t'ai peint dans ton fauteuil' [It was when I painted you seated in your chair]. And Ferdinand is cognisant of his own bodily loss in the encounter. In a statement doubly resonant in a work of adaptation, Ferdinand states when looking at Adèle's first reproduction of his initial masterpiece: 'C'est troublant de se voir ainsi reproduit. C'est moi et ce n'est pas moi' [It's hard to see yourself reproduced like that. It's me and it's not me]. If Ferdinand feels a sense of corporeal loss from the first of Adèle's reproductions, this loss is almost complete by the adaptation's close when Adèle paints entirely in his stead, acknowledging her works as her own. In yet another act of bodily reflection and displacement which entails still more personal diminution, Ferdinand rails at God in the closing words of the programme: 'Vous nous avez créé à votre image, c'est que vous êtes petit, bien petit' [You made us in your image which shows how small, how very small you are].

Ferdinand's identity is annulled in the adaptation in a way it was not in the source text. But neither is the creative body of Adèle any less problematic. The adaptation repeatedly depicts it as essentially derivative in nature. Rennequin walks in on her painting work already signed by her husband, discovering the truth of her authoring the paintings which her husband passes off as his own. They argue over what her identity really is. In words which deny her very existence, Adèle stammers: 'moi, je ne suis...' [I am not/I am just...], the incomplete sentence, the negative and the grammatical ellipsis pointing to the void at the heart of her creative body. Rennequin emphasises that lack by completing her sentence 'qu'un faussaire' [You are nothing more than a forger] even as she weakly replies in a comeback still devoid of her own identity 'que sa femme' [I am just his wife]. Both potential closes to the sentence diminish her as a physical and creative body, hinging as they do on the 'que' [just]. As if to underline the absence that is the body of both Ferdinand and Adèle, Rennequin contemplates the painting created by both of them, before taking a brush dipped in red, to bar it with a large cross. In Zola's 'Madame Sourdis' Adèle and Ferdinand fashion creative, complementary bodies for themselves in their translational relationship; in the 1979 adaptation, a piece far more anxious about creative ownership and ontology than its source text, the bodies of both are marked by a fundamental absence. Venuti, as this chapter has suggested, may urge the translator to make him- or herself visible, but 'Madame Sourdis' and *Madame Sourdis* underline how difficult it may be to delineate between creative identities in the processes of translation and mediation.

If anything, the creative bodies circulating in the television adaptation are visibly more shifting, multiple and collective than those in Zola's source text. The adaptation opens with a screen which proclaims '*Madame Sourdis*. D'Après le roman d'Emile Zola' [*Madame Sourdis*. Based on the Zola story]. The television series immediately proclaims itself as an adaptation and affixes textual ownership of the adaptation's source to Zola. Yet this source text is one which denies the very possibility of singular textual ownership. The telefilm's direction is undertaken by Caroline Huppert, a director who underlines the creative identity she fashioned for herself from the experience. While biographical readings of texts are not without their problems, Huppert implicitly positions her telefilm to be read in such terms. Huppert, in what was her first telefilm undertaken at the age of twenty-eight, uses Zola's name and adapts his words to find a televisual identity for herself in a series of works about women empowering themselves. As Adèle nurtures and ultimately realises the creative dreams which she has repressed and silenced, Huppert states: 'Faire un film, c'était un rêve secret, que je n'osais pas m'avouer tant cela semblait improbable' [Making a film was a secret dream of mine, a dream I dared not utter out loud, so unlikely an outcome did it seem].[43] Zola's creative body enables Huppert to fashion an adaptive creative product. In keeping with Zola's short story, the adaptation and dialogue stem from a collaboration between Huppert herself and her then husband Laurent Heynemann. Not only does their marital collaboration echo something of Zola's source text, but Heynemann's more recent work on the highly successful *Chez Maupassant* series underlines his predilection for tales in which textual and personal ownership shifts and is shared in complex collaborative arrangements. Heynemann's *L'Héritage* [The Inheritance] (2007), in the first series of *Chez Maupassant*, depicts a man passing off another's child as proof of the potency of his own incapable body. The child, who is not of his loins, allows him to trigger an inheritance enabling him to reinforce his incapable physical body in social and material terms. Heynemann's *Ce cochon de Morin* [That Pig Morin] (2008) in the same collection contemplates the shifting bodies of friends superseding each other in relation to the same woman. Morin steals a kiss from an unwilling girl on a train and is saved from legal proceedings only by his friend's more expert kissing of her in the same situation. The more successful kiss leads to seduction and the girl's silence on Morin. And the bodies translating and translated into *Madame Sourdis* are not just those of the source author and his director and screenwriter. Pierre Clémenti, the actor who plays the part of the dissolute artist Ferdinand, was chosen by Huppert precisely because the role translated, in television, the life for which his body in reality was known. Huppert states:

> Et le rôle du mari, le peintre génial mais alcoolique et débauché, je l'ai proposé à Pierre Clémenti, qui était très connu, hélas pas forcément pour des bonnes raisons, la drogue, la prison... A cause de ça, sa carrière était dans le creux de la vague.[44]
>
> [I offered the role of the husband, the engaging but debauched, alcoholic painter to Pierre Clémenti who was, sadly and for the wrong reasons — drugs and prison — very well known... His career was in the doldrums precisely for those reasons.]

Clémenti's body and reputation as an actor translated the character Huppert sought to create, in some senses blurring the delineation between character and actor. In the 1979 *Madame Sourdis* adaptation, Zola's words about the mediated, collaborative nature of authorship are themselves mediated by the translating bodies and influences of Huppert and Heynemann, their creative staff and their cast of actors.

And yet more creative bodies circulate in *Madame Sourdis* as the television adaptation visibly adapts the canonical works, techniques and bodies of core Impressionist painters. Ferdinand's first painting has much of Manet's *Déjeuner sur l'herbe* (1862–63) about it, with its dressed *pion* and undressed classical nude in a sheltered country location. The adaptation might also be seen ekphrastically to reproduce Degas's 1876 *Dans un café* (*L'Absinthe*). Disgruntled and undone by his wife's progressive replacement of his own artistic body with her own, a bearded, dark Ferdinand, a man as known for his bohemian personality as the painting's original masculine figure, painter Marcellin Deboutin, orders an absinthe in a local café. The adaptation offers a static shot whose pose, colours, content and despondency echo those of Degas's canvas. But it does so playfully, excising the female body in the picture. Adèle at that very moment paints at home, her brushstrokes excising the corporeality of the artist upon whom we gaze. Clearly positioned as an Impressionist painter, Adèle is placed in outdoor scenes whose subject matter and composition (sunsets, water scenes, shifting foliage in different lights) serve as an entirely appropriate backdrop to the debates Rennequin and Adèle have on Impressionism itself. The adaptation, though, is able, in experimental aesthetic terms, to embody some of the Impressionist techniques its eponymous heroine espouses, compensating for elements of the source text which it has cropped. Thus, Adèle walks home at sunset in a sequence disconcertingly flooded in blue as the environmental conditions and play of light alter the innate colour of the objects on and around her body. Impressionism was repeatedly criticised for the 'bleuissement' [pervasive blueness] of its canvases and significantly the 1967 adaptation of *L'Œuvre* also draws on this technique, substituting the conventional fade-to-black scene transition with a more disconcerting fade to blue in the closing scenes of the piece as Christine pushes Claude to slander his painting. *L'Œuvre*, as this chapter has suggested, is, as a piece of television, interested in the liquefying play of light on objects. A glaring, painful shot up at the sun eating into the outlines and materiality of the sky and its foliage is immediately followed with a reverse vertical shot exploring the play of the same light on the water below, the shots' reflective verticality confining the lovers even in this rare moment of apparently open-air freedom. *Madame Sourdis* though, in its televisual form, is more interested in other Impressionist techniques. Impressionist *décentrage* makes an appearance in the jarring scene transition to the sequence where Ferdinand, initially unrecognisable, lies below the camera, facing away, his body partially cropped, downing a bottle of alcohol in a raucous party game. The adaptation reproduces in televisual form not just some of the techniques of Impressionism but also some of its most famous canvases and creative bodies. 'Madame Sourdis' and *Madame Sourdis* thus collectively probe the porous boundary between the source author and re-creative artist, asking where one stops and the other begins, multiplying the creative bodies at play in the re-creative process.

Venuti's value to Adaptation Studies is clear. He pushes for a closer relationship between the theoretical bodies of thought supporting both Translation and Adaptation Studies and he places the physical body of the re-creative artist at the core of the processes in both disciplines. His underlining of both translation and adaptation as hermeneutic actions undermines the persistent logic of the fidelity criticism which Adaptation Studies has struggled with in various ways. Adaptations cannot easily and unproblematically be written off as an inferior copy of their superior canonical source if they are approached as subjective interpretations created by people for people. Venuti's call for translators to become visible in the works they mediate and create has particular purchase in the sphere of adaptation as a consequence precisely because, when enacted in the adaptive medium, it pushes the adaptation to be evaluated as an interpretative, personal artefact and not as the original itself. If Venuti's approach has core purchase across Adaptation Studies, it has specific resonance in relation to the case study texts of this chapter in both their literary and televisual forms. While the television adaptations of 'Madame Sourdis' and *L'Œuvre* both initially seem to obfuscate their acts of adaptation, placing Zola's text in the foreground as creative body, both anticipate Venuti's call to make their acts of recreation visible. They italicise the machinery of the adaptive process, underscoring that what they can offer of the source body of Zola's text is partial, remediated and refracted via the prism of their own creative personality. They make visible the negotiation between the body of the source text and that of the translating adaptive medium in complex works which ask useful questions of Venuti's theoretical approaches. Collectively, Zola's 'Madame Sourdis' and *L'Œuvre*, when read in conjunction with their television adaptations, probe the porous boundary between source author and translator/textual mediator, asking where one stops and the other begins. They embrace a vision of textual production and mediation which introduces an intriguing plurality into Venuti's largely binaristic call for the translator to make his or her body visible in relation to that of his or her source. What this chapter's case studies underline and make visible is the shifting, porous, overlapping, compelling re-creative bodies from whose complex interactions art is created.

Notes to Chapter 2

1. Zola, *Ecrits sur l'art*, p. 313.
2. Both adaptations are available via the Centre du consultation, Inathèque, Bibliothèque nationale de France, <http://www.inatheque.fr/consultation/centres-de-consultation-paris.html> [accessed 3 November 2019].
3. Venuti, *Translation Changes Everything*, p. 179.
4. Ibid.
5. Venuti, *The Translator's Invisibility*, p. 1.
6. Ibid., p. 7.
7. Venuti, *Translation Changes Everything*, p. 34.
8. The history of translation underlines that Venuti is the latest in a long line of theorists and translators who have sought to pin down the position of the translating body in relation to the body of the source text or source author. Writing in the seventeenth century of his translation of Virgil's *Aeneid* (1697), English poet and translator John Dryden explicitly sought to position his translating body as close to that of the source author as possible: 'I thought fit to steer betwixt the two extremes of paraphrase and literal translation; to keep as near my author as I could, without losing all his graces, the most eminent of which are the beauty of his words' (cited in *Theories of Translation: A Collection of Essays from Dryden to Derrida*, ed. by Rainer Schulte and John Biguenet (Chicago: Chicago University Press, 1992), p. 174). Dryden, though, makes clear that the source author's body must speak to the era of the translator: 'I have endeavoured to make Virgil speak such English as he would himself have spoken, if he had been born in England, and in this present age' (cited in Susan Bassnett, *Translation Studies* (London: Routledge, 2002), p. 64). Alexander Fraser Tytler, author of the first systematic study in English of the translation process, *The Principles of Translation* (1791), is both comparably corporeal and strikingly similar in his conclusions, despite being fundamentally opposed to aspects of Dryden's work. He argues that translation must resuscitate the author in a new language and context and that the translator's body must 'adopt the very soul of his author, which must speak through his own organs' (cited in Bassnett, *Translation Studies*, p. 67). Comparably, Edward Fitzgerald, the nineteenth-century translator best known for his version of *The Rubaiyat of Omar Khayyam* (1858), justified the great liberties he took with his Persian source, the 'improvements' he claimed to have made to what he saw as a comparatively lowly source, in corporeal terms. He declared that a text must live at all costs 'with a transfusion of one's own worst life if one can't retain the original's better' (cited in Bassnett, *Translation Studies*, p. 73). Bodies, and more specifically the relationship of that of the source text or author with that of the translator, have driven key moments of translation theory and history as translators assess the complex personal presence they glean from their attempts to convey the body of their source.
9. Ernest Alfred Vizetelly, 'Preface', in Emile Zola, *His Masterpiece*, trans. by Ernest Alfred Vizelly, Project Gutenberg ebook, <http://www.gutenberg.org/files/15900/15900.txt> [accessed 7 September 2017].
10. Emile Zola, *L'Œuvre*, in *Œuvres completes*, ed. by Henri Mitterand, 15 vols, (Paris: Cercle du Livre Précieux, 1966–69), v, 423–747 (p. 452); *His Masterpiece*, trans. by Vizetelly (no pagination; all further quotations from this translation therefore without a page reference).
11. Tamara Chaplin, *Turning on the Mind: French Philosophers on Television* (Chicago: University of Chicago Press, 2007), p. 44.
12. Venuti, *Translation Changes Everything*, p. 34.
13. Cardinal's cropping here offers a teasing and inverted intertextual allusion to the famously cropped feet of the trapeze artist in the top right-hand corner of Manet's canonical *Bar aux Folies-Bergère* (1882).
14. Venuti, *Translation Changes Everything*, p. 37.
15. Zola, *Ecrits sur l'art*, p. 147.
16. Ibid., p. 81.
17. Lawrence Venuti, 'Genealogies of Translation Theory: Jerome', *Boundary 2*, 37.3 (2010), 5–28 (pp. 6–7).

18. Zola, *Ecrits sur l'art*, p. 313.
19. Cited in Lecomte-Hilmy, 'L'Artiste de tempérament chez Zola et devant le public', p. 87.
20. Susan Harrow, *Zola, The Body Modern: Pressures and Prospects of Representation* (Oxford: Legenda, 2010), p. 14.
21. For a discussion of this quotation, see Harrow, *Zola, The Body Modern*, p. 73 (Harrow's translation).
22. The square brackets indicate my translation of the section relating to blood which the Vizetelly translation omits.
23. Roger Pearson translates the passage the Vizetelly translation omits thus: 'That's the part that's always thrilled me more than all the rest, the belly. The very sight of one makes me want to do impossible things. It's so lovely to paint, like a sun!', Emile Zola, *The Masterpiece*, trans. by Roger Pearson (Oxford: Oxford University Press, 1993), p. 236.
24. Emile Zola, 'Le Moment artistique', *L'Evénement*, 4 May 1866.
25. Pearson's translation translates the section the Vizetelly translation omits thus: 'Christine gave herself up to him entirely, and he possessed her entirely, from her throat to the tips of her toes, holding her in an embrace so close as to make her flesh melt into his own', Zola, *The Masterpiece*, trans. by Pearson, p. 140.
26. Christine is not alone in her reflective doubling of the male artist. Sandoz's relationship with his wife Henriette works in a similarly symmetrical way. Henriette's actions mirror those of her husband. Thus at their dinner party, 'Henriette [...] disparut; et l'on entendit le bruit léger de ses pas au premier étage: depuis le mariage, c'était elle qui soignait la vieille mère infirme, s'absentant ainsi à plusieurs reprises dans la soirée, comme le fils autrefois'/'Henriette [...] disappeared; and her light footfall was heard on the first floor. Since her marriage it was she who tended the old, infirm mother, absenting herself in this fashion several times during the evening, just as the son had done formerly' (p. 595). Zola continues, underlining Henriette's reflective parity of the creative body of her husband, 'Henriette reparut, et les yeux de Sandoz ayant cherché les siens, elle lui répondit d'un regard, elle eut ce sourire tendre et discret, qu'il avait lui-même jadis, quand il sortait de la chambre de sa mère'/'Henriette came back, and Sandoz's eyes having sought hers, she answered him with a glance and the same affectionate, quiet smile that he had shown when leaving his mother's room in former times' (p. 595).
27. Emile Zola, *Correspondance*, ed. by B. H. Bakker, 10 vols (Montreal: Les Presses de l'Université de Montréal; Paris: CNRS, 1978–95), v, 278–79.
28. Emile Zola, *Les Rougon-Macquart*, ed. by Henri Mitterand, 5 vols (Paris: Gallimard 1960–67), IV, 1354.
29. Ibid., p. 1355.
30. Mitterand cited in Zola, *L'Œuvre*, p. 427. A variety of critics have produced an insightful range of work affixing elements of Claude's life and flesh, as well as that of the artists around him, to real, historical creative bodies. They seek the original bodies behind Zola's fictional translations. Robert J. Niess's work, *Zola, Cézanne and Manet: A Study of L'Œuvre* (Ann Arbor: University of Michigan Press, 1968), states its intent to 'attempt to measure with some exactness the scope of the biographical elements of the book and to assay its "real life" content' (p. 26). Another attempt to access the materiality of these real artistic bodies is made in Brady's appropriately titled *L'Œuvre d'Emile Zola*. For Pierre Daix, Cézanne and Manet are the real bodies Claude most visibly translates: 'Zola a accouplé, ravaudé, rapetassé des morceaux de Manet et des morceaux de Cézanne qui détonnent abominablement' [Zola brought together, stitched together, took small parts of Manet and Cezanne in a horribly clashing way] (Pierre Daix, 'Introduction', in Zola, *L'Œuvre*, p. 425). The notice to this edition of the novel goes further, ascribing material moments and traits in these artists' life to Claude as creative body: 'Claude Lantier [...] doit un peu de son portrait physique, de sa timidité maladroite, de son intransigeance, de ses brusques décisions à Cézanne. Mais plusieurs épisodes de sa carrière rappellent Edouard Manet (son passage dans l'atelier de Berthou — Thomas Couture — l'envoi de "Plein air" au Salon des Refusés [...]), Claude Monet (son séjour à Bennecourt), André Gill (sa déception devant le sort qui a été réservé à sa toile, au dernier Salon), et même l'écrivain Duranty (pour la scène finale de l'enterrement)' [Claude Lantier owes some of his appearance, of his awkward shyness,

of his intransigence, of his brusque decisions to Cézanne. But several points in his life are reminiscent of that of Edouard Manet (his time in the atelier Berthou — Thomas Couture — the presentation of the painting Plein Air at the Salon des Refusés [...]), others are reminiscent of Claude Monet (the time spent in Bennecourt), others of André Gill (his disappointment at the treatment of his canvas at the final salon) and even of Duranty (the closing scene at the funeral)] (ibid., p. 739). Nor is the urge to assign real bodies to the characters of the novel new. Paul Alexis read the novel and wrote: 'Et Flaubert, et Cézanne, et moi, et nous tous! *Notre* jeunesse à tous est dans ce livre' [And what of Flaubert, and Cezanne and of me? All of us in fact! Our young lives are all in this book] (cited in Zola, *Œuvres complètes*, ed. by Mitterand, v, 1385–86). From the novel's publication, a whole host of real creative identities have been proposed as the artistic bodies behind Zola's translational fiction. For more on this reading of Zola's translation of real artistic bodies, see Griffiths, *Zola and the Art of Adaptation*, pp. 37–57.
31. Cited in Zola, *L'Œuvre*, p. 1359.
32. Ibid., p. 1358.
33. Ibid., p. 1353.
34. Niess, *Zola, Cézanne and Manet*, p. 61.
35. Claude Monet, letter to Zola cited in Zola, *Les Rougon-Macquart*, ed. by Mitterand, IV, 1387.
36. Adolfo Fernandez-Zoïla, 'Le Système écriture-peinture et le figural dans *L'Œuvre*', *Cahiers naturalistes*, 66 (1992), 91–103 (p. 92).
37. Ernest Alfred Vizetelly, *With Zola in England*, <http://onlinebooks.library.upenn.edu/webbin/book/lookupname?key=Vizetelly%2C%20Ernest%20Alfred%2C%201853–1922> [accessed 5 September 2017].
38. For an intriguing reading on the reception of Zola in England in the late nineteenth century and the unexpected reasons for altering his texts in translation, see Anthony Cummins, 'Emile Zola's Cheap English Dress: The Vizetelly Translations, Late-Victorian Print Culture, and the Crisis of Literary Value', *Review of English Studies*, 60 (2009), 108–32. Cummins argues that Vizetelly's father deliberately promoted the scandalous nature of Zola's texts, promising uncut access to them, even while cutting elements of them. The subsequent prosecution and imprisonment of Vizetelly the elder for crimes against morality was, Cummins argues, driven by concerns about mass literacy. The extension of reading skills amongst the poor following educational reform meant that the wrong people would be reading Zola. Zola, in the hands of the newly educated masses, was pornographic. Yet he circulated, Cummins points out, in his French original form in England entirely unproblematically. For in the hands of the educated, in the hands of those with a reading knowledge of French, he became cultural — the reading equivalent of a grand tour. That Vizetelly junior felt himself constrained in his translations by the culture for which he was translating is clear from his reticence in translating *Fécondité*. He writes in his preface, 'Moreover, absolute freedom of speech exists in France, which is not the case elsewhere. Thus, when I first perused the original proofs of M. Zola's work, I came to the conclusion that any version of it in the English language would be well-nigh impossible' (Vizetelly, preface to *Fecundity*, <http://www.gutenberg.org/files/10330/10330-h/10330-h.htm#link2H_4_0001> [accessed 13 September 2018]).
39. In his preface to *Rome*, for example, he writes: 'At present then I only desire to say, that in spite of the great labour which I have bestowed on this translation, I am sensible of its shortcomings, and in a work of such length, such intricacy, and such a wide range of subject, it will not be surprising if some slips are discovered. Any errors which may be pointed out to me, however, shall be rectified in subsequent editions' (Vizetelly, preface to *Rome*, <https://www.gutenberg.org/files/8726/8726-h/8726-h.htm#link2H_PREF> [accessed 13 September 2018]).
40. 'But, of course, both Rougon and Macquart are genuine French names and not inventions. Indeed, several years ago I came by chance upon them both, in an old French deed which I was examining at the Bibliothèque Nationale in Paris. I there found mention of a Rougon family and a Macquart family dwelling virtually side by side in the same village. This, however, was in Champagne, not in Provence. Both families farmed vineyards for a once famous abbey in the vicinity of Epernay, early in the seventeenth century. To me, personally, this trivial discovery meant a great deal. It somehow aroused my interest in M. Zola and his works. Of the latter I

had then only glanced through two or three volumes. With M. Zola himself I was absolutely unacquainted. However, I took the liberty to inform him of my little discovery; and afterwards I read all the books that he had published. Now, as it is fairly well known, I have given the greater part of my time, for several years past, to the task of familiarising English readers with his writings. An old deed, a chance glance, followed by the great friendship of my life and years of patient labour' (Vizetelly, preface to *The Fortune of the Rougons*, <https://www.gutenberg.org/files/5135/5135-h/5135-h.htm#link2H_INTR> [accessed 13 September 2018]).

41. Vizetelly, preface to *The Fat and the Thin*, <https://www.gutenberg.org/files/5744/5744-h/5744-h.htm#link2H_INTR> [accessed 13 September 2018].
42. Emile Zola, 'Madame Sourdis', in *Contes et nouvelles* (Paris: Gallimard, 1976), pp. 1124–56 (p. 1134); *The Attack on the Mill*, trans. by Douglas Parmée (Oxford: Oxford University Press, 1984), pp. 310–43) (p. 320).
43. Domininque Attal and Dominique Baron, 'Entretien avec Caroline Huppert', <www.groupe25images.fr/up/files/gazette/LC32CHUPPERT.pdf> [accessed November 2014].
44. Ibid.

CHAPTER 3

❖

Interpersonal Transactions: Zola, Nord and *L'Argent*

Having looked, in Chapter One, at the audience as body and, in Chapter Two, at the body of the translator/adaptor, this current chapter works to pluralise its vision of the creative bodies at play in the adaptive process. Taking Zola's 1890 novel *L'Argent* and its adaptation at the hands of director Jacques Rouffio and others for Antenne 2 in 1988, it evaluates the utility of translation theorist Christiane Nord in the sphere of Adaptation Studies.[1] Nord's concept of translation as an interpersonal rather than an intertextual process has powerful implications for both the study and reception of adaptations as creative artefacts.[2] Instead of pushing us to seek the source in the re-creative work as the sole marker of quality, Nord instead leads us to contemplate the people, both hidden and visible, whose creative identities shape the artistic process in myriad ways. Nord's translation theories have particular purchase when applied to Zola's *L'Argent*, and its subsequent reinterpretations for both the novel and its adaptation probe the interpersonal networks via which art is created. *L'Argent*, though, in its translated and adapted forms, does not just underscore the utility of Nord's theories to Adaptation Studies. It also permits us to evaluate them, probing their fault lines. In the play of personal influences and multiple identities that shape the linguistic and cultural transformation of texts, Nord suggests that the translator serve as mediator, ethically and loyally managing his or her responsibility to each of the people involved in the translation process. Zola's *L'Argent* and, to an extent, the translations and adaptations of it, unpick the challenges of said mediation as enunciated by Nord. Collectively Zola, Antenne 2's adaptation and Nord underline the creative yet complex interpersonal transactions from which art, be it translated or adapted, is born.

Nord's vision of translation as interpersonal process carried out by people for people needs some introduction, absent as Nord is from the sphere of Adaptation Studies. Adaptation Studies, like Translation Studies, has long had a residual fascination with 'fidelity' as swathes of critics ask how a target text can best engage with or replicate the style and content of its source text. Fidelity, though, for Nord is a reductive concept, limited and ultimately unhelpful in its focus on text-to-text relations, for it ignores the role played by people in these processes of textual transit and transformation. In place of the text-to-text approach of fidelity, Nord proposes an interpersonal vision of translation. Nord, like Ernst-August Gutt —

the theorist around whom Chapter One revolved — is a Functionalist translation theorist. She conceptualises translation as a communicative process which, aimed as it is at a target audience, needs, above all, to meet the needs of that audience. However, if the audience is king for Gutt, Nord is clear that there are multiple other creative personalities at play in the translational interaction, personalities who shape the matter of the translation and whose needs must also be met: the text initiator/commissioner, the source author, the translator, as well as the target text user, to mention but a few. The translator, for Nord, serves as the nexus between all these individuals and is duty bound to mediate and be loyal to their various needs. Designating her theory under the word 'loyalty', Nord writes:

> As an interpersonal category referring to a social relationship between individuals who expect not to be betrayed in the process, loyalty may replace the traditional intertextual relationship of 'fidelity', a concept that usually refers to a linguistic or stylistic similarity between the source and the target texts, regardless of the communicative intentions and/or expectations involved.[3]

For Nord it is the translator who mediates the 'social relationship between individuals' that is translation, serving as a powerbroker.[4] Nord is under no illusion that this interpersonal mediation is an easy thing, but it is, she argues, something necessary to attempt. The value of Nord's theory to Adaptation Studies is threefold. First, it italicises the complex web of intersecting creative influences and people from which adaptations spring. It situates adaptations as communal creative artefacts in which authorship is a complex personal negotiation. Second, by foregrounding the personal, it clearly casts adaptations as subjective artefacts, allowing them to be read as hermeneutic pieces, rather than being assessed as absolute copies of an earlier source. Indeed, Nord urges translators to make clear their personal strategies in their published translations by means of prefaces and the like, in order that translators only be judged according to those personal strategies and intents. Third, Nord's vision of adaptations as subjective, hermeneutic pieces implicitly recognises that there are as many different translations and ways to translate as there are translators, and that the way a translator chooses to translate is defined by his or her time and context. For Nord, people in different eras and nations or culture groups drive the translational process and are key to any understanding of it.

Zola's *L'Argent* initially appears to run counter to Nord's interpersonal vision, focusing on events rather than people. It works to adapt near-contemporary economic reality in the form of the Krach of the Union Générale in 1882. It recounts the stratospheric rise of its hero Aristide Saccard via the company he forms to extract wealth from overseas territories in exchange for the offer of infrastructure. Saccard builds his company on fraudulent stock market speculation, reaching stratospheric heights before crashing spectacularly on the stock exchange. In its paratextual material, the Cercle du Livre Précieux edition of the novel inserts periodic photographs of newspaper articles on events leading up to and following the crash of the Union Générale.[5] In so doing it positions Zola's text as the fictional reworking of this financial maelstrom. Numerous critics have worked to assess the fidelity of Zola's financial translation in technical terms, seeking the source, the money, behind it. Philippe Gille writes, for example, 'les chiffres me paraissent les mêmes' [the financial figures seem to me to be the same].[6] Figures, though, in this novel, lie. The 'actions' issued by the Banque Universelle are a case in point. There is no core, static, real money or substance behind them. Instead, Zola's novel dramatises the ways in which substance and value are created for them in the interpersonal fictive financial transactions through which Saccard, Zola's fictional financier, leads them. They are sold and resold using a series of *prête-noms*, acquiring a vast value which ultimately has no basis in reality or substance behind it. Zola writes in relation to the bank of 'le surchauffement mensonger de toute la machine, au milieu des souscriptions fictives, des actions gardées par la société pour faire croire au versement integral'/'the deceptive overheating of the machine, the fictitious subscription of shares and their retention by the Bank, in order to make people believe that they had really been taken up' (p. 531/198).[7] Claiming, at his financial apogee, to have grasped the wealth in its materiality, Saccard uses the metaphor of gold:

> Enfin, comme il s'y efforçait depuis tant d'années, il la possédait donc, la fortune, en esclave, ainsi qu'une chose à soi, dont on dispose, qu'on tient sous clé, vivante, matérielle! Tant de fois le mensonge avait habité ses caisses, tant de millions y avaient coulé, fuyant par toutes sortes de trous inconnus! Non, ce n'était plus la richesse menteuse de la façade, c'était la vraie royauté de l'or, solide.

> [At last, as had been his endeavour for so many years, he had made fortune a slave, a thing of his own, a thing one can dispose of, keep under lock and key, alive and real. So many times had falsehood dwelt in his coffers, so many millions had flowed through them, escaping by all sorts of unknown holes! But this was no longer the deceptive splendour of the façade; it was real sovereignty substantially based upon full sacks of gold.] (pp. 540–41/208–09)

But he fails to understand his own metaphor, to realise that gold's value is only ever metaphorical, predicated as it is on circulation and exchange between people. Saccard may talk of solidity and materiality in relation to gold but its one physical presence in the novel, in the form of the smelter Kolb's gold ingots, underscores such solidity and materiality as an impossibility. Kolb's gold is not static, cannot be static if it is to have value. Hence the novel focuses on it in an endless state of transition as Kolb melts down currency to form ingots which subsequently return to him as currency for the process to start afresh. Zola writes in liquid, ungraspable terms of:

> Ce ruissellement d'or, du matin au soir, d'un bout de l'année à l'autre, au fond de cette cave, où l'or venait en pièces monnayées, d'où il partait en lingots, pour revenir en pièces et repartir en lingots, indéfiniment, dans l'unique but de laisser aux mains du trafiquant quelques parcelles d'or.

> [This streaming of gold, from morning till night, from year's end to year's end, in the depths of that cellar, whither the gold came in coins, and whence it went away in ingots, to come back again in coins and go away again in ingots indefinitely, with the sole object of leaving in the trader's hands a few particles of the precious metal.] (p. 418/86)

Zola's novel, then, underlines that the quest for an origin in financial terms is a fruitless one, for money, the novel makes clear, may never truly be accessed as a static point of origin or source. It is, as an artefact, markedly missing from the novel so obsessed by it, existing only as a symbolic value whose meaning is accreted by means of ceaseless circulation or transaction between people.

In *L'Argent*, though, Zola adapts not just the money and events of the Krach, but, in a manner which maps onto Nord's interpersonal approach, the people behind it. Having tantalised his reader with endless character conversations about Prussian statesman Otto von Bismarck (1815–98) in *Nana*, Zola finally introduces him in *L'Argent* as a character in its fiction.[8] Deliberately blurring the boundary between his source, reality and his fictional recreations, Zola has the real historical figure, Bismarck, contemplate his fictional creation, Saccard: 'Lorsque Saccard, triomphal, traversa la pièce, ayant à son bras Mme de Jeumont, et suivi du mari, le comte de Bismarck s'interrompit de rire un instant, en bon géant goguenard, pour les regarder curieusement passer'/'When Saccard in his triumph crossed the room with Madame de Jeumont on his arm and the husband following behind, Count von Bismarck for a moment ceased laughing like a good-humoured, playful giant, and gazed at them inquisitively as they passed' (p. 544/210). Saccard, though he may be fictional, allows the novel to translate the real presence of Emperor Napoleon III, albeit always off stage. Saccard pays an exorbitant price to attend a ball with Madame de Jeumont, the married woman whose favours Napoleon III enjoyed earlier in the plot (p. 542/208). The novel clearly parallels the fates of Saccard and Napoleon. Bell states, 'at precisely the same moment the Banque Universelle [Saccard's creation] opens the doors of its sumptuous new headquarters and inaugurates its most successful period of existence', the Second Empire hosts the Exposition Universelle and enjoys comparable success.[9] Zola writes:

> Et cette exaltation des titres de l'Universelle, cette ascension qui les emportait comme sous un vent religieux, semblait se faire aux musiques de plus en plus hautes qui montaient des Tuileries et du Champ-de-Mars, des continuelles fêtes dont l'Exposition affolait Paris.
>
> [And this exaltation of Universal shares, this ascension which carried them up as if on a divine wind, went on to the accompaniment of the yet louder and louder music that arose from the Tuileries and the Champ de Mars and of the endless festivities with which the Exhibition intoxicated Paris.] (p. 539/208)

Saccard positions the emperor as his reflective double. Thus, as the crowds celebrate Napoleon III and the empire which has proved so fertile for Saccard's machinations, Saccard feels as though the celebrations are for him (p. 539/208). And, numerous critics suggest, Bismarck and Napoleon III are far from the only real people in Zola's fictional translations. Edward J. Ahearn situates Saccard's rival Jewish financier, Gundermann, as James de Rothschild.[10] Both attain an immense fortune, are recognisable in their Jewish faith and are driven by their sense of duty to their large immediate family. Zola's characters, he suggests, have models in reality. The paratextual material of the Cercle du Livre Précieux edition takes him at his word, both going in quest of and offering a range of images of the real personalities behind Zola's fictional characters. Hence it inserts immediately after the novel's first description of Gundermann a photo captioned 'Le Baron James de Rothschild (Modèle de Gundermann)' [The Baron James de Rothschild (Model for Gundermann)] (p. 407). Comparably, Zola's initial description of the princesse d'Orviedo, a character who divests herself of everything, such is her charitable zeal, is immediately followed with a photograph of a contemporary noble whose philanthropy followed similar paths (p. 370). The photograph is entitled 'La duchesse de Galliera (Modèle de la princesse d'Orviedo)' [The Duchess of Galliera (Model for the Princess of Orviedo)].[11] A Nadar photograph of Procureur général Chaix D'est-Ange is offered as the model for Delcambre (p. 609), as well as an unassigned drawing of Ernest Picard, an opposition deputy (p. 468). Numerous critics and critical editions approach Zola's novel as an interpersonal adaptation of nineteenth-century people.[12]

In its reworking of Zola's novel for television, Antenne 2's 1988 version of *L'Argent* is as insistently interpersonal. Its depiction of the historical figure Bismarck is a case in point. Bismarck appears only fleetingly in Zola's novel, a towering figure both literally and metaphorically who, for Zola's contemporary audience, needs no introduction, so readily comprehensible is his referential source. If Zola adapts near-contemporary reality for his audience, the television adaptation is instead a period piece recreating a temporally distant past. It needs to give its audience far greater communicative clues, to use Gutt's term as explored in Chapter One, in order to allow them access to Bismarck in personal and/or historical terms. The adaptation's Bismarck is thus introduced on screen with an image of the Prussian flag behind him.[13] He both speaks and writes his own full name as he appears on screen, engaged as he is in autographing an image of himself as a gift for the French imperial family. The resemblance of the actor playing Bismarck, Jacques Dacqmine, to the real historical figure is reinforced by the point-of-view shot of this gift. Dacqmine, playing Bismarck, looks at and signs an image of the real Bismarck. The point-of-view shot functions as a complex identificatory moment in a reflective sense. Dacqmine, playing Bismarck, stares at Bismarck in a point-of-view shot which, in technical terms, makes him the historical figure he can never be. The layers of identity in this shot are complex and shifting in interpersonal terms. Dacqmine plays the part of a real historical figure, Bismarck, as well as Zola's reading of him in *L'Argent*. The lines Dacqmine utters are often Zola's — his dialogue matches that of his novelistic forebear almost exactly. Yet the referents around him in the scene relate to Bismarck as historical figure. The character strokes, for instance, a huge dog. His historical forebear was known for his love of dogs, animals which often accompanied him on his governmental trips, functioning, some argue, as a means to unsettle his foreign counterparts and coming to be known in his home nation as 'Reichshunde' [dogs of the Empire]. And into this shifting interpersonal negotiation of identities must also be factored the visible presence of Dacqmine himself. He may have been selected because of his resemblance to his historical predecessor and clothed and made up to emphasise that resemblance. Yet he remains clearly visible as Jacques Dacqmine, the readily identifiable prolific French character actor perhaps best known for playing lords, rulers and authority figures in cinema, theatre and television. (In his first television appearance, he played King Conrad; in almost his penultimate appearance he played Charles X.) Dacqmine, a well-known French actor, strains televisual credibility by playing Bismarck in French with an inconsistent and intermittent Germanic accent to gesture to the foreignness of his source text: Bismarck himself. Yet if Dacqmine's Prussian accent undermines the authority of his character, Dacqmine's legible typecasting precisely as a man of authority for a French contemporary television audience reinforces it. Antenne 2's *L'Argent*, via Dacqmine's Bismarck, underscores the multiple, intersecting levels of interpersonal interactions from which it is formed.

Dacqmine is far from the only actor in *L'Argent* whose previous roles and televisual identities speak to Nord's interpersonal vision of re-creative art. The career of Claude Brasseur, the actor playing Saccard, is a case in point. Symbolically, Brasseur also played Sganarelle, the shape-shifting character who appeared across Molière's plays in different personal forms. Specifically Brasseur featured in Marcel Bluwal's 1965 telefilm *Dom Juan ou Le Festin de Pierre*. Brasseur's Sganarelle ruthlessly dissects characters and the action for the audience in a manner which anticipates Brasseur's Saccard and his Naturalist ability to cut to the core of individuals and their motivations. The seventeenth-century servant's love of money — he famously bewails his loss of wages as the ground swallows up his demonic master, barely leaving him behind — anticipates the love of lucre which will drive Brasseur's Saccard in a pact which is no less destructive. Intriguingly, whilst Brasseur's Sganarelle closes the play watching the ground swallow his master, Brasseur's Saccard closes his adaptation, in a scene which has no equivalent in the novel, promising precisely to reclaim the ground from the force which has swallowed it (he pitches for investment in the Netherlands to reclaim land from the water in a reprisal of remorseless financial activity which Caroline Hamelin clearly characterises as demonic). These previous televisual identities which continue to resonate within Brasseur's subsequent onscreen identities not only find expression in the shape-shifting Sganarelle but are also in many ways incarnated in his role as Arlequin in Bluwal's 1967 telefilm *Le Jeu de l'amour et du hasard*. Brasseur plays the part of a valet dressed up as his master Dorante in a role where his previous identity (that of Arlequin) has to remain visible as he performs as Dorante in order for the play to function. This notion of the cumulative, concurrent creative identities constantly at play within the roles Brasseur plays is further reinforced by his role as François Vidocq in the 1971 ORTF series *Les Nouvelles Aventures de Vidocq*. Playing the lead role, Brasseur's interpretation of the famous criminal turned criminalist perfectly predicts the thin line which, as Saccard, he treads between criminality/social pariah and success/core social kingpin or creator. Moreover, Brasseur as Vidocq offers a telling example of the inter- or multi-personal nature of television acting in two key respects. First, the part is an oft-repeated one as the story has a long history in France, both in literature and in television and film.[14] Brasseur's role was inevitably inflected by previous incarnations of the historical figure. But Brasseur as Vidocq is inter- or multi-personal in a second key facet. He is not only inflected interpersonally by the identities of his previous incarnations in literature and moving images, his role also contains within it the identity of the actor he replaced in Bluwal's series: Bernard Noël. Bluwal's series started in 1967 starring Noël; Brasseur took over in 1971 in Bluwal's new version of the series subsequent to Noël's illness and death. Bluwal thus charged Brasseur not only with playing the part of Vidocq but also Noël as Vidocq. He claims in an interview that there are deliberate similarities between Noël and Brasseur as Vidocq.[15] Just as Saccard in Zola's *L'Argent* is inflected by his previous incarnations in Zola's *La Curée*, a part which he both continues and alters, the actor who plays him for the adaptation offers an incarnation inflected by his previous parts and their shifting, varying prominence in the mind of those who view the series. Zola's characters have their published and traceable genealogies in the family tree which accompanies the Rougon-Macquart series and the television actors who star in the novel's adaptations have their own very visible televisual genealogy, inflected as their performances are by a shifting range of their previous roles. The adaptation thus adds further layers and dimensions to the interpersonal vision offered by Nord in its play on the multiple, shifting identities of its actors.

If Nord's list of the network of people who must be analysed in the translation process is extended to the sphere of adaptation, then the figure of the director must feature on it. The director Jacques Rouffio is one of the key personalities shaping *L'Argent* as a piece for television. Though Rouffio's filmography is not extensive — he made only a handful of films and even fewer television pieces in his own directorial right — the personal tropes which characterise his creative corpus in both thematic and stylistic terms are visible in *L'Argent*. His 1978 feature film *Le Sucre* and his last piece for television in 2007, the adaptation of Maupassant's short story 'Miss Harriet', make clear the thematic and aesthetic personality of much of his corpus and bind both pieces to his version of *L'Argent*. In thematic terms, *Le Sucre* is a clear predecessor of Rouffio's *L'Argent*. Both underscore his interest in money and the stock market, particularly in its hidden shadowy transactions. *Le Sucre* focuses on a 1974 financial scandal relating to the stratospheric stock market rises for sugar as a core commodity and the questionable banking practices related to it, while Rouffio's later offering *L'Argent* unpicks the fraudulent practices behind Saccard's Banque Universelle and its attempt to woo investors in order to extract wealth from a far-off oriental land as it funds industry, infrastructure and development. Both adaptations (*Le Sucre* is based on a novel by Georges Conchon) explore the skulduggery behind French stock market booms in their chosen eras.[16] Both relate to real events and work, as adaptations, to underscore Rouffio's interest in where reality as source text stops and the fictional translations begin. The paratextual material accompanying both adaptations is key to my line of argument here. Rouffio's *Le Sucre* is available on DVD, accompanied by a documentary featuring Rouffio and the creative personnel behind the film and directed by Pierre-Henri Gilbert. Rouffio's *L'Argent* aired on Antenne 2 with an introduction from the Bourse itself, a brief interview with Rouffio and a reminder that the adaptation will be followed by the show *L'Histoire immédiate*, 'consacrée ce soir à la crise financière mondiale' [focusing this evening on the global financial crisis]. In both sets of paratextual material, Rouffio features physically as an authority figure, shaping the adaptation on offer via the vector of his personal interests and knowledge. In both,

Rouffio sets out, in keeping with Nord's theories, his interpretative strategy in paratextual material which functions almost as a filmed preface. Both adaptations pursue a sense of reality. Just as the Cercle du Livre Précieux edition of Zola's *L'Argent* pitches the nineteenth-century novel as a direct adaptation of reality, offering contemporary photographs and images of news reports to help the reader access Zola's source, Gilbert's documentary accompanying *Le Sucre* does likewise. It offers direct screen shots of the news articles on the sugar shortages which both reported on and helped fuel the soaring commodity prices behind the scandal. Intriguingly, the screen shots of these real news articles infiltrate the fictional body of the film. That they are intended to provide a reality effect is clear. But Zola's *L'Argent* teaches the reader precisely to be wary of the reality which newspaper articles offer. The novel uses its fictional newspaper *L'Espérance* to underline that the truth it offers is fluid and ultimately fictional. *L'Espérance*, bought by Saccard to support his financial endeavour, publishes the truth he dictates rather than the reality around it (p. 427/96).[17] The paratextual material to Rouffio's *L'Argent* pushes for a similar reality effect. The interview preceding the programme takes place in the Bourse that was the backdrop to the financial cataclysm which Zola's novel fictionalises. Rouffio's adaptation may depict that nineteenth-century cataclysm but the current affairs programme following it, the introduction announces, details and parallels it with the global financial crisis affecting Rouffio's contemporary audience. This juxtaposition of period drama and current affairs in the televisual flow, to use Raymond Williams's term, offers interpretative clues to the contemporary viewer as per Gutt's theory in Chapter One, making it relevant to them. It also marks Rouffio's adaptation as real, as an adaptation of reality both past and contemporary in a manner which is temporally complex. But the sense of reality cultivated by *L'Argent* is no less problematic than that of *Le Sucre*. Reality, for Saccard, in Zola's *L'Argent* is always a fictional, subjective, complex construct. He fabricates a truth tailored to the needs of his potential investors in order to liberate the cash which will make elements of his lies come true. A recurrent musical motif accompanies Saccard's fabrications of truth, coming to serve as a theme music for the adaptation. Intriguingly, this musical motif, with its associations with fabrication and falsity, plays through the factual interview which precedes the adaptation. It perforates the divide between factual interview and fictional adaptation. Thus the factual interview preceding the adaptation may seek to ground reality as the text behind Zola's novel and the adaptations made of it, but the musical refrain infiltrating it ultimately underlines the porous boundary between reality and fictional reworking of it. In keeping with Nord's interpersonal vision of reproductive art, the shaping force of Rouffio's personality on the works he directed is visible both within his television adaptation and in the paratextual material he uses to foreground his adaptive strategy.

Rouffio's personal influence as one of the network of identities shaping the recreation of Zola's source text is also visible in aesthetic terms in *L'Argent*. Rouffio's work is characterised by a core visual claustrophobia and tendency to crop objects, conversations and shots. In Rouffio's *Miss Harriet*, his adaptation of Guy de

Maupassant's short story of the same name for the series *Chez Maupassant*, only half of the character Sapeur's conversation as he chats to the painter protagonist is available to the viewer. It is cropped by the scene which starts *in medias res*. Narrative cropping is a core feature of the adaptation of *L'Argent*. In some places it serves merely to accommodate the needs and mores of the contemporary viewer, underscoring how dominant the viewer is in the interpersonal pact that is adaptation. All the anti-Semitism detailed in Zola's novel disappears.[18] Cropping at times takes place to make the sheer expanse of Zola's novel fit the more claustrophobic space of television. Thus the endless mass of investors in Saccard's bank are all cut bar one, the blindly faithful office worker at *L'Espérance*, who comes to represent the whole. Other moments of cropping are core to the adaptation's message. As Saccard speaks to the bank's advisory board his words are blotted out by the musical refrain which associates them with the falsity and fiction so ceaselessly identified with his financial endeavours. Saccard's words thus speak and signify for the viewer even when being silenced. Language in this adaptation is cropped to powerful effect. Saccard alters his brother's opposition to his financial endeavour to support simply by cropping his statement. His brother states: 'Que mon frère fasse ce qu'il veut mais qu'il ne compte jamais sur moi' [My brother can do what he likes but he should never count on me]. Saccard abbreviates it to 'Que mon frère fasse ce qu'il veut' [My brother can do what he likes]. The adaptation's most resonant moment of narrative cropping occurs in the first episode of this three-part adaptation. Saccard confesses his life story to Madame Caroline. The adaptation does not allow his words to be heard for it plays a musical refrain over them. We watch Saccard speak but his words are lost to us. This act of silencing is resonant in multiple spatial ways. In spatial terms, it expands our comprehension of Saccard, revealing in fragments his innately interpersonal identity as he speaks of the names and personae under which he has lived: Saccard, Sicardot, Rougon. Yet, far from offering Saccard space, liberation and release in the confession of all these identities, the sheer expanse of Saccard's identities entraps him. His previous identities and signatures permit the moneylender Busch to corner Saccard. Saccard's previous identities in the adaptation confine the very space of his life. As if to underscore this, the adaptation constrains the space of both his protagonist and his production in telling ways. Extreme high-angle shots are frequent in this adaptation. Such shots take place frequently in the Bourse and again when Saccard dances with Mme de Jeumont having been toasted as 'Le roi de Paris' [The King of Paris]. They make a mockery of the toast for they trap him in a shot from above which reduces him in physical size as the camera bears down on him. There is, throughout the adaptation, a refusal of an expansive spatial aesthetic. Rather than offering long-shot establishing images of authentic period buildings which allow the viewer to revel in their authenticity and give space to the past as artefact, the adaptation insistently forecloses the period buildings it shoots. Its use of the Bourse building is a case in point. It features at the start of each of the three episodes in three close-focus images which, one after the other, inch closer to the Bourse building, cropping its integrity and refusing to situate it in broad spatial terms. The shots function almost as a point-of-view shot as they zero in on the object of Saccard's obsession: the stock exchange and the money it generates. In physical and metaphorical terms, the adaptation makes the spatial restraint of television in its era still smaller, cultivating a spatial aesthetics which functions as something of an authorial signature across his corpus.[19] Rouffio, in keeping with Nord's interpersonal model, visibly shapes the adaptation to which he puts his name.

If claustrophobia is one of Rouffio's signature tropes, so too is inexorability. In his adaptation of Maupassant's 'Miss Harriet', the tale of a frustrated spinster's love for a painter, he refuses to allow the viewer to contemplate an ending other than that toward which the adaptation moves so intently. In the early stages of his Maupassant adaptation, the gravedigger digs, creating a space the likes of which the English spinster will come to fill, having been spurned by her love. A maid struggles to winch a bucket from a well and Miss Harriet crosses the scene. By the adaptation's close, she will have become the obstruction in the well, having committed suicide in it. Prediction too lies at the heart of Rouffio's *L'Argent*. The episodes of this three-part series close with a continuity voiceover directly addressing the viewer, predicting what might happen and exhorting them to tune in at the same time next week in order to find out more:

> Saccard sera-t-il finalement écrasé par son ennemi mortel? Est-il prêt à tout sacrifier pour se perdre dans le vertige de cet ultime combat? Est-ce vraiment la fin de cet aventurier de l'argent? Réponse dans la troisième et dernière partie de *L'Argent*. Mercredi à 20h 35.
>
> [Will Saccard ultimately be destroyed by his mortal enemy? Is he ready to sacrifice everything and throw himself into this final battle? Is this really the end of the road of his adventures on the Stock Exchange? Find out in the third and final part of *Money*, Wednesday at 8.35.]

The adaptation's continuity announcer points relentlessly to the adaptation's close. The same instinct clearly guides the introductory segment to each of the episodes. A repeated collage of clips from the adaptation as a whole serve as the opening for each instalment. The clips, repeated at the start of each episode, offer segments of action from across the three episodes. They trace Saccard's inexorable rise and fall, starting with shots of the Bourse, before juxtaposing Saccard being hailed as 'Le roi de Paris' with Gundermann's prediction of Saccard's destruction at the hands of the very financial passion which has created him. The function of this repeated opening segment is two-fold. First, it ties the viewers into the narrative to come, offering them snippets of the action they will view if they tune in again next week. Yet, perhaps more importantly, this repeated opening clip forecloses a host of narrative possibilities, limiting the audience's room for interpretation, pointing inexorably to the adaptation's ending specifically in the form of Saccard's ruin. It ties us into an ending before the adaptation has even begun. It forecloses the adaptation's space. Space, though, in the field of canonical literary adaptation is arguably always already foreclosed because of the source's knownness to many of its viewers. For if the viewer knows the source text, he or she knows the adaptation's ending, unless the director deviates from it. Rouffio's piece engages with that sense of the *déjà connu*, by starting his adaptation with flash forwards to precisely where it will close. Such prediction and narrative foreclosure reflect Rouffio's signature aesthetic more broadly. In Nord's list of the personalities shaping re-creative art, Rouffio clearly signs his name on his adaptation of Zola's *L'Argent*.

In Nord's reading of the interpersonal nature of re-creative art, the re-creating artist is duty bound to be loyal to the intentions of the source author. In this instance, Rouffio's and Zola's creative intents overlap. Zola's novel is as inexorable in its trajectory as Rouffio's adaptation of it. The book, from the outset, underlines the inevitability of Saccard's failure in a variety of ways. Flushed with success, Saccard emerges, having set up the Banque Universelle and dreaming of its future triumphs. His eyes fall on Madame Méchain, the woman who, with Busch, buys up bad debt and bankrupt shares. He focuses on the bag in which she transports her spoils. She buys them driven by her belief that:

> La déroute était fatale, que le jour du massacre viendrait, où il y aurait des morts à manger, des titres à ramasser pour rien dans la boue et dans le sang. Et lui [Saccard] qui roulait son grand projet d'une banque, eut un léger frisson, fut traversé d'un pressentiment, à voir ce sac, ce charnier des valeurs dépréciées, dans lequel passait tout le sale papier balayé de la Bourse.
>
> [Ruin was inevitable, that the day of massacre would come, when there would be dead to eat, shares to pick up for nothing, from amid the mire and the blood. And Saccard, who even then was revolving a grand banking project in his mind, gave a slight shudder, and felt a presentiment at sight of that bag, that charnel-house, as it were of depreciated stock, into which passed all the dirty paper swept away from the Bourse.] (p. 347/13–14)

This premonition clarifies and strengthens in his mind in his second contemplation of this bag: 'il croyait comprendre qu'elle [Mme Méchain] menaçait d'attendre aussi longtemps qu'il serait nécessaire, pour y enterrer à leur tour ses actions à lui, quand la maison croulerait'/'And he understood, so he fancied, that she meant to wait as long as might be necessary in order to bury his own shares in it, when the fall of his enterprise should come' (p. 441/111). The premonition, announced at the novel's outset, is fulfilled at its close. Standing in the Bourse, having realised the scale of his defeat, Saccard looks up:

> Et il fut tout de suite debout, en reconnaissant en haut, à la galérie du télégraphe, penchée au-dessus de la salle, la Méchain qui dominait de son énorme personne grasse le champ de bataille. Son vieux sac de cuir noir était posé près d'elle, sur la rampe de pierre. En attendant d'y entasser les actions dépréciées, elle guettait les morts, telle que le corbeau vorace qui suit les armées.
>
> [And in a moment he was on his feet again; for up above, looking down upon the hall from the telegraph galley, he recognised La Méchain, her huge fat person dominating the ghastly battle-field. On the stone baluster beside her lay her old black leather bag. Pending the arrival of the time when she might fill it to overflowing with the worthless shares, she was watching the dead, like a voracious raven that follows armies until the day of massacre.] (p. 604/274)

The inevitability of Saccard's failure is inscribed in other ways. The novel opens with characters discussing the financial fall of Schlosser. Schlosser's failure in the

Bourse predicts that of Saccard, even while he mounts the nascent Universelle. Zola describes Schlosser, in terms which apply to Saccard, as: 'un filou de la même bande, de l'éternelle bande qui exploite le marché, comme les voleurs d'autrefois exploitaient une fôret'/'a sharper of the same band, the eternal band which "works" the market, in the same way as the robbers of olden time "worked" a forest' (p. 621/293). Refusing to allow its reader to believe in anything but Saccard's inevitable failure, Zola's novel traps the reader in the inexorability of his fall. The space of the audience is as constrained in Zola's novel as it is in Rouffio's adaptation.

To call the adaptation 'Rouffio's', though, is both to mislead and to obfuscate the multiplicity of creative identities at play in Nord's vision of reproductive art. The opening credits to the television adaptation underscore the sheer range of creative personnel whose personalities both infuse the adaptation and wrest, in differing measures, a portion of presence for themselves in it. Venuti may call for the translator to make him- or herself visible in the singular, as Chapter Two suggested, but what *L'Argent* underlines in adaptive form is that Venuti's vocabulary, if applied to the context of television, needs to be pluralised in keeping with Nord's vision. *L'Argent*, in television form, is an interpersonal adaptation formed at the hands of a variety of television personnel. Nord situates the translator as a nexus, mediating between all of these different personal agents. Her view of the translator as mediator, however, is far from unproblematic, as a consideration of Saccard in *L'Argent* underlines. Saccard sets himself the task of mediating the desires of all those who invest in his translational project, yet, as those desires clash and conflict, he cannot. He cannot simultaneously satisfy Hamelin's desire to protect the Catholic faith (p. 393/61), Caroline's desire to bring health and prosperity to the people of the Orient (pp. 390–91/58), his advisory board's desire to make exorbitant fortunes (p. 410/77), the Beauvilliers' desires to safeguard aristocratic forms of power (p. 515/192) and the urges of industrialists and workers to better themselves physically and socially (p. 527/194). The desires of those in the transactional process depicted in the novel do not intersect. Moreover, Saccard might be seen to underscore the difficulties of requiring the translator to serve as a comparably disinterested force charged with loyally mediating the needs of others. Saccard, as a character, is anything but disinterested. If he mediates the desires of those around him, he does so for his own personal benefit both in financial terms and to further his very personal battle to the financial death with his arch rival Gundermann. Saccard probes the disinterestedness implicitly at the heart of the loyalty Nord suggests, gesturing towards the potentially clashing visions of those involved in the process as well as the innate self-interest of the central mediating figure in different forms.

L'Argent probes Nord's interpersonal vision of translation in a second respect. Nord's loyalty, for all its interpersonal approach, still focuses on the translator as an integral body, a central mediator ultimately responsible for the translation of an earlier source. There is a singularity to her vision of the translator's body precisely in the responsibility she accords him or her, even amongst the plurality of shaping forces surrounding it. Zola's *L'Argent* and its adaptation offer a vision of the re-creative artist in more insistently interpersonal terms, as a creative space both enabled by and lost to the desires of the agents around it. Translators, in Zola's *L'Argent*, are not integral beings. The novel features a literal translator: Sigismond, the polyglot who translates both orally and in written form in the course of the novel. Sigismond's body, though, is an interpersonal one. It is materially maintained and cared for in its perpetual sickness by his brother Busch (p. 365/32). It is intellectually supported by Karl Marx as Sigismond seeks to function as a conduit for Marx in both linguistic and translational terms, burning both ends of the candle to write a masterplan for society's reinvention without capitalism (p. 361/28). Sigismond's identity as a translator is further pluralised by its doubling with the character of Saccard. Sigismond, the Marxist who ought to be the polar opposite of Saccard in his unbridled capitalism, is insistently positioned as his double. Both are incarcerated in rooms, one for health reasons and one for legal reasons. Both feverishly pass their nights scribbling plans for regeneration, albeit plans working in very different directions (pp. 654/233; 649/316). Sigismond plots to divest capital of its power, Saccard to harness, exploit and increase it. Both work on desks of bare white pine; both expire, one literally and one financially, almost concurrently (p. 655/324). Picking up on this link, Rouffio has Saccard answer Caroline's surprise at his friendship with a Marxist with the following words: 'J'aime les gens capables de se faire tuer pour leur passion, même si ce n'est pas la mienne' [I like people who are willing to destroy themselves for their passion, even if that passion does not correspond with mine]. If Sigismond is a literal translator, Saccard functions as a metaphorical translator, translating his vision of the Orient and its development to encourage investors to buy into his personal project. Saccard's metaphorical translation of the Orient is clearly a corporeal one. People invest in him because of his body. Pilleraut states of Saccard's body: 'Tenez! Tant que je verrai ce monsieur-là solide à son poste, avec son air de gaillard qui veut tout manger, j'achèterai'/'Look here! As long as I see that gentleman yonder at his post, looking as though he wants to devour everything, I shall go on buying' (p. 574/244). Saccard's body dominates the narrative, which revolves around his attempt to ratify it by pushing people to invest in his person. Saccard's relationship with the mass is both reflective and narcissistic for he wants them to invest in his very being. From a position of fragmentation in the opening chapter when his peers refuse to see or to acknowledge him (p. 336/2), Saccard constructs an ideal identity for himself and releases it, via publicity, to the masses, masses conceived of repeatedly in aquatic, narcissistic terms. We see elements of this mass streaming to the Bourse: 'Des quatre carrefours, ouverts aux quatre angles de la place, des flots ininterrompus de voitures coulaient, sillonnant le pavé, au milieu des remous d'une cohue de piétons'/'From the four crossways at the four corners of the Place, streams of vehicles poured in uninterruptedly, whisking across the pavement amid an eddying mob of foot passengers' (p. 345/11). They are, for Saccard, 'un flot ininterrompu des gens, l'éternelle foule à exploiter, les actionnaires de demain'/'an endless flow of people, the eternal crowd of future victims, the investors of to-morrow' (p. 368/34). These investors bring Saccard narcissistic joy. Their investment and acclamation not only validates Saccard, it seems also to augment his physical being:

> Un instant, Saccard, avant de quitter la salle, se haussa, comme pour mieux embrasser la foule autour de lui, d'un coup d'œil. Il etait réellement grandi, soulevé d'un tel triomphe, que toute sa petite personne se gonflait, s'allongeait, devenait énorme.
>
> [For a moment, Saccard, before leaving the hall, straightened himself to his full height, as if the better to survey the crowd around him. He had really grown so magnified by his triumph that all his little person expanded, lengthened, became enormous.] (p. 586/256)

Saccard's body though, for all its dominance, ultimately does not belong to him, so interpersonal is it in its creation. It is indebted to the faceless multitude of investors who simultaneously make it possible and impossible in its innate borrowed-ness. Saccard's circulation of his identity brings presence in this interpersonal transaction, but so too, inevitably in psychoanalytic terms, does it simultaneously entail absence. The fluid mass of investors escapes from the grasp of Saccard, seeping beyond his control. And, when the crowd has ceased to reflect him, turning instead to contemplate the power of his rival, Saccard falls, wondering how best to create and recirculate himself anew. Bodies, specifically translating bodies, are innately, multiply interpersonal artefacts in Zola's *L'Argent*. Their borders and boundaries are neither integral nor easily grasped and Zola's *L'Argent* asks questions of the central agency Nord ascribes to the body of the translator.

Saccard's body as translator is interpersonal not only within the book, but also beyond it. If critics have, as this chapter has already suggested, offered real life models for characters in this book, the figure of Saccard is more multiple and shifting in its sources than any of his fictional counterparts in the novel. Saccard has been identified by critics as an adaptation of the banker Bontoux: 'Saccard, comme Bontoux, acquiert le contrôle de journaux financiers; comme Bontoux, il fait dépasser à ses actions le cours fabuleux de 3000' [Saccard, like Bontoux, took control of financial newspapers, like Bontoux he pushed his shares above the magic 3000 franc mark].[20] The paratextual material of the Cercle du Livre Précieux edition, however, offers a competing model for Saccard. It features an André Gill caricature of 'Le Financier Jules Mirès' [The Financier Jules Mirès], subtitling it 'un des modèles de Saccard' [one of the sources for Saccard] (p. 427). The plurality of the subtitle is key to Saccard's identity, for Saccard is both of these men and yet neither of them. He is, Zola underlines, a plural adaptation in interpersonal terms, a man whose origins are ultimately unfixable in their multiplicity and fluidity. The plurality of Saccard's identities outside the novel is mirrored by their multiplicity within it. Within the novel Saccard is a fictional continuation of the character of the same name who featured in Zola's *La Curée*, a character ostensibly fixed in his identity by both the family tree which Zola publishes alongside his novels and by the reader's comprehensive understanding of Saccard's genetic inheritance at this stage in Zola's Rougon-Macquart series. But *L'Argent* unveils Saccard as a dizzying multitude of people. Contemplating Saccard's handwriting, Busch unveils the lie of his identity in *L'Argent*, revealing him as Sicardot, the man who despoiled a young woman, leaving her destitute and pregnant with nothing but the promissory note

Busch now owns (p. 360/23). And Saccard's identities do not stop there. For Sicardot too is an assumed name. It is a name taken to cover the Rougon surname which his brother fears he will sully, a name taken to efface Saccard having been on the wrong side of the coup d'état which brought his reflective double Napoleon III to power. Napoleon III, though, does not fix or anchor the fictional Saccard's personality in reality. He cannot, for he is as shifting an identity as his fictional counterpart. Napoleon III models himself on the power and standing of his forebear and namesake, Napoleon Bonaparte. In a dizzying conflation of identities, Zola writes: 'Et ce que les croisades avaient tenté, ce que Napoléon n'avait pu accomplir, c'était cette pensée gigantesque de la conquête de l'Orient qui enflammait Saccard'/'And it was this gigantic thought of conquering the East, the scheme which the Crusaders had attempted and which Napoleon had been unable to accomplish, that inflamed Saccard' (p. 392/59). Saccard's victories are equated with those of Napoleon Bonaparte: 'Ce fut sa grande journée, celle dont on parle encore, comme on parle d'Austerlitz et de Marengo'/'It was his grand day, the day which people still speak of, as they speak of Austerlitz and Marengo' (p. 586/256). Saccard himself states:

> Ce que Napoléon n'a pu faire avec son sabre, et ce que nous ferons, nous autres, avec nos pioches et notre or. [...] Napoléon est bien revenu de l'ile d'Elbe. Mois aussi, je n'aurai qu'à me montrer, tout l'argent de Paris se lèvera pour me suivre; et il n'y aura pas, cette fois, de Waterloo.
>
> [What Napoleon was unable to do with his sword, we shall do with our pickaxes and gold! [...] Napoleon came back from Elba, remember. I, also, shall only have to show myself, and all the money of Paris will rise to follow me: and this time there will be no Waterloo.] (p. 649/322)

However, in situating Saccard as a would-be Napoleon Bonaparte, the narrative simultaneously equates him once again with the self-proclaimed Napoleon III, the leader who sought to capitalise on his illustrious predecessor, the leader so malleable that he appeared to be everything to everyone and, consequently, ultimately no one at all. Bell writes:

> Napoleon III's political power is linked to his ability to assume convincingly in the eyes of the beholder various positions from which he seems to represent the different interest groups. He is a Republican for the Republicans, a protector of the working class for the workers [...], a defender of the interest of small retailers, a liberal when necessary [...] and so forth as far as everyone wishes to go. The emperor, then, is capable of assuming every position in turn; he is a figure of constant substitution, standing for everything and (at the same time) for nothing in particular.[21]

Identities are innately interpersonal in Zola's *L'Argent* in a way which both speaks to and nuances Nord's critical framework.

Just as Nord's list of the identities shaping translations is plural, so too is the range and depth of identities shaping adaptations. This chapter has assessed the formative influence of the television adaptation's director, amongst other creative identities in the television process. But it is also necessary to consider the ways in which the adaptation engages not just with Zola's source text but Zola as a person. In teasing scenes which encourage the knowing audience member to revel in a sense of the *déjà connu*, the director adapts Zola as a body of work, referencing the author from his collective output. The adaptation's intertextual relationship with Zola's novel *Nana* is pronounced. A shot focusing on a portrait of Bismarck is soon followed by characters offering contrasting readings of the Prussian leader as they debate his identity. Their debate repeats that twice repeated in the pages of *Nana*. Describing Sabine's reception, Zola, in *Nana*, depicts a society fascinated by Bismarck, with the guests recurrently discussing him.[22] The debate is reprised almost in its entirety at Nana's subsequent dinner party. The same words and thoughts circulate, but in different mouths and a starkly different social group.[23] The adaptation of *L'Argent* not only reprises this reprisal, it also adds a lesbian relationship for the baronne Sandorff, a relationship which echoes that of Zola's Nana. The baronne Sandorff, a woman immune to all men, finds solace, as Nana did with Satin, in the arms of a working-class woman, in this case her servant. In an adaptation which takes the viewer to the opera to see Offenbach, the presumed source in parodic form of the musical offerings in *Nana*, Saccard, Daigremont and others sit at a table and share refreshment.[24] While their conversation is financial, it includes details of Daigremont's intention to go to the Variétés that night in response to gossip that 'la fille qui joue Vénus a un cul extraordinaire' [the girl playing Venus has an incredible arse].[25] Zola's Nana, who played precisely the part of Venus on stage, is a tangible presence in Antenne 2's reworking of *L'Argent*. The adaptation, though, interacts with Zola's fictional corpus beyond *Nana* in the *Rougon-Macquart* series. In adapting from Zola's work broadly, it testifies to the innate seriality of that fiction. As Saccard adapts various arguments and identities in his quest to fashion himself in *L'Argent* and indeed in *La Curée*, Zola adapts the identity of his protagonist across his cycle, creating new fiction from him. Corinne Saminadayar-Perrin underlines Saccard's status as a fertile adaptive source, appearing and reappearing across the novels of the *Rougon-Macquart* series in adapted and re-adapted form.[26] Indeed, he ends the novel *L'Argent* precisely by starting to reinvent himself anew. Saccard and this novel, *L'Argent*, are the latest incarnations of a Zola character constantly being reborn, a character whom the adaptation urges us to read interpersonally, in relation to his previous incarnations in Zola's work.

Antenne 2's adaptation, though, in adapting Zola's person, in some senses takes the reader directly back to Zola's *L'Argent*, a novel which arguably features a variety of Zola figures. A range of critics see Saccard and his flair for fiction as a Zola figure embedded in his own novel.[27] That Saccard is an artist in words and fiction is repeatedly underlined by the text: he speaks 'à larges traits, avec sa parole ardente qui transformait une affaire d'argent en un conte de poète'/'with broad touches and glowing words, which transformed a pecuniary affair into a poet's tale' (p. 412/79). Zola adds, 'Il gesticulait, il était debout, se grandissant sur ses petites jambes; et, en vérité, il devenait grand, le geste dans les étoiles, en poète de l'argent que les faillites et les ruines n'avaient pu assagir'/'He gesticulated as he spoke, erect, and stretching his little legs till he really became taller, his arms waving among the stars, like the inspired bard of Money, whose poetic flight, no failure, no ruin had ever been able to check' (p. 531/198). If Saccard might be seen to be a Zola figure, Jordan more clearly merits the same description. In a manner which echoes Zola's biography, the impoverished young man making ends meet via his journalism finds success at the novel's close:

> Après tant d'années de travail ingrat, son premier roman, publié d'abord dans un journal, lancé ensuite par un éditeur, avait pris brusquement l'allure d'un gros succès; et il se trouvait riche de quelques milliers de francs, toutes les portes ouvertes devant lui désormais.
>
> [After so many years of thankless toil, his first novel, issued at first as a newspaper serial, and then in book form by a publisher, had suddenly proved a big success; and he now found himself in possession of several thousand francs.] (p. 617/289)

The adaptation has the older Zola figure, Saccard, help the younger Zola figure, Jordan, with his debts. Saccard does so because he explictly sees himself in Jordan: 'Cet argent que je vous donne, c'est à moi que je la donne. Ce Saccard d'autrefois qui crevait de faim avec sa femme' [The money I'm giving you, I am actually giving it to myself. To the Saccard of earlier times who struggled to make ends meet with his wife]. The television adaptation, like Zola's novel, adapts elements of Zola's person in the interpersonal play of its own creation. It engages with Nord's interpersonal model and the importance it affords to the source author.

The adaptation, though, like Nord clearly privileges the persons of the audience in the interpersonal transactions of its offering. Nord is a Functionalist at heart (albeit one who offers a moderated version of Functionalism in response to criticisms of the movement) and her Functionalism speaks powerfully to the plot of Zola's novel in its focus on meeting the requirements of the audience. Saccard, as Functionalist as they come, adapts the mission of his Banque Universelle to suit the needs and desires of respective audiences. Thus, to Georges Hamelin the devout Catholic he pitches it as a pious endeavour to restore the Pope's power (p. 393/61). To Hamelin's humanitarian sister, he pitches it as financial salvation for both the brother and oriental lands she loves so dearly (pp. 390–91/58). To the charitable princesse d'Orviedo he sells it as means to benefit Christians (p. 420/88), to the more venal Huret he packages it as a means to secure personal wealth and gratification (p. 416/84). Rouffio, like Saccard, adapts his message to his audience. He makes extensive cuts to the complex nineteenth-century financial detail which Zola includes in the novel and which he realises the twentieth- and now twenty-first-century viewer might not have, instead offering a beginner's guide to the stock market in Zola's era. He does so via a conversation between Saccard and the *agent de change* Mazaud's son, a conversation which has no precedent in his source novel. Overhearing Mazaud's discussion with Saccard about the way in which his arch enemy Gundermann is seeking to trigger a stock market fall in order to undo the Banque Universelle, Mazaud's son asks how the market works. Saccard explains it for both him and the adaptation's contemporary audience, offering, to use Gutt's terms from Chapter One, communicative clues to ensure viewer comprehension. Rouffio's Saccard is no less Functionalist than his literary forebear and the director in whose work he appears. In selling the core concept of the Banque Universelle to his investors, Saccard commissions a range of texts which both meet their needs and lead them to invest. He asks Jantrou to write an editorial in favour of the Pope in the paper Saccard owns, *L'Espérance*. A surprised Jantrou retorts 'Je ne vous croyais pas si catholique' [I had no idea you were so Catholic], to which Saccard responds that he does not give a damn about the Pope. He points out, though, that the majority of his customers are Catholic and, in taking their side, he makes millions for the venture. Scene transitions underscore the flexibility of Saccard's Functionalism. The episode cuts from Saccard's repeated claims that he does not give a damn about the Pope to a new scene with him promising Georges Hamelin that the Banque Universelle will be the bank of the Catholic faith, responsible for safeguarding the Pope's power. Saccard makes the promise in order to access Hamelin's plans and surveys of the Orient, plans necessary to the creation of the Banque Universelle. His oral text of the Universelle is as shifting and multiple as the audiences for which it is destined. It is shaped entirely for the needs and desires of those consuming it, needs and desires Saccard has to satisfy in order to trigger investment and his own gratification. The dialogues between the translation school of Functionalism and the protagonist of *L'Argent* are intriguing.

In some senses the adaptation is as Functionalist as its protagonist. It shapes itself to cater for the contemporary mores of its twentieth-century audience. As has already been suggested, it cuts the anti-Semitism rampant in the novel. It cuts the political critique of a Second Empire whose politics and inner workings have become as alien to its audience as they were known and close to Zola's contemporary reader. It not only explains the nineteenth-century financial system to its viewers via Saccard's dialogue with Mazaud's son as explored above, it also accommodates it to the financial situation of the adaptation's contemporary era. Rouffio in his introductory interview to the adaptation seeks to underline the economic pertinence of Zola's message to the contemporary era: 'Nous sommes dans un cas qui est le même que celui du film' [We are in a situation which is the same as that in the film]. That Zola's novel is ripe for adaptation at Rouffio's hands in the late 1980s is clear in economic terms. Having abandoned the *dirigisme* of the early 80s, the French economy moved to encourage private entrepreneurs, growth and innovation. 'The promotion of the competitiveness of private firms', Robert Boyer writes, '[was] at the core of the economic strategy of all French governments since the mid-1980s'.[28] Saccard, entrepreneur par excellence, driven by competition in a duel to the financial death with Gundermann, embodies these economic policies. Moreover, Rouffio recreates Zola in the image of 1980s economic policy in another key respect. Writing on the Americanisation of French economic models and structures, a process he situates as originating well in advance of the advent of Nicolas Sarkozy, Boyer writes:

> The economic slowdown observed in France since 2002, instead of being the expression of a long legacy of Colbertism and statism, is in fact evidence of the strong interdependence between French and American macroeconomic activity. This interdependence extends to financial markets — the French stock market reacts more to American markets than to domestic ones.[29]

It is not for nothing then that in scenes which have little connection to the original novel, Saccard plots at the adaptation's close to save himself from Gundermann's attack by having a lavish order for Universelle stock telegraphed from the New York Stock Exchange when his enterprise is seemingly at its lowest ebb. Zola's novel was less geographically specific in this respect. That the order never comes, Daigremont's relative in New York having perfidiously changed his mind, perhaps bears witness to the at times thorny nature of Franco-American relations in the contemporary era. The adaptation reworks not just the Zolian past but also the economic values and history of the era for which it adapts. It shapes itself to the knowledge and values of its contemporary audience.

However, the adaptation addresses its mass of viewers not just in its values and references, but also within the fabric of its images and dialogue. It does so by means of a series of direct address shots. Gundermann turns both to look at and to talk to us in the course of the action. While direct address shots were common in early silent film, acting styles rapidly evolved, requiring actors, for the most part, to behave as if, in André Antoine's terms, a fourth wall existed, separating them from the audience.[30] They were required to perform their fictions without acknowledging the intended recipients of those fictions. While direct address shots have all but disappeared from cinema, remaining in use only in works which seek to disconcert the viewer, they are commonplace, as Chapter One suggested, in the non-fictional output of television: news, chat and game shows, advertisements, outputs which talk directly to us. Antenne 2's *L'Argent*, though, is not non-fictional television output and its use of direct address is both comparatively unusual and revealing. In each of the three opening credit sequences Gundermann, his face initially in a static cameo shot, turns to the audience to state: 'Je suis Gundermann, de la Banque Gundermann. Vienne, Paris, Londres, Berlin, Frankfort. Je n'aime pas M. Saccard. M. Saccard n'est pas un banquier sérieux. Il est bon qu'on le ruine pour lui apprendre le sérieux' [I am Gundermann, of the Gundermann Bank. Vienna, Paris, London, Berlin, Frankfurt. I don't like Mr Saccard. Finding himself ruined will teach him a lesson]. In the course of the adaptation, Gundermann, in a comparable stance, turns to address us yet again in relation to Saccard: 'Je vais le laisser prendre son élan, s'aggrandir, croire au succès. Et, à ce moment là...' [I am going to let him gather momentum, get bigger, believe that he is succeeding. And then...]. The functions of these moments of direct address are multiple. They make clear the duel to the financial death which the adaptation situates at its core. They underline Gundermann's status as the silent and soon to be triumphant personal power behind events in the adaptation's financial world. More importantly, though, such moments of direct address make clear the adaptation's dependence upon our presence and they refuse to allow us to enjoy our usual more distanced, voyeuristic relationship with the text. The adaptation not only harnesses us to its artistic production, it playfully underlines that it does so. As Saccard needs the investment and engagement of faceless masses in his project for it to be deemed a success, so this television adaptation points to the audience as generative force, to the anonymous masses it needs in order to mount and maintain its production.[31]

To contemplate Zola's *L'Argent* and its 1988 television adaptation via the prism of Christiane Nord's translation theory is to come face to face with the interpersonal network from which adaptations are generated. Nord's value to Adaptation Studies lies in her insistence that translation is an interpersonal and not an intertextual process, in her belief that translations are done by people for people. Nord's interpersonal vision of translation enables a reading of adaptations as hermeneutic artefacts, authorising the critic to move away from a quest for a source text to focus instead on the creative networks of people via whom the text has successively been refracted in order to exist in televisual form. Nord's reading is powerful in the sheer range of its interpersonal vision, in the multitude of agents it depicts as potentially shaping the translated text, be they commissioners, editors, proof readers, typesetters or the like. Her theory creates the space for an exploration of the shaping influence and identities of the musical director, producer, actors, continuity announcers and paratextual interviewers who contribute to the adaptation. Functionalist as her theory is, it also requires us to contemplate the shaping force that is the audience in the television adaptation, to unpick the ways in which the abstract, invisible, yet highly potent body that is the audience shape the very creative artefact designed for their consumption. The television adaptation both tailors its output for that audience and acknowledges the interpersonal transaction that provides the core of its existence via its direct address shots. The television adaptation, though, not only provides a powerful case study to which to apply Nord's theory, it also offers intriguing insights as to the limits and difficulties of said theory. Nord's notion of the translator as loyal mediator to the needs and the desires of the agents around him or her is both a laudable and a necessary one. Read in association, though, Zola's *L'Argent* and the television adaptation of it show that such a task is no mean feat. They underline the conflicting, often irreconcilable desires of different agents of translation and suggest that the disinterest implicitly required by Nord of the translator in her vision of loyal translation might at times conflict with the instincts of individual identity. Moreover, *L'Argent* in both novel and television form underscores the need for Nord's theory to be still more multiple and interpersonal in its conceptualisations of the translator as an individual figure. Nord may situate the translator as an integral, responsible and ultimately powerbroking individual mediating the wishes of those around him or her, but both versions of *L'Argent* question the very possibility of talking of the translator as a singular, integral being. They offer instead a vision of bodies innately and fluidly indebted to those around them. They underline that the borders and boundaries of the creative personalities engaged in these acts of fictional recreation across media and time are shifting, porous entities. In the interpersonal transactions of *L'Argent*, an interwoven web of creative bodies is made partially and variably visible in the complex negotiation that is its process of adaptation.

Notes to Chapter 3

1. Rouffio's adaptation is available at the Centre du consultation, Inathèque, Bibliothèque nationale de France, <http://www.inatheque.fr/consultation/centres-de-consultation-paris.html> [accessed 3 November 2019].
2. Nord, *Translating as a Purposeful Activity*.
3. Christiane Nord, 'Function Plus Loyalty: Ethics in Professional Translation', *Génesis: Revista Cientifica do ISAG* (2006–07), 7–17 (p. 10).
4. Nord writes, 'the acceptability of translation purposes is limited by the translator's responsibility to all her or his partners in the cooperative activity of translation. Loyalty may oblige translators to reveal their translation purposes and justify their translational decisions' ('Function Plus Loyalty', p. 10). Elsewhere she writes: 'As the only one in the communicative "game" of translation who (by definition) knows both the source and the target cultures, translators play a powerful role. They could easily deceive their partners without anybody noticing — sometimes even just by "faithfully" translating [sic!] "what the source text says" [...]. Seen in this way, loyalty may be a corrective in the powerplay between client, author, target receivers, and the translator' (Christiane Nord, 'Manipulation and Loyalty in Functional Translation', *Current Writing*, 14 (2) (2002), 32–44 (p. 36)).
5. Emile Zola, *L'Argent*, in *Œuvres complètes*, ed. by Henri Mitterand, 15 vols (Paris: Cercle du Livre Précieux, 1966–69), VI, 311–675 (pp. 472, 591, 651). Unless otherwise stated, subsequent references are to this edition and will be made in the text.
6. Philippe Gille, '*L'Argent*, par Émile Zola', *Le Figaro*, 13 March 1891, cited in Zola, *L'Argent*, p. 323.
7. All English translations of Zola's novel *L'Argent* are, unless otherwise stated, taken from Emile Zola, *Money*, trans. by Ernest Alfred Vizetelly (New York: Mondial, 2007).
8. Emile Zola, *Nana*, in *Œuvres complètes*, ed. by Henri Mitterand, 15 vols (Paris: Cercle du Livre Précieux, 1966–69), IV, 11–363 (p. 64).
9. David F. Bell, *Models of Power: Politics and Economics in Zola's Rougon-Macquart* (Lincoln, NE: University of Nebraska Press, 1988), p. 125.
10. Edward J. Ahearn, 'Monceau, Camondo, *La Curée*, *L'Argent*: History, Art, Evil', *French Review*, 73.6 (2000), 1100–15 (p. 1107).
11. Palais Galliera, 'Marie Brignole-Sale, Duchesse de Galliera', <http://www.palaisgalliera.paris.fr/fr/palais-galliera/le-palais/marie-brignole-sale-duchesse-de-galliera> [accessed 16 December 2018].
12. For intriguing readings of how such photographs may be seen as fictional constructs rather than offering a tangible reality, see, inter alia, Peter Burke, *Eye Witnessing: The Uses of Images as Historical Evidence* (London: Reaktion, 2001), and Lynn Hunt and Vanessa R. Schwartz, 'Capturing the Moment: Images and Eyewitnessing in History', *Journal of Visual Culture*, 9 (2010), 259–71.
13. Such use of images as visual shorthand is frequent in Antenne 2's *L'Argent*. Sigismond, the Marxist translator, has an image of his master and friend Karl Marx on his bedside wall, a portrait visible before he has enunciated both his collectivist ideas and his relationship with Marx himself. Georges Hamelin has an image of a Pope on the wall of his home, an image which indicates the religious fervour which will drive him to collaborate with Saccard before he has uttered said fervour. Jantrou buys for his office wall at the newspaper *L'Espérance* one of Manet's now famous series of paintings of the execution of the Emperor Maxmilian created in 1867–69. In scenes which playfully enact some of the key techniques of the Impressionism with which Manet was associated, the camera visually crops aspects of the canvas as the delivery men move it into the office. The painter who famously cropped images at the borders and boundaries of his canvas in order to indicate his canvases' status as a slice of life, able only to gesture at the vast fresco of reality which exceeds their confines, is himself cropped in television form. Some of Manet's most famous instances of cropping appear in his canonical *Bar aux Folies-Bergère* (1882): the trapeze artist at the top right hand of the canvas is visible only in the referential green shoes and the reflection of the barmaid is only partial, sliced as it is by the edge of the work.

Antenne 2's *L'Argent* teasingly adapts this other Manet canvas in the scene in which the Emperor Maximilien canvas appears. Like the customer and client in *Bar aux Folies-Bergère*, Saccard and Jantrou stand opposite each other, separated by a counter or tabletop. Their relationship is as transactional as that between Manet's barmaid and client as Jantrou prostitutes himself ethically to the highest bidder and is as buy-able as the barmaid, whom Manet links in terms of colour palette with the products for sale in front of her. Moreover, the mirror which dominates the Manet painting, casting much of it as mirror reflection, finds a counterpart in this scene in the adaptation. Jantrou, the man who sells himself to his boss Saccard, contemplates Saccard and the Manet painting behind him. He does so with a mirror behind him, a mirror which both references Manet's composition and subject matter in *Bar aux Folies-Bergère* and Manet's work in the direct form of the Maximilian painting reflected in it. Rouffio's scene about a man, Jantrou, who is known for his cultural allusions and visible erudition is itself culturally allusive via its playful, erudite allusions to a range of Manet's canvases. Space in Rouffio's adaptation both reflects on and interacts with the characters who occupy it and it does so specifically in pictorial terms.

14. A multi-part silent film of the memoirs of this key French historical figure appeared in instalments in 1909 and 1911. A further silent film was released in 1922. The first sound film adaptation of it appeared in 1938, while an American version graced screens in 1946 and a science fiction version of it appeared in 2001. In 2017 a version starring Vincent Kassel was in pre-production. Vidocq also features in a scene of the video game *Assassins Creed Unity*.
15. Michel Bitzer, 'Du bagne à la sûreté', *Le Républicain lorrain*, 18 August 2012, <https://www.republicain-lorrain.fr/actualite/2012/08/12/du-bagne-a-la-surete> [accessed 2 October 2018].
16. Georges Conchon, *Le Sucre* (Paris: Broché, 1977).
17. Reality is, as a source, as *Le Sucre*'s accompanying documentary suggests, always already veiled by text. The documentary offers the viewer a screen shot of the script from which Rouffio worked, a script complete with his annotations. Yet behind this layer of text lie others. The documentary screenshots Rouffio's typed notes from his extensive interviews with stock market personnel, research which not only mirrors that of Zola for *L'Argent* but also echoes, in filmic form, the photographs of Zola's preparatory dossiers in the edition of the Cercle du Livre Précieux. It also screenshots the cover of Conchon's novel. Reality, in Rouffio's works, is an object always already covered by layers of translation, interpretation and notation.
18. Zola's Saccard contemplates his Jewish competitor in banking, Gundermann, and the narrative conceptualises his thoughts thus: 'Ah! Le juif! Il avait contre le juif l'antique rancune de race, qu'on trouve surtout dans le midi de la France; et c'était comme une revolte de sa chair même, une répulsion de peau qui, à l'idée du moindre contact, l'emplissait de dégoût et de violence, en dehors de tout raisonnement, sans qu'il pût se vaincre. [...] cette race maudite qui n'a plus de patrie, plus de prince, qui vit en parasite chez les nations, feignant de reconnaître les lois, mais en réalité n'obéissant qu'à son Dieu de vol, de sang et de colère'/'Ah! The Jew! Against the Jew he harboured all the old racial resentment, to be found especially in the South of France; and it was something like a revolt of his very flesh, a repugnance of the skin, which at the idea of the slightest contact, filled him with disgust and anger, a sensation which no reasoning could allay, which he was quite unable to overcome. [...] the cursed race without a country, without a prince, which lives as a parasite upon the nations, pretending to recognise their laws, but in reality only obeying its Jehovah — its God of robbery, blood, and wrath' (pp. 402–03/70). Rouffio's cropping of the clear thread of anti-Semitism in the novel is clearly a functionalist accommodation to tailor the narrative to the needs and social values of the contemporary audience he targets.
19. Intriguingly, Rouffio's problematisation of space of the Bourse resembles that of Zola. The novelist's hero Saccard is driven by an urge to conquer the Bourse as a physical space. In his peregrinations Saccard repeatedly returns to the Bourse. However, while the narrative may revolve around the space of the Bourse, that space cannot be possessed. It repeatedly disintegrates under the narrative's gaze. It dissolves in the rain as Sigismond predicts its ultimate demise: 'elle [la bourse] y était toujours, mais très vague, au fond de la nuit tombante, comme fondue sous le linceul de pluie, un pâle fantôme de Bourse près de s'évanouir en une fumée grise'/'it was still

there, though very vague and dim in the depths of the twilight, looking, in fact, as if it were melting away under the rain, like a pale phantom Bourse on the point of vanishing into grey mist' (p. 563/232). Caroline's final image of the space of the Bourse is one enunciated precisely in terms of the dust and powder, the presence becoming absence: 'Le crépuscule tombait, le ciel d'hiver, chargé de brume, mettait derrière le monument comme une fumée d'incendie, une nuée d'un rouge sombre, qu'on aurait crue faite de flammes et des poussières'/'The twilight was falling. Behind the building a ruddy cloud hung in the fog-laden wintry sky — a cloud like the smoke of a conflagration, charged with the flames and the dust of a stormed city' (p. 628/300). *L'Argent* focuses claustrophobically on the Bourse, a place which even in its omnipresence is ever in the process of becoming an absence.

20. André Wurmser, cited in Zola, *L'Argent*, p. 323.
21. Bell, *Models of Power*, p. 125.
22. Zola, *Nana*, p. 64.
23. Ibid., p. 95.
24. See Griffiths, *Zola and the Artistry of Adaptation*, p. 62.
25. Rouffio's use of Offenbach in the form of a visual of a poster for the composer's *La Périchole* is telling. The structure of *La Périchole* gestures to that of *L'Argent*. Don Andres de Ribeira intervenes in the life of an impoverished couple, seeking to make La Périchole his mistress. Saccard does likewise in relation to Georges and Caroline Hamelin. La Périchole's aria in the third act, which contains the line 'tu n'es pas beau, tu n'es pas riche' [you are neither handsome nor rich], echoes Zola's own description of Saccard as a short, ugly man whom this novel will ultimately bankrupt.
26. Corinne Saminadayar-Perrin, 'Fiction de la bourse', *Cahiers naturalistes*, 78 (2004), 41–62.
27. See, among others, Robert Lethbridge, 'Zola et Haussmann: une expropriation littéraire', in *La Curée de Zola ou 'La Vie à outrance'*, ed. by David Baguley (Paris: Sedes, 1987), pp. 85–96 (p. 92).
28. Robert Boyer, 'Who's the Comeback Kid? France, Germany, Italy', *International Economy* (2003), 8–11 (p. 11), <www.international-economy.com/TIE_F03_Euro3.pdf> [accessed 21 March 2014].
29. Ibid.
30. Antoine, *Mes souvenirs sur le Théâtre-libre*.
31. Sarah Cardwell studies the impact of direct address shots in *Moll Flanders*, a 1996 television production, situating them as a highly unusual feature whose self-reflexivity is a feature of post-1990 adaptive production in British television. Her arguments resonate with *L'Argent* and indicate that such a trend intriguingly extends beyond Britain and the timeframe she analyses (Cardwell, *Adaptation Revisited*, pp. 160–84).

CHAPTER 4

❖

The Art of Deformation: Zola, Berman and *Une page d'amour*

Fidelity criticism is predicated on a belief that it is both possible and desirable to replicate a text in near perfect form in a different medium. The critical framework of twentieth-century translation theorist Antoine Berman suggests that translation practice habitually runs counter to this belief as translators deform, to use Berman's words, the texts they recreate, shaping them ethnocentrically, consciously or subconsciously, to the lexicon, look and lure of their target era and audiences. Such deformation, Berman argues, is a negative thing but it may be avoided if those re-working texts reflect ethically on their acts of deformation, seeking to mitigate them. Berman's theoretical framework speaks to the discipline of Adaptation Studies in general, and to Zola's 1878 novel *Une page d'amour* and its 1980 television reworking of the same name directed by Elie Chouraqui in particular.[1] Collectively Zola and Chouraqui anticipate, evaluate and counter the model of deformation which Berman sets out. Both Zola's novel and Chouraqui's recreation of it are adaptations of earlier sources: Zola's novel adapts reality, while Chouraqui's television adaptation explicitly and reflectively works from Zola's novel. Both Zola and Chouraqui deform their source, shaping it ethnocentrically to the requirements of their era, audience and medium. But they both, anticipating Berman's model, reflect on what they have changed and deformed, meta-textually incorporating those changes into their works. They make space for what they alter, omit and cannot do, contemplating in highly self-reflexive ways their adaptive strategies. They resist in complex ways the deformations which power them. But both Zola and Chouraqui offer an important counterpoint to Berman's vision of deformation as innately negative. When read together, they underscore the creative power of deformation and its potential artistry. They wrest a complex fidelity to their sources in the self-consciously deforming pieces they craft from them.

Berman, a translation theorist, features fairly fleetingly in Adaptation Studies, yet his utility to the discipline is pronounced.[2] Whilst his work focuses on translation, it does probe the interstices between translation and adaptation.[3] There is, Berman recognises, a small measure of adaptation in any act of translation, and adaptation sits as an outlying form of translation in his work. The power of Berman's thought, though, in the sphere of Adaptation Studies, lies, as this chapter's introduction suggested, in his fascination with fidelity, his exploration of how sources are shaped and deformed in adaptation by the ethnocentric urges of those recreating them. Berman recognises the traditional dominance of fidelity as a critical framework, despite efforts to unseat it: 'à propos de la traduction, on parle depuis toujours de *fidelité* et d'*exactitude*' [when talking about translation, people have always talked about fidelity and exactness].[4] But he also recognises the way in which fidelity as a framework of assessment runs counter to adaptive practice on the ground as artists, consciously and subconsciously, shape the work they recreate to the ethnocentric demands of their target audience, moment and medium. Such ethnocentric deformations, Berman argues, transcend time. They are the 'internalized expression of a two-millenia-old tradition'.[5] They also transcend, in his view, nation as he underlines the 'ethnocentric structure of every culture, every language'.[6] Such deformations are, Berman believes, to be resisted and the first step in resisting them is to be taken by identifying them. Berman, thus, writes an indicative list of said deformations: rationalisation, clarification, expansion, ennoblement and popularisation, impoverishment (qualitative, quantitative), the destruction of networks and patternings. Berman challenges artists who translate (and by extension also adapt) not only to identify the deforming, ethnocentric tendencies of their work but to reflect ethically on them and find ways to counter them.

Zola's 1878 novel *Une page d'amour* and Elie Chouraqui's 1980 adaptation of it anticipate, evaluate and query Berman's vision of deformation in print and television. Both works need some introduction. Zola's *Une page d'amour*, the eighth and comparatively rarely studied novel in the Rougon-Macquart cycle, depicts the fortunes of widowed Hélène Grandjean, as she lives in near solitude on the outskirts of Paris with her daughter Jeanne, having moved from Marseille. A sickly child, Jeanne guards her mother's affections jealously, fighting off the attentions of both the merchant Rambaud, attentions encouraged by his brother the *abbé*, and those of the married doctor who attends her, Dr Deberle. When her mother succumbs to Deberle, Jeanne dies of a chill, consumed by her jealousy. Chouraqui's adaptation of Zola's novel, a heritage piece which revels in the detail and decor of its source text, aired on France 3 in October 1980 in its Saturday night drama slot. Repeated subsequently on Direct 8 (2005), the adaptation is now commercially available on DVD.

Chouraqui's adaptation both seeks to be faithful to Zola's novel and deforms it in keeping with Berman's model. The adaptation seeks fidelity in three complementary directions. First, in its paratextual material, it highlights the Zola novel from which it derives, labelling itself as a work 'd'après le roman d'Emile Zola' [inspired by Emile Zola's novel]. Chouraqui positions his adaptation as the continuation of Zola as source. The director opens his adaptation where Zola's novel finishes, starting with a scene which commences with all the elements of the novel's close: Jeanne unwell in bed, a stormscape and a hunt for a doctor. Second, the adaptation works from Zola as source author above and beyond his plot in *Une page d'amour*, adapting his philosophy of life and the influence of heredity behind and throughout his work as a whole. In Zola's novel, Hélène's husband dies unexpectedly upon their arrival in Paris.[7] In the adaptation he dies in a mad house, a victim to the genetic flaw or *fêlure* which characterises Zola's Rougon-Macquart family in the twenty novels he wrote about them. Chouraqui adapts Zola's underpinning vision of heredity and the central philosophies of the novelist's work. Third, the telefilm explicitly seeks to offer us Zola's nineteenth-century era. It is a period piece, filmed in period locations and period dress, packed with artefacts from the era with which it seeks to reconnect. It insists on its heritage status, inserting intertitles in the action which proclaim the action to take place in varying seasons of the year 1895 in the locality of Passy, a suburb of Paris. The use of such intertitles itself adds to the piece's heritage authenticity, dating as such a technique does to the era of silent film when such shots were a necessity. They provided information which could not be offered visually in film before the advent of sound. In its paratextual material, its adaptation of Zola's broader philosophy and its heritage authenticity, Chouraqui's piece seeks fidelity to Zola as source.

Zola's *Une page d'amour* has its own source which it seeks, like Chouraqui, to replicate as faithfully as it can: reality. Zola seeks to transcribe the reality of the Parisian landscape in his fiction, structuring his novel around five visions of a small section of the city in different light conditions and seasons. These panoramic visions of Zola's contemporary landscape and its spaces dominate the narrative. Zola's narrative underscores the scale of its task, depicting the Parisian space it seeks to capture in print as both vast and ever in the process of becoming still more vast. The space of Paris expands before the narrative gaze in descriptions in which the verb *s'élargir* [to widen, to stretch] occurs and re-occurs in a variety of forms. Gazing on the Parisian expanses below Helene's window, Zola writes: 'La plaine semblait s'élargir, une mélancolie montait de ces deux millions d'existences'/'the stretch of plain seemed to expand, and a sadness rose up from the two millions of living beings' (p. 1106/221–22). Hélène, responding to the space her illicit love offers her, gazes at the panoramas of Zola's landscape and revels in their expanse: 'elle gardait la conscience des vastes étendues qui se déroulaient sous elle, derrière la nuit dont elle s'aveuglait. Une voix haute montait, des ondes vivantes s'élargissaient et l'enveloppaient'/'she retained some consciousness of the vast expanse which stretched beneath her, beyond the darkness that curtained her sight. A loud rumbling arose, and waves of life seemed to surge up and circle around her' (p. 1054/138). The source space Zola's *Une page d'amour* seeks to capture is panoramic and endless.[8]

But if Zola and Chouraqui seek to adapt their source faithfully, both, in keeping with Berman's model, deform the very source they seek to proffer. Chouraqui adapts a 240-page novel into a telefilm of an hour and a half. His adaptation deforms Zola's novel and it does so for the ethnocentric reasons which Berman's theory enumerates, driven by Chouraqui's 1980 context. Chouraqui cuts many of the subplots of Zola's novel entirely. Those which disappear largely do so for reasons of time. Both the historical context of the Second Empire, so core to Zola's suite of novels, disappears as do some of the lesser-known nineteenth-century intertextual references which shape Zola's *Une page d'amour*. They disappear for they are not as readily accessible to the 1980s viewer as they were to the readers of Zola's novel, and Chouraqui does not have the televisual time to contextualise and explain. His annexation of the historical specificity of Zola's era is particularly visible in this adaptation which, in its historical artefacts, time slot, costuming and long, ponderous takes proclaims itself to be a period piece. In Zola's novel, Zéphyrin, the sweetheart of Hélène's maid, is a soldier, a poignant reference to the military misadventures which characterised the Second Empire, misadventures fresh in the mind of Zola's readers as they consumed the novels just a few short years after the fall of the empire. In Chouraqui's adaptation, re-named as Pierre, he is a civilian, working in a neighbouring household, important only for the love scenes he has with Hélène's maid, love scenes which speak the desire Hélène herself represses in relation to Henri Deberle. Zola used Zéphyrin to refract political history. Chouraqui uses Pierre to refract personal, sexual histories, displacing and deforming the specificity of nineteenth-century history which was so important to Zola's novel.

Chouraqui displaces and deforms some of the literary intertexts with which Zola's novel interacts for similarly ethnocentric reasons. Zola's *Une page d'amour* interacts intensively with Alfred de Musset's play *Un caprice* (1837), a text which disappears in Chouraqui's adaptation in its entirety. Musset's play, in which a young innocent (Mathilde) is married to an unfaithful man (Chavigny), offers a tangled plot in which a well-meaning friend, Madame de Léry, tries to bring the couple back together. In Zola's novel, Juliette Deberle picks and directs Musset's play as an item to be performed at one of her soirées (p. 1134/266). In its web of intrigue, it metatextually references the novel in which it appears, tying characters still more closely to their allotted roles. Juliette chooses Malignon to play the part of Chavigny, the unfaithful male who seduces and allows himself to be seduced on a seemingly regular basis. However, shortly before her extra-marital meeting with Malignon, Juliette herself stands in for him, reading his part in a role which anticipates her imminent fall into adultery (p. 1135/267). Musset's Madame de Léry steps in to reconcile Chavigny and his abandoned wife. Comparably, Hélène, Juliette's latest friend, rushes to the love nest where Malignon and Juliette are set to meet, seducing Henri when he subsequently arrives both before she wants to and in order to cover the truth of Juliette's intended infidelity (p. 1147/286). By seducing Henri, Hélène paradoxically preserves his marriage with Juliette, ultimately excluding herself from a space in his affections.[9] Zola's novel uses its nineteenth-century audience's awareness of Musset's play to drive its plot to its inevitable conclusion, a conclusion which is always already known for the reader in their intertextual knowledge. Chouraqui's adaptation removes Musset's text in its entirety, deforming the source text it adapts.

Chouraqui's adaptation not only deforms Zola by cutting subplots and intertextual references, he also cuts the nineteenth-century Parisian panoramas around which Zola's novel is structured. He does so because they are no longer available to him as authentic real spaces. Zola's protagonist may not be able to access the Parisian skyline she watches so intently from her elevated window above it but her counterpart in the adaptation finds herself still more constrained in spatial terms, for the director cuts Paris in its entirety. The effect is to make the space of

Chouraqui's *Une page d'amour* both smaller and more enclosed than its counterpart novel. With the exception of the enclosed garden and brief storm-swept foray to get the doctor when Jeanne is ill, Hélène's world becomes an entirely interior one in television. Two scenes reminiscent of Zola's predilection for elevated perspectives, detailed vision and expansive panoramas in the novel do feature in the adaptation. But both parody the vision and space so characteristic of Zola's panoramas. In the first Pauline, a character who wilfully chooses blindness as she ignores her future husband's infidelity with her sister (Deberle's wife), looks down from a walled terrace to the garden below. The small, enclosed space of the garden is blocked and obscured by a wall of torrential rain preventing it from being accessed in any form. In the second potentially panoramic scene, Jeanne and Lucien Deberle hide in the shared room of Lucien's parents safe in the knowledge that they will not be troubled there, such is the abeyance into which the Deberle's conjugal relations have fallen. Blind to the truth of their world, they plot a future which can never be — Jeanne plans to live to a ripe old age so that her mother need never sleep alone. Inverting the direction of the novel's vision as it looks out onto the world in a panoramic sweep, the camera instead pans almost full circle around the internal circumference of the room, focusing on the closed world of blindness within, on the children who hide from the hapless and harassed English nursemaid with such skill. The panoramic Parisian landscape so important to Zola's novel is insistently disallowed in Chouraqui's adaptation.

But Chouraqui is far from unthinking about the changes he makes to Zola's novel. He reflects on them in ways which speak to Berman's theory, integrating those reflections into the fabric of his televisual fictions. He does so specifically in his play on windows and his analysis of time. Windows are key to Zola's Naturalist project, standing as metaphors for his intent to offer his readers a window onto his near contemporary world. In Zola's novel, Hélène sits at her elevated window, trying, with her novelist creator, to make sense of the Parisian landscape they both contemplate. Chouraqui's adaptation is not able to recreate the nineteenth-century Paris-scape which his adaptation, in its period trappings, implicitly promises. It no longer exists in its integrity. He cuts it from his adaptation. But Chouraqui metaphorically reflects on that act of cutting in the play on windows around which his adaptation is structured. Chouraqui repeatedly offers his viewer windows onto Zola's world but he will not allow them to be accessed. They are filmed from angles which deny the viewer the ability to see through them. They are blocked by curtains, nets and characters. The opening scene in which Hélène seeks Henri in his capacity as a doctor speaks volumes in this respect. The scene is filmed through the glass window. This window, far from allowing vision, blocks it, covered as it is by torrential rain which warps and obscures the characters peering through it (Pierre, Hélène and Henri). If windows in Zola's fiction offered access to reality as source, serving as a metaphor for the naturalist project, windows in Chouraqui's adaptation block Zola as source, underscoring the complex ways in which the adaptation warps and distorts him. The adaptation blocks this opening scene aurally as well as visually, drowning out the sound of the conversation which takes place. It does so using both the torrential rain and the increasing volume of the Bach cello music which forms the musical accompaniment to the telefilm. The adaptation is not a window onto Zola's contemporary world. It is a blocked, obscured, partial window onto a period text, a text both offered and foreclosed by its images. Via his use of windows, Chouraqui reflects on his adaptation's deformation of the Zola source it simultaneously proffers and denies.

Chouraqui's contemplation of time works in a similar vein, allowing the director to reflect on the way that the nineteenth-century era he offers in his period piece is shaped, altered and re-made to meet the needs of his twentieth-century television audience. The adaptation may seek to return to the past but that past is inevitably of the adaptation's present. It underscores the circularity of time, circling both past and present. Words, images, objects and scenes return in it. The adaptation closes as it started, with Hélène remembering in dream the opening scene of Jeanne's recovery. Jeanne is ill three times in the course of the adaptation in scenes so similar in their location, dialogue and personnel that the adaptation compels their comparison. The first brings Hélène and Deberle together, the second cements their love and the final scene testifies to its containment. Henri is ejected from the room (as Rambaud was previously) and three doors are shut on him — the first by Helene, the second by Rosalie and the third by Henri himself. In the adaptation's circular temporal structures, Hélène and Henri find time only in spatial and temporal interstices. In the only fast movement of the camera in the intentional ponderousness of the adaptation, Hélène and Henri embrace in a doorway after Jeanne's illness. They later have their first kiss in the darkness of a closed door. The abbé Jouve, however, will not allow these spatial and temporal interstices. He rights the time of Hélène's clock (it is fifteen minutes slow) and subsequently the lovers' time disappears. He closes the door space in which the couple previously kissed, shutting Henri Deberle out at the adaptation's close. Hélène, seeking to reassure Jeanne in relation to the space and time of their relationship, promises Jeanne shortly before her demise that 'tout va recommencer comme avant'/'everything will be as it was'. Her words are telling. They speak not to Jeanne's future — Jeanne will shortly die and occupy no physical space in the future to which her mother alludes. Rather they reflect the circular time which will subsequently trap Hélène. In post-adaptive time, according to the programme's closing voice-over, Hélène will marry the man her daughter identifies as the double of her unhappy father and Hélène's life, in its endless sameness and repetitious serial rhythms, will turn and return on itself. Indeed the action closes with the piece's only flashback as, in Hélène's dream, it remembers the opening of the adaptation when Jeanne recovers.[10] In ways which speak to Berman's claim that adaptations adapt ethnocentrically for their own time, Chouraqui's adaptation underlines that the heritage time it offers is simultaneously of and for its own time, circling both past and present.

Time in Zola's novel is not circular. In contrast it is starkly linear. Zola's *Une page d'amour* insistently points to and moves towards its own ending from the outset, refusing to allow the reader the space to contemplate any other denouement. The novel's end may be glimpsed in summary form in Zola's early descriptions of Paris.

Predicting the fire and desire which will ignite Hélène, leading to the cold, snowy landscape of Jeanne's funeral and the glacial numbness which is to be her mother's life, Zola characterises Hélène's contemplation of the landscape thus:

> Et les tours de Notre-Dame, toutes dorées, se dressaient [...] au-delà desquelles la rivière, les constructions, les massifs d'arbres, n'étaient plus que de la poussière de soleil. Alors, éblouie, elle quitta ce cœur triomphal de Paris, où toute la gloire de la ville paraissait flamber. Sur la rive droite, au milieu des futaies des Champs-Elysées, les grandes verrières du palais de l'Industrie étalaient des blancheurs de neige; plus loin, derrière la toiture écrasée de la Madeleine, semblable à une pierre tombale, se dressait la masse énorme de l'Opéra.
>
> [The golden towers of Notre-Dame sprang up like boundary-marks of the horizon, beyond which river, buildings and clumps of trees became naught but sparkling sunshine. Then Hélène, dazzled, withdrew her gaze from this the triumphant heart of Paris, where the whole glory of the city appeared to blaze. On the right bank, amongst the clustering trees of the Champs-Elysées she saw the crystal buildings of the Palace of Industry glittering with a snowy sheen, farther away, behind the roof of the Madeleine, which looked like a tombstone, towered the vast mass of the Opera House.] (p. 1012/69)

The narrative leads its reader inexorably to forthcoming events and to the annihilation of Hélène's life as she knows it. Bringing together her mother and Henri in the opening illness, Jeanne unknowingly undoes their clothing, gesturing to the physical love which will subsequently occur between the two:

> Le châle était complètement tombé de ses épaules, découvrant la naissance de la gorge. Par derrière, son chignon dénoué laissait pendre des mèches folles jusqu'à ses reins. Elle avait dégagé ses bras nus, pour être plus prompte [...] n'ayant plus que la passion de son enfant. Et devant elle, affairé, le médecin ne songeait pas davantage à son veston ouvert, à son col de chemise que Jeanne venait d'arracher.
>
> [The shawl had slipped off her shoulders, and her hair had become unwound, some wanton tresses sweeping down to her hips. She had left her arms free and uncovered, that she might be the more ready, she had forgotten all, absorbed entirely in her love for her child. And on his side the doctor, busy with his work, no longer thought of his unbuttoned coat, or of the shirt-collar that Jeanne's clutch had torn away.] (p. 974/9)

Time, in its inexorability, in its linearity, traps both the characters and the reader in the inevitability of Zola's ending.[11] Time, thus, works intriguingly differently in Zola's novel and its adaptation. Zola proffers a temporal structure which is linear as his work moves relentlessly to its intended close. The adaptation looks to Zola's past and seeks to offer it to us, but the past is for and of our present. Thus the temporality of the adaptation is circular, moving as it does constantly between both poles, underscoring the ethnocentric alterations which Berman argues are innate to the adaptive process.

Chouraqui's self-reflexivity about his adaptive act and the changes he makes to Zola as source in many ways take him back to Zola. The nineteenth-century novelist's adaptation of reality is one which dramatises its fault lines and limitations, making art from them. As per Berman's model, Zola deforms his source. Zola seeks to translate the reality of the Paris landscape but what he embeds in his descriptions is the impossibility of so doing. His characters and his narrative contemplate the landscape, seeking to grasp it in words and vision, yet it cracks, fissures and breaks before them. Hélène spends hours trying to make sense of the city before her, studying it in different lights, seasons and times of day. In liquid descriptions which echo the Impressionists' study of light, the paradoxical vocabulary of cracking and breaking stand out: 'A l'horizon, sur le lac dormant, de longs frissons couraient. Puis, le lac, tout d'un coup, parut crever; des fentes se faisaient, et il y avait, d'un bout à l'autre, un craquement qui annonçait la débâcle'/'Prolonged quivers were darting over the sleeping lake of mist on the horizon. Suddenly it seemed to burst, gaps appeared, a rending sped from end to end, betokening a complete break-up' (p. 1009/65). Inserting very clear rips, fissures, breaks and holes in his descriptions of Paris, Zola disrupts and refuses the landscape which nevertheless exists and finds presence in his fiction: 'plus haut, des dômes et des flèches déchiraient le brouillard, dressant leurs silhouettes grises, enveloppés encore des lambeaux de la brume qu'ils trouaient'/'up above domes and steeples rent the mist, rearing grey outlines to which clung shreds of the haze which they had pierced' (pp. 1006–07/62). Intriguingly, in a play on presence and absence, Zola's descriptions of Paris focus repeatedly on dust — the matter endlessly in the process of absenting itself. He writes: 'Ce jour-là, dans le ciel pâle, le soleil mettait une poussière de lumière blonde'/'The sun filled the pale atmosphere that day with a golden dust' (p. 997/45), focusing later on 'ce blond soleil de février, pleuvant comme une poussière d'or'/'the pale yellow February sunshine that rained down like golden dust' (p. 1004/56). Zola's landscapes acknowledge their limits both by cropping the edges of their word canvas and by breaking the physical matter at their core, offering the reader dust in its place: 'les tours de Notre-Dame, toutes dorées, se dressaient comme les bornes de l'horizon, au-delà desquelles la rivière, les constructions, les massifs d'arbres n'étaient plus que de la poussière de soleil'/'the golden towers of Notre-Dame sprang up like boundary-marks of the horizon, beyond which rivers, buildings, and clumps of trees became naught [but the sparkling dust of sunshine]' (p. 1012/69). Fires metaphorically burn through Zola's translations of the city scape. The city before Hélène's and Jeanne's eyes is 'éclairé par les nuées saignantes, pareil à quelque ville des légendes expiant sa passion sous une pluie de feu'/'illumined by blood-red clouds, like some city of an old-world tale expiating its lusts under a rain of fire' (p. 1059/147). Such fires reference the nascent desire which burns ever more strongly in Hélène — Henri has just declared his love to her and she will shortly succumb to her sexual passion for him. But they also turn the city, the proffered source text behind Zola's adaptation, into ash. Zola's landscapes in *Une page d'amour* both reflect and comment on the Naturalist project, on their ability to capture reality in words. Zola deforms the source text he seeks to adapt into print but comments and reflects on his deformation in his images, achieving a complex, creative power and artistry in so doing.

Zola thus offers his readers not a naive belief that Naturalism can adapt reality in either its entirety or its integrity, but rather a thoughtful vision of the fictional game that is Naturalism in its intent to adapt reality as source. He playfully inscribes such a vision in his writing. He depicts a Paris-scape thus: 'des camions et des fiacres traversaient le pont, gros comme des jouets d'enfant, avec des chevaux délicats qui ressemblaient à des pieces mécaniques'/'drays and cabs crossed the bridge, mere child's toys in the distance, with miniature horses like pieces of mechanism' (p. 1010/68). Realism might, it seems, be child's play. He cannot, in his fictional landscapes, give us reality, for the reality his prose offers is always already artistic, always mediated by the filter of his fiction. He inscribes that artistry knowingly and visibly on his descriptions, compelling his reader to reflect on it. In the Deberle garden, 'on apercevait l'étroit jardin en toilette d'hiver, pareil à une grande sépia traitée avec un fini merveilleux'/'a full view could be had of the little garden, which, in its winter guise, looked like some large sepia drawing, finished with exquisite delicacy' (p. 1174/327). As Hélène gazes at Paris, the narration encodes the landscape thus: 'une lumière coulait, limpide et froide comme une eau de source, mettant Paris sous une glace où les lointains eux-mêmes prenaient une netteté d'image japonaise'/'there came a stream of light, pure and cool as the waters of a spring; and Paris once more shone out as under a glass, which lent even to the outlying districts the distinctness of a Japanese picture' (p. 1205/379). Zola contemplates the landscape next to Jeanne's grave: 'Plus loin, à droite, les grands arbres du quai étaient des merveilles. On aurait dit des arbres de verre filé, d'immenses lustres de Venise, dont des caprices d'artistes avaient tordu les bras piqués de fleurs'/'In the distance, to the right, the lofty trees on the quay seemed to be spun of glass, like huge Venetian chandeliers, whose flower-decked arms the designer had whimsically twisted' (p. 1207/382). Zola's novel offers us not reality as accessible source, but reality visibly deformed, albeit beautifully and with artistry, by the novelist's own craft. Zola's novel is as self-reflexive in its adaptation as Chouraqui's reworking of it. Both works, as per Berman's framework, reflect on their deformations of their sources, integrating that process of deformation into their adaptations precisely as a means to resist it.

Berman's approach to resisting deformation of his source takes a different form from those of Zola and Chouraqui. Berman argues that translation or adaptation should welcome the foreign, translating as literally as possible in order to let the foreign be foreign and the source have its own voice in its recreated form. He argues against naturalising translations and adaptations, pushing for them to gesture clearly to their provenance. Whilst this vision is specifically set out in his *La Traduction et la lettre ou L'Auberge du lointain*, it runs through Berman's thought consistently, most visibly perhaps in the source voices Berman allows audibly to speak in his theoretical frame. When writing on fidelity as a critical school, for example, Berman cites and reuses the words of Wilhelm von Humboldt:

> Chaque traducteur doit immanquablement recontrer l'un des deux écueils suivants: il s'en tiendra avec trop d'exactitude ou bien à l'original, aux dépens du goût et de la langue de son peuple, ou bien à l'originalité de son peuple, aux dépens de l'œuvre à traduire.[12]
>
> [Each translator inevitably comes up against one of two obstacles: either he tries to replicate exactly the original, sacrificing the cultural tastes and language of

his audience, or he tries to stick too closely to what makes his audience distinct, at the expense of the work being translated.]

Berman's citation of another thinker is far from insignificant, for he seeks to underline the thinkers and sources from whom he crafts his theory of translation, the foreign texts and others whom he welcomes and hosts in his work. Berman cites frequently and foregrounds his acts of citation, underscoring the adaptive influence of earlier texts on the fabric of his philosophy and the place of others in his own voice. He paraphrases Bakhtin, enacting Bakhtin's message about cumulative, palimpsestuous voices in that very act of paraphrasing:

> This is the central problem posed by translating novels — a problem that demands maximum reflection from the translator. Every novelistic work is characterized by linguistic superimpositions, even if they include sociolects, idiolects, etc. The novel, said Bakhtin, assembles a *heterology* or diversity of discursive types, a *heteroglossia* or diversity of languages, and a *heterophony* or diversity of voices.[13]

Berman explores the multiple voices which feed into his creative identity and product, the multiple voices from which he adapts his theoretical framework. He engages with the polyphony of his own work.

Zola, as a writer, anticipates the diversity of voices at the heart of Berman's theory, a diversity which, this chapter will argue, is also characteristic of Chouraqui's *Une page d'amour*. The nineteenth-century novelist highlights the wide range of intertextual and intermedial voices which speak in his fiction. That Zola adapts a whole host of other sources and voices in his fiction is, as I have suggested elsewhere, clear.[14] These sources and voices underscore the impossibility of fidelity as a critical space. Adaptations of Zola's work may be judged by their ability to convey Zola's voice as integral, ontological presence. Zola's voice, though, far from being ontological and integral, is itself a knowing translation and adaptation of earlier influences and authors. Intriguingly, while intertextuality is often associated with the broadening of the individual text as it opens itself to an apparently endless play of earlier texts, art forms, authors and moments, Zola's intertextual references in *Une page d'amour* confine the space of the novel, ceaselessly underlining the impossible nature of the love that drives and defines Hélène and the inevitability of the ending which awaits her. Zola's intertexts do not allow artistic escape but rather ensure textual confinement. Hélène's perusal of Walter Scott's *Ivanhoe* is a case in point. Hélène reads the novel about a man who, like Henri, has two women in his life — Lady Rowena and the beautiful Rebecca. Hoping that the novel's happy ending will be her own, Hélène identifies herself with the noble lady who will marry the novel's eponymous hero at the work's close. Hélène dreams of Henri:

> Elle songeait invinciblement au chevalier Ivanhoe, si passionnément aimé de deux femmes, Rebecca la belle juive, et la noble lady Rowena. Il lui semblait qu'elle aurait aimé avec la fierté et la sérénité patiente de cette dernière. Aimer, aimer! Et ce mot qu'elle ne prononçait pas, qui [...] vibrait en elle, l'étonnait et la faisait sourire.

[Yet she remained entranced, dreaming unceasingly of the knight Ivanhoe, loved so passionately by two women — Rebecca, the beautiful Jewess, and the noble Lady Rowena. She herself thought she could have loved with the intensity and patient serenity of the latter maiden. To love! To love! She did not utter the words, but they thrilled her through and through in the very thought, astonishing her, and irradiating her face with a smile.] (p. 1007/63)

However, Hélène's quest to identify herself with Rowena and her successful love undoes itself. Zola underlines its impossibility in grammatical terms. His use of a past conditional, 'aurait aimé', underlines the no-place in temporal terms of this love. Hélène's love as Rowena has not taken place and indeed even now she cannot voice it, however much the words resound in her soul. Hélène, in any case, is not Rowena. Zola works hard to twin her fate with that of Rebecca, the woman who loves so passionately and so impossibly. As Rebecca sits at the elevated window narrating to the injured Ivanhoe the details of the landscape and battle below, so Hélène gazes at Paris from the sickroom on high that she has shared with Henri, processing the details of the landscape below in textual descriptions which frequently have recourse to the vocabulary of war.[15] Describing the rooftops, Zola writes: 'Il y en avait d'énormes, nageant de l'air majestueux d'un vaisseau amiral, entourées de plus petites qui gardaient des symétries d'escadre en ordre de bataille'/'Some of them were very large, sailing along with all the majestic grace of an admiral's ship; and surrounded by smaller ones, preserving the regular order of a squadron in line of battle' (p. 1055/140). Comparably, the narrative contemplates fragments of light which attack the landscape 'avec son poudroiement continu de fusée'/'like the constant firing of a rocket' (p. 1056).[16] Hélène, unlike Rebecca, is alone in her contemplation of the landscape, her love even more isolated and impossible than that of Scott's character. As Rebecca leaves the country at the close of *Ivanhoe*, escaping both persecution and her love, so Hélène will go into exile in Marseille. Zola's heroine may wish for the fate of Rowena, but, implicitly allying her with the beautiful Rebecca, Zola refuses her that fate.[17] The intertextual use of Scott's novel by Zola, far from opening the novel to a play of textual possibility, underlines, in no uncertain terms, the impossibility of Hélène's love, the lack of space from which it will perish in the pages of Zola's writing.

Zola's novel though is not just an intertextual piece, but also an intermedial piece which demonstrates the infiltration of painterly techniques into the literary space of the text. Rodolphe Walter deems *Une page d'amour*'s five descriptions of Paris to be a series painting in words some ten years before Monet painted such a thing on canvas, working, like Zola on a set image but in different light conditions.[18] Zola's championing of the Impressionists and their core philosophies is key to his attempt to adapt the visual reality of Paris into his prose. Nathan Kranowski argues that *Une page d'amour*'s panoramic descriptions underscore Zola's artistic intentions to paint in words, to study light and colour as the Impressionists did.[19] Light, as it is so often in Impressionist painting, is an essentially fluid phenomenon in Zola's descriptions of Parisian reality, eating into the fixity of the reality his prose details. Describing Paris, Zola writes that 'un coup de soleil lui faisait rouler des flots d'or'/'A flash of sunshine came, and it would roll in waves of gold' (p. 1007/62).

This liquid light eats into outlines of the landscape, blurring them and offering in their place only the fleeting impression so characteristic of the canvases of the movement: 'on voyait des quartiers dont les lignes mollissaient et tremblaient, comme si on les eût regardés à travers quelque flamme invisible'/'the outlines of some districts grew faint and quivered as if they were being viewed through an invisible flame' (p. 1010/68). The people in the midst of this light are reduced to mere indications: 'En bas, sur la vaste place et sur les trottoirs, aux deux côtés de la Seine, [Hélène] distinguait les passants, une foule active de points noirs emportés dans un mouvement de fourmilière'/'Down below, on thoroughfare and pavement on each side of the Seine, she could see the passers-by — a busy cluster of black dots, moving like a swarm of ants' (p. 1010/68). Reality, both Zola and the Impressionists underline, is subjective, refracted through the consciousness of its viewer. Jeanne stares at Paris and the novel, in its vocabulary, mediates the landscape through her childlike perspective: 'A mesure que le rayon s'élargissait, des hachures roses et bleues peinturluraient l'horizon, d'un bariolage d'aquarelle enfantine. Il y eut un flamboiement, une tombée de neige d'or sur une ville de cristal'/'As the gush of light streamed across the sky, touches of pink and blue appeared on the horizon, a medley of colour suggestive of a childish attempt at water-colour painting. Then there was a blaze, a fall of golden snow, as it were, over a city of crystal' (p. 1156/298). Zola offers a similarly subjective word painting of reality from the perspective of Jeanne's mother Hélène, describing the same landscape from the same window but from the viewpoint of a different person. In so doing he works to underscore the unbreakable bond between Jeanne and her mother Hélène, offering us further insight into Hélène as heroine. Hélène stares at the city:

> La Seine, entre ses berges que les rayons obliques enfilaient, roulait des flots dansants où le bleu, le jaune et le vert se brisaient en un éparpillement bariolé; mais, en remontant le fleuve, ce peinturlurage de mer orientale prenait un seul ton d'or de plus en plus éblouissant; et l'on eût dit un lingot sorti à l'horizon de quelque creuset invisible, s'élargissant avec un remuement de couleurs vives, à mesure qu'il se refroidissait.
>
> [The Seine, whose banks the oblique rays were enfilading, was rolling dancing wavelets, streaked with scattered splashes of blue, green and yellow; but farther up the river, in lieu of this blotchy colouring, suggestive of an Eastern sea, the waters assumed a uniform golden hue, which became more and more dazzling. You might have thought that some ingot were pouring forth from an invisible crucible on the horizon, broadening out with a coruscation of bright colours as it gradually grew colder.] (p. 1057/143)

Hélène's vision echoes that of Jeanne, cited above, in vocabulary (the use of *peinturlurer* and *barioler*), in colour scheme (the central focus on gold) and in its youthful naivety. Hélène may be a generation older than her daughter but by referencing the orient in her vision of the landscape, Zola links her vision of the city to that of her daughter, who attends a fancy dress party in Japanese costume and dances. Hélène, Zola implies, is no more worldly and mature in emotional terms than the daughter implicitly referenced in this description in which she is not actually present, the daughter who will crush the nascent passion with Henri of which Hélène dreams as she stares at Paris.[20] Zola's Paris-scapes in *Une page d'amour* adapt the philosophies and techniques of the Impressionists as well as the landscape which is at the heart of Zola's text.

And Impressionist canvases are not the only intertexts from the world of visual arts on which Zola draws. *Une page d'amour* adapts and translates Fragonard's *Les Hasards heureux de l'escarpolette* (known in English simply as *The Swing*) (1767). It does so to underscore in intertextual terms the confined, constricted space of Hélène's life, love and eventual destiny. In the Deberle garden Hélène soars to the skies, pushed by the paternal Rambaud (p. 1003/55). The moment reflects the brief taste of freedom, abandon and exhilaration Hélène will subsequently experience in her affair with Henri. This swing scene reflects not only Hélène's fate, though, it also twins that fate, in an inter-artistic moment, with the heroine of Fragonard's painting. Zola, the writer so famed for his relationship with his painterly confrères, implicitly references Fragonard's painting in a number of ways. The garden's foliage and depiction of its green space as a seductive secluded area echoes that in Fragonard's titillating painting. As Fragonard's female figure is watched as she swings by a network of animate and inanimate gazes (the cupid, the man beneath her skirt, the viewer), so Hélène, trapped in a comparable network of gazes, swings in a moment of abandon. Fragonard's heroine loses her shoe in a painterly gesture to the virtue she has either already lost or will soon give up. Hélène, still chaste, is undressed differently. Zola writes: 'Hélène montait; à chaque envol, elle gagnait de l'espace [...] une natte de son chignon se dénouait'/'Hélène went higher, each ascent taking her farther [...] but a plait of her hair slipped down' (pp. 1003–04/55). Comparably, the skirt she has tied around her ankles with string refuses its restriction: 'Malgré la ficelle qui les nouait, ses jupes flottaient et découvraient la blancheur de ses chevilles. Et on la sentait à l'aise'/'Despite the cord which bound them, her skirts now waved about [revealing the paleness of her ankles] and you could divine that she was at her ease' (p. 1004/55; Vizetelly's translation cuts the supplied passage). Like the hidden viewer in Fragonard's painting, the reader peeps beneath Hélène's skirts, witnessing in this reflective moment the prediction of the infidelity Zola will not allow her to avoid. Far from opening the novel up to the space of intertextual play, Zola cites other texts and mediums to foreclose Hélène's life.[21]

Chouraqui's adaptation, at first glance, appears less intermedially capacious than its source text. No equivalent to the Impressionist techniques so intriguing to Zola may be located in the telefilm for it blocks the Parisian landscape in its entirety. So too does it cut Zola's ekphrastic rendering of Fragonard's painting, depriving Hélène even of her moment of airborne freedom and showing only Jeanne swinging sullenly in her mother's place. The adaptation, though, introduces its own painterly intertext into its gallery of images. Seeking her mother, Jeanne walks into the maid Rosalie's work space to discover her carrying out her ablutions. Rosalie sits, the focus of the scene, with her naked back to us, her legs apart. In a moment highly reminiscent of Degas's bathing scenes, the shot of Rosalie's naked body is neither sensual nor romanticised. The adaptation's interest is not in the beauty of her body, but rather in the play of her muscles as she reaches to wash herself, in the contortions of her muscles as she carries out this most prosaic of acts, her legs splayed and her skirt around her waist.²² The adaptation's reference to Degas seals Hélène in the claustrophobic space of her life. In filming Rosalie in a state of undress, the adaptation gestures towards the undressing of Hélène herself in her sexual relationship with Henri, a relationship so stifled it never appears on screen. Their sexual relations are presumed but televisually disallowed. And, alienating Hélène still further from her ephemeral moment of sexual freedom, the adaptation displaces all sexuality from her body onto that of her servant. Subsequent to her bathing, Rosalie will leave to flirt and caress Pierre in the Deberle garden while Hélène and Henri sit at the opposite end of the garden, laughing and chastely holding hands. In intermedial relations which resonate with the palimpsest of voices making up Berman's translation theory, the adaptation uses art to deny her any sexuality, allowing her to love physically only in refracted form in the words and caresses of others.

The adaptation's intermedial borrowings extend to the sphere of music as Chouraqui's piece, like Zola's novel, draws creative power from its italicisation of the polyphony of creative voices from which it crafts itself. As if to highlight his alterations to and foreclosing of Zola's voice, Chouraqui plays on the wandering nature of words as speech slips between characters, authors and owners, its meaning mutating as it passes to new contexts and mouths. Rosalie sits at the central table in Hélène and Jeanne's home, peeling vegetables for dinner. She sings 'Belle qui tiens ma vie' [Beautiful one who holds my life] by Thoinot Arbeau (1520–95), a song of impossible love:

> Belle qui tiens ma vie
> Captive dans tes yeux
> Qui m'as l'âme ravie
> D'un sourire gracieux,
> Viens tôt me secourir
> Ou me faudra mourir. (bis)
>
> Pourquoi fuis-tu mignarde
> Si je suis près de toi,
> Quand tes yeux je regarde
> Je me perds dedans moi,
> Car tes perfections
> Changent mes actions. (bis)
>
> Tes beautés et ta grâce
> Et tes divins propos
> Ont échauffé la glace
> Qui me gelait les os,
> Et ont rempli mon cœur
> D'une amoureuse ardeur. (bis)
>
> Mon âme voulait être
> Libre de passions,
> Mais Amour s'est fait maître
> De mes affections,
> Et a mis sous sa loi
> Et mon cœur et ma foi. (bis)

Approche donc ma belle
Approche, toi mon bien,
Ne me sois plus rebelle
Puisque mon cœur est tien.
Pour mon mal apaiser,
Donne-moi un baiser. (bis)

Je meurs mon angelette,
Je meurs en te baisant.
Ta bouche tant doucette
Va mon bien ravissant.
À ce coup mes esprits
Sont tous d'amour épris. (bis)

Plutôt on verra l'onde
Contre mont reculer,
Et plutôt l'œil du monde
Cessera de brûler,
Que l'amour qui m'épasse
Décroisse d'un seul point. (bis)

Beautiful one who holds my life
Captive in your eyes,
Who has ravished my soul
With a gracious smile.
Come to my aid
Or I must die.

Why do you flee, dainty one,
If I am near you?
When I behold your eyes
I am lost inside myself
Because your perfection
[so affects my behaviour].

Your beauty and your grace
And your divine ways
Have melted the ice
Which was freezing my bones
And have filled my heart
With a loving ardour.

My soul wanted to be
Free of passion,
But love became master
Of my affections
And put under its law
My heart and my faith.

Come near, my lovely one,
Come near, my [dear one],
Do not resist me further
For my heart is yours,
To relieve my ills
Give me a kiss.

> I die, my Little Angel,
> I die when kissing
> Your mouth so sweet.
> My very lovely one,
> With that touch my spirits
> Are completely lifted in love.
>
> Sooner will waves
> Flow backwards
> And sooner will the moon
> Cease to shine
> Before the love which conquered me
> Wanes a single iota.[23]

Rosalie's song, in a multifaceted moment of ventriloquism, speaks for multiple characters in words which are never her own, belonging as they do to Arbeau. Her song predicts the action and is both for and about Hélène. Arbeau's text gestures to Hélène's icy untouchable beauty and foreshadows the imprisonment that is her life as a result of this love which holds her 'captive'. It both references her captivity in the system of desiring gazes which surrounds her and the sickness and death (of Jeanne) which will drive her. The song speaks Hélène's sexual desire for Henri Deberle, referencing both his profession and the impossible unsatisfied desire the couple share in the line 'pour mon mal apaiser'. It also speaks Deberle's pursuit of her ('Approche donc ma belle | Approche, toi mon bien, | Ne me sois plus rebelle'). So too does it speak Jeanne's jealous passion for total possession of her mother and her affections. Indeed, having cut to a static shot of Jeanne as Rosalie sings, the adaptation plays with the vocabulary of the song and specifically the line 'la glace qui me gelait les os', integrating it into the adaptation as Hélène re-enters the action scolding her daughter for having 'les pieds glacés' [frozen feet]. Rosalie's song, with its insistent 'ou me faudra mourir', points relentlessly to Jeanne's death, heartbroken at her mother's infidelity. Words slip between mouths within the adaptation, their meaning different in each mouth and in relation to each character.[24] The adaptation, like Berman, makes itself a home for the voices of other artists and creators. Like Zola, it emphasises its inability to capture and translate the voice of its source, instead embracing a plurality of intermingling, sonorous voices from which it makes art.

If Rosalie's intradiegetic song, Arbeau's 'Belle qui tiens ma vie', is important, the extradiegetic presence of Bach's Cello Suites 1–6 is still more resonant in Chouraqui's adaptation. Angered by her future husband Malignon, Pauline disappears to play Bach's Cello Suites, her artistry filling the Deberle household. However, Bach's suites, extradiegetically, form the soundtrack to the adaptation. They begin as Hélène leaves her rooms to seek the services of Henri Deberle for the sick Jeanne and are thereafter associated with the plight of the two lovers. They surge when Juliette announces that she will holiday without her husband, unwittingly allowing Henri the space to pursue his illicit love for Hélène. They also play when Jeanne seeks her mother in their empty rooms, informing the audience where that mother is: consummating her passion for Henri. The adaptation's choice of music is far from unconsidered. The cyclical structure of Zola's five-part novel with its serial contemplation of the same space in the Parisian landscape, a circularity which echoes the enclosure of Hélène's life, has its counterpart in these musical studies which Bach intended as a systematically conceived cycle. Bach inserted intermezzos, or *galanterie* movements, in the form of pairs between the sarabandes and the gigues. Moreover, Bach's suites, like Hélène's life, revolve around and find ephemeral beauty in the repetition of a sense of sameness. Bach's prelude to the first suite and the sarabande to the fifth take the form of arpeggiated chords with no actual melody. They repeat the same pattern with only the chord changing. Hélène's life may change chord with the eruption of Henri into her affections, but its patterns are fixed in many respects. She is as entrapped in musical terms as she is in every other way in this adaptation, an entrapment which, Chouraqui's piece suggests, will dominate her post-filmic life. The cello suites play in Hélène's impossible dream at the close of the telefilm as the camera dips into her consciousness shortly before Jeanne's death and the repetitions of Bach's music continue after the television image has faded to black. Bach's music has become the soundtrack to the circles and cycles of Hélène's life. The impact of music in Zola's *Une page d'amour* has not gone unconsidered. William J. Berg and Laurey K. Martin write:

> *Une page d'amour* illustrates Zola's preoccupation with the arts, his interest in questions of knowledge and communication, and his fascination with possible exchanges between artistic media; the novel reflects various art forms (notably literature, music and painting) in its composition, themes, and style.[25]

Writing on the five descriptions of Paris, they continue: 'Zola suggested their musical nature in one of his preparatory outlines for the novel; he referred to them as "five or six large-scale landscape descriptions, coming back like a song, always the same"'.[26] Bach's suites, in their repetitions create beauty from sameness. They give voice to the musical analogies in Zola's novel. They testify, in musical terms, to the entrapment of his heroine. They harmonise with the intertextual multiplicity, the range and resonance of voices in Berman's theory.

The adaptation's commitment precisely to this range and resonance of voices which Berman identifies is underscored by the way in which it compensates for the intertextual references which it has cut from Zola's novel. Musset, in Chouraqui's adaptation, may have disappeared, but in his place the adaptation inserts a different, more readily accessible intertext. Using another book within this adaptation of a canonical book, Jeanne reads what is presumed to be Perrault's tale of *Barbebleue* [Bluebeard] (1697) to Rambaud, the would-be suitor for her mother's hand. Rambaud, the man characterised by his beard (he shaves it off to please Jeanne), owes much to his fairy-tale counterpart. While Zola's Rambaud is a good, albeit unexciting man, the adaptation's version of him is far more explosive and volatile in his speech. 'Quelquefois il me fait peur' [Sometimes he scares me] states Hélène to his brother, after one of Rambaud's early outbursts. Jeanne, like her mother, fears the overpowering strength of this man whom the adaptation tellingly films in close up, allowing his large body to overpower the screen and the shot (he is played by Jean-Pierre Castaldi, a physically imposing actor). She struggles to release her hand from his powerful embrace and resists as he twirls her around, shouting in relation to his beard: 'ça pique, ça pique!' [it stings, it stings!]. Though Barbebleue has no place as such in Zola's novel, the stuff of fairy tale does. Contemplating the children's fancy dress ball, the narrative states: 'On aurait dit le gala d'un conte de fée, avec des amours déguisés pour les fiançailles de quelque prince charmant'/'The scene realised to the mind the merrymaking of a fairy-tale to which trooped Cupids in disguise to honour the betrothal of some Prince Charming' (p. 1050/132). Fairy tale, in any case, is always, theorist Julie Sanders suggests, metatextually resonant in a work of adaptation for it functions as a potential metaphor for the adaptive process itself, representing an endlessly earlier body of narrative worked and re-worked across time for new moments and contexts.[27] It is a culturally recognisable source whose intertextuality the adaptation asks its viewer to recognise as it traps Hélène not in the literal death Barbebleue metes out to his wives, but in the spiritual death of a marriage to a man she does not love as history repeats itself by offering her another loveless marriage. Barbebleue may massacre his wives, but the metaphorical violence done to the adaptation's heroine by such a marriage is enacted by the abrupt severance of the adaptation. No view of Hélène's life post-Jeanne is offered. No view of her marriage is offered. Rather, having cut to black, the adaptation offers an abrupt voiceover, a technique alien to the rest of the adaptation, to describe in highly cursory terms, the non-life that is Hélène's post-marriage. The adaptation, like Zola, uses a variety of intertextual voices to deprive Hélène of her agency and voice. It changes Zola's chosen intertexts, deforming them as per Berman's model. But in deforming Zola it paradoxically takes us back to him, echoing the intricate intertextual play on texts of contemporary relevance to the novel's consumption.

Deformation lies at the heart of Berman's reading of translation and adaptation and is, to Berman's mind, something to be countered as strongly as possible. Zola's *Une page d'amour* and Chouraqui's adaptation anticipate, explore and evaluate Berman's critical framework. They reflect ethically on the ways in which they deform the sources they seek to recreate in new media. But they mitigate their acts of deformation in novel ways. They contemplate the changes they make to their sources self-reflexively, integrating them into the fabric of their fictions as they reflect both on the limits and potentialities of their adaptations. They show and make art from what they cannot do. Moreover, and perhaps most importantly, both Zola and Chouraqui challenge Berman's assumption that deformation is an innately bad thing. Zola's novel acknowledges that it can only capture partial, fragmented, fleeting and subjective slices of the reality of which it goes in quest. But it is more powerfully realist in its adaptation precisely as a result of such an acknowledgement, testifying to the compelling complexity and ungraspable expansiveness of its source. Chouraqui's adaptation acknowledges that it deforms Zola, cutting elements of him and updating him ethnocentrically for a 1980s televisual context. But in deforming Zola, Chouraqui simultaneously takes us back to Zola as he weaves a powerfully polyphonic range of intertexts adapted to resonate with his contemporary audience. Chouraqui may deform Zola, but he crafts a complex fidelity to him in so doing, even while wresting a no less complex creative potency and originality for himself. Linked by their polyphonic texts, which welcome the voices of others, Zola, Chouraqui and Berman diverge in their reading of adaptation and deformation of source texts. For Berman, with his more central focus on translation, deformation is to be avoided at all costs. For Zola and Chouraqui, working squarely in the field of adaptation, it is precisely in the complexities of deformation that fidelity, creativity and art may be found.

Notes to Chapter 4

1. Chouraqui's adaptation is widely available on commercially released DVD (2017).
2. See, for example, Kate Griffiths, 'Radio and the Space of Adaptation: Diana Griffiths's *Madame Bovary* (Radio 4, 2006)', *Dix-Neuf*, 18 (2014), 211–23.
3. Berman writes: 'la *Phèdre* antique et celle de Racine, l'*Antigone* de Sophocle et celle d'Anouilh.... Là encore, la frontière entre une traduction "libre" qui recule devant certaines particularités du texte (et donc le modifie) et la transformation avouée n'est pas nette' [The *Phèdre* of antiquity and that of Racine, Sophocles's *Antigone* versus that of Anouilh.... The boundary between a 'free' translation which shies away from certain specificities of the text (and therefore modifies it) and overt transformation is not distinct] (Berman, *La Traduction et la lettre ou l'auberge du lointain*, p. 37).
4. Ibid., p. 74.
5. Antoine Berman, 'Translation and the Trials of the Foreign', trans. by Lawrence Venuti, in *The Translation Studies Reader*, ed. by Venuti, pp. 240–53 (p. 242).
6. Ibid.
7. Emile Zola, *Une page d'amour*, in *Œuvres complètes*, ed. by Henri Mitterand, 15 vols (Paris: Cercle du Livre Précieux, 1966–69), III, 959–1220 (p. 981); *A Love Episode*, trans. by Ernest Alfred Vizetelly (London: Hutchinson, 1895), p. 20.
8. Zola's panoramas may be vast but, paradoxically, they trap his heroine Hélène in a tiny, claustrophobic life. Hélène may see the ever-broadening expanses of Paris from her window, but she never fully accesses them either in mind or body. Paris remains a stranger to her psychologically. Neither she nor her daughter comprehend it: 'elles continuèrent à regarder Paris, sans chercher davantage à le connaître. Cela était très doux, de l'avoir là et de l'ignorer. Il restait l'infini et l'inconnu. C'était comme si elles se fussent arrêtées au seuil d'un monde dont elles avaient l'éternel spectacle, en refusant d'y descendre'/'So they continued to gaze on Paris, troubling no further to identify any part of it. It was very delightful to have it there before them, and yet to know nothing of it, it remained the vast and the unknown. It was as though they had halted on the threshold of a world which ever unrolled its panorama before them, but into which they were unwilling to descend' (p. 1014/72). The windows, so ubiquitous in Zola's fictions, and their panoramic descriptions serve to offer Hélène access to this world and simultaneously to block it. Not only is Hélène's vision of Paris from the window blocked, but so too are her rare experiences of the city itself as she descends into it. The action unfurls in a series of interior, closed spaces such as the screened gold and black salon and the hothouse in the Deberle household, rooms in which characters repeatedly have recourse to the vocabulary of 'étouffement' [suffocation]. Even the few outdoor spaces to which Hélène has access are as closed as their internal counterparts. Hélène repeatedly traverses the Passage des eaux, 'un étrange escalier étranglé entre les murs des jardins voisins'/'a strange steep lane, like a stair case pent [squeezed in] between garden walls' (p. 988/33), '[un] étroit couloir'/'narrow alley', bordered by gardens whose doors 'elle n'avait jamais vues ouvertes'/'she had never seen open' (pp. 992/38–39). A claustrophobic space in and of itself, the Passage des eaux seemingly shrinks as Hélène moves through it: 'A droite et à gauche, les murs se resserraient, allongés démesurément par la nuit'/'The walls, right and left, grew closer, seemingly prolonged by the darkness' (p. 1128/257). The novel's other external space, the Deberle jardinet, proves no more open: 'Une simple grille le fermait sur la rue [...], seulement, un tel rideau de verdure avait grandi là, que de

la rue aucun regard ne pouvait pénétrer; des lierres, des clématites, des chèvrefeuilles se collaient et s'enroulaient à la grille, et, derrière ce premier mur de feuillage, s'en haussait un second, fait de lilas et de faux ébéniers. Même l'hiver, les feuilles persistantes des lierres et l'entrelacement des branches suffisaient à barrer la vue'/'The garden [...] was separated from the Rue Vineuse by a plain iron railing, but against this grew a thick green hedge, which prevented the curious from gazing in. Ivy, clematis, and woodbine clung and wound around the railings, and behind this first curtain of foliage came a second one of lilacs and laburnums. Even in the winter the ivy leaves and the close network of branches sufficed to shut off the view' (p. 997/44–45).

9. Zola's use of Musset's play underscores the fascination of the novel as a whole with the world of theatre and playacting. Not only does the novel open with a series of repetitious conversations about theatrical performances, but the theatre pervades the novel in metaphorical form (p. 979/18). A marionette performance is the cause of much excitement at the children's ball (p. 1044/127). Juliette Deberle goes to the church as she would a theatrical performance, reserving seats for her friends. Henri appears to view her brief passion for religion as he would a passion for theatre as he comes to collect her: 'Lui, très grave, avait la mine correcte d'un mari qui venait chercher ces dames chez Dieu, comme il serait allé les attendre dans le foyer d'un theatre'/'the expression on his face was sober [...] the same, indeed, as if he had been waiting for them in the lobby of a theatre' (p. 1070/162). He is, in any case, himself playing a part in this novel as he dissembles his affection for his wife's friend. Assessing Jeanne's refusal to allow Henri near her mother, Zola continues: 'elle les forçait à une contrainte continuelle, à une comédie d'indifférence dont ils sortaient plus frissonnants'/'she forced them into a constant constraint, a comedy of indifference from which they emerged more tense than ever' (p. 1088; translation taken from Emile Zola, *A Love Story*, trans. by Helen Constantine, (Oxford: Oxford University Press, 2017), p. 136, for its maintaining of Zola's theatrical imagery).

10. Flashbacks are more numerous in Zola's novel. They are used to give textual space to Hélène's first marriage (p. 1009/65). They are also used to underscore Hélène's all-consuming desire for Henri as she lives and relives his declaration of love for her (p. 1052/138). Moreover, Zola's compulsive return to the section of Parisian landscape before Hélène's window comes to function as something of a flashback as the sameness of the location pushes both the intra- and extra-diegetic viewer to assess time as a phenomenon as the seasons in the novel's year pass and shape the colours, outlines and features of the landscape on offer.

11. In keeping with Zola's novel, Chouraqui does underline time's ability to compress and enclose Hélène in the adaptation. The adaptation's plot, told from start to end with no deviations, takes place in one calendar year, 1895, and in one place, Passy. The adaptation thus adapts some of the tenets of Classical French seventeenth-century tragedy to confine Hélène in the narrative and the inevitability of her fate. It obeys the unity of time (albeit making one day into one year), place (situating everything in Passy) and action (the adaptation never deviates from its study of Hélène's love). It might also be seen to obey, in modern televisual form, the notion of *bienséance*, for the sex Zola details is presumed but not seen on his adaptive screen. Hélène's love is not spoken directly, it reverberates only in speech about other matters. Ventriloquising Jeanne, Hélène speaks her affection for Henri. Her words to explain Jeanne's discomposure in front of Henri are simultaneously her own: 'Elle est impressionnée c'est tout' [she's shy, that's all]. 'Par moi?' [Because of me?], Henri replies. To which she responds, 'Elle n'a pas l'habitude des visages nouveaux' [She's not used to seeing new faces]. Henri reciprocally expresses his affection for Hélène via Jeanne, holding the girl's hand in a scene shortly before he will endeavour to hold that of her mother. Characters in the adaptation are trapped not only by the machinations of Jeanne, they are also enclosed in temporal terms, in dramatic structures which foster a sense of constriction.

12. Berman, *L'Epreuve de l'étranger*, p. 9.
13. Berman, 'Translation and the Trials of the Foreign', pp. 251–52.
14. See Griffiths, *Zola and the Artistry of Adaptation*.
15. Walter Scott, *Ivanhoe* (Ware: Wordsworth Editions, 2000), p. 242.
16. This translation, which maintains the military vocabulary of the source, is taken from that by Constantine, *A Love Story*, p. 98.

17. For more on Hélène's misreading of reality and indeed of *Ivanhoe*, see Corinne Kubler, 'Intertextualités zoliennes', *Cahiers naturalistes*, 63 (1989), 168–81. While *Ivanhoe* occupies a smaller space in the adaptation (it lies on Hélène's lap in the Deberle garden and triggers a brief discussion), the adaptation is even more categorical in its refusal to allow Hélène the happy ending Scott's novel promises. Hélène, in the adaptation, is not allowed to speak the textual love to which she aspires. Juliette, the woman who will, like Rowena, win Ivanhoe/Henri, takes the book from Hélène, summarising the story, reading its text in her own voice, before slamming it shut and keeping it in her grasp.
18. Rodolphe Walter, 'Emile Zola et Claude Monet', *Cahiers naturalistes*, 26 (1964), 51–61.
19. Nathan Kranowski, *Paris dans les romans d'Emile Zola* (Paris: Presses universitaires de France, 1968).
20. Zola's landscapes translate not just contemporary Paris, but also the emotional landscape of Hélène's life, gesturing towards the nascent passion which will develop in the course of the novel in their insistent personification of a cityscape gendered and clothed in the feminine. The landscape takes on the hues and textures of Hélène's flesh: 'Sur la rive droite, le quartier des Tuileries avait le rose pâli d'une étoffe couleur chair'/'Up on the right bank a pale pink, flesh-like tint suffused the Tuileries district' (p. 1009/66). And as her body will unclothe itself for the sex scene with Henri which we never see, the landscape predicts her sexual fall with her lover from the outset, disrobing and casting aside its feminine clothing in landscapes which form something of a metaphorical striptease: 'Cependant les eaux baissaient toujours. Elles n'étaient plus que de fines mousselines étalées; et, une à une, les mousselines s'en allaient, l'image de Paris s'accentuait et sortait du rêve'/'However, the watery mist was quickly falling. It became at last no more than a fine muslin drapery, and bit by bit this muslin vanished, and Paris took shape and emerged from dreamland' (p. 1009/66).
21. Specific critics, moreover, have sought to establish further intertextual parallels between individual paintings and key textual sequences and their aquatic imagery in *Une page d'amour*. For William Berg, Berthe Morisot's *Femme et enfant au balcon* (1874) is reproduced ekphrastically in the pages of Zola's novel. From an elevated viewpoint a darkly dressed mother and her young daughter gaze, like Hélène and her daughter whilst in mourning, at the city below. As Hélène and Jeanne never seek to access or to comprehend the city below, so Morisot's protagonists are separated from the metropolis by the bars of the balcony, by the metaphorical blockage which so frequently restrains and restricts the female space in this painter's work. Indeed Morisot's heroine does not even appear to look at the landscape before us: her gaze is directed elsewhere just as Hélène, even while watching the ever-changing vista of Paris never fully sees it, focusing instead on the puzzling, obscured vista of her own psyche. Zola's intermedial relationship with Morisot thus, even while it opens *Une page d'amour*'s narrative space to a different art form, simultaneously closes his text by reiterating Hélène's endless enclosure in both her personal and textual space (Berg, *The Visual Novel*, p. 102).
22. Intriguingly, in her 2006 adaptation for theatre of *Thérèse Raquin*, Marianne Elliott utilised a comparable bathing shot reminiscent of Degas showing Thérèse cleansing herself of the offstage murder of Camille. For further details see Griffiths, *Emile Zola and the Artistry of Adaptation*, p. 135.
23. Thoinot Arbeau, 'Belle qui tiens ma vie', 'Beautiful One Who Holds my Life', trans. by David Samuel Barr, <https://lyricstranslate.com/en/belle-qui-tiens-ma-vie-beautiful-one-who-holds-my-life.html> [accessed 10 October 2018].
24. Not only are words not fixed in the adaptation but so too the borders and boundaries between core characters prove permeable. Hélène's dead husband and her prospective suitor — the brother of the abbé Faujas — are a case in point. Hélène's husband died of madness. Her prospective suitor, whom she will marry in post-adaptive time, suffers from nervous complaints, insomnia and unease. Underscoring that Hélène's future marriage will be a replica of her past, l'abbé Jouve promotes the marriage with the multiply resonant words 'votre mari était comme mon frère' [your husband was like my brother], signalling unwittingly both the closeness of their relationship and the similarity of their dispositions. Words, in the adaptation, move in multiple directions, seeping beyond the possession and intended meanings of their original speaker.

Identities prove porous as the television adaptation engages in an extended play on displacement as a trope. Hélène's relationship with Henri is driven by a sexual desire which is never spoken or shown in its physical incarnation. The adaptation displaces it onto their offspring. Henri and Hélène make charged chit-chat in a social group in the garden as the governess seeks their children Jeanne and Lucien. The camera cuts to the parental bedroom, the children lying in the bed their respective parents would like to occupy together. A comparable act of displacement occurs when Hélène and Henri's love is consummated off-screen. The camera offers a scene of a naked Rosalie bathing, the flexing muscles of her nude body referencing those of her mistress at the same time off-screen. Such displacement might be seen to take us away from Zola as source author and creative body yet actually they lead us back to him on a meta-creative level, for the nineteenth-century novelist has his heroine kiss Jeanne on the exact spot Henri kissed said daughter in order to connect with him. Malignon and Juliette arrange to meet in Malignon's love nest, yet Jeanne, in her bid to save Henri's marriage from infidelity, prevents their infidelity, paradoxically coming to lie with Henri in the extra-marital bed from which she barred Juliette. Despite her jealousy of Juliette, Hélène simultaneously loves her as an extension and representation of the man to whom she is married. Words and bodies are replaced and displaced in intricate and inextricable ways in the work of Zola and his reincarnation in television form.

25. William J. Berg and Laurey Kramer Martin, *Emile Zola Revisited* (New York: Twayne, 1992), p. 132.
26. Ibid., p. 135.
27. Sanders, *Adaptation and Appropriation*, pp. 82–93.

CHAPTER 5

Germinal and the Politics of Patronage: Zola, Lefevere and the BBC

Chapter Four focused on the ethnocentric alterations innate to the adaptive process, arguing that source texts are inevitably shaped in adaptive form to the time and tendencies of their target era or audience. This current chapter maintains a focus on culture. It asks if, in our debates on fidelity, we need to look further than the source text and consider the formative force of those commissioning adaptations, the dominant poetics of the time and prevailing ideologies of adaptation. It seeks to question the fixity of the term 'fidelity' as a critical framework, underscoring that it has meant very different things in different historical eras. The chapter takes as its core the theorist André Lefevere (1945–96), a towering figure in the field of Translation Studies. Lefevere's vision of translations or adaptations as artefacts shaped and rewritten by the culture for which they are destined, a culture which in turn they seek to influence in different ways, has powerful purchase when applied to the BBC's 1970 five-part adaptation of *Germinal*, dramatised by David Turner. It is, as a television programme, visibly shaped by the adaptive poetics of the BBC, by BBC cultural values as embodied by the corporation's charter, by contemporary economics as well as politics and the need to maintain a distinct audience in the face of competition from ITV. So too is it shaped by the state of BBC technology at the time and by contemporary debates on or opposition to the cultural and moral value of BBC creative outputs. This television translation of Zola's *Germinal* bears the hallmark of the BBC as cultural entity, as 'patron', to use one of Lefevere's key terms, as much if not more so than that of its source author. But its value to Adaptation Studies does not end there. BBC adaptations have long been associated, Robert Giddings and Keith Selby argue, with a certain sense of authenticity, with a faithfulness to their source.[1] However, when contrasted with the BBC adaptation with which this monograph opened, *The Paradise* (2012), and viewed in the evolving poetics of BBC adaptation more broadly, this 1970 version of *Germinal* underscores, in very visible ways, the different meanings of fidelity in different BBC eras and different BBC contexts. Fidelity is an evolving, shifting concept, shaped by the time, culture and context in which it is wielded. It is, as Lefevere suggests, never neutral but rather always ideological in its use and specific construction.[2] Fidelity means, as the BBC's 1970 *Germinal* makes clear, very different things in very different times and cultures. And to hold fidelity up as an absolute marker of critical success or lack thereof in relation to an adaptation is, Lefevere suggests, to fail to engage with its innate mutability across time and space.

Zola's 1885 novel *Germinal* needs little introduction, such is the fame and reach of this work about the plight of miners in northern France as they strike to improve their lot in life. Galvanised to strike by the arrival of the book-thirsty and recognition-hungry idealist Etienne Lantier, a member of Zola's blighted Rougon-Macquart family, the novel traces the hardships of mining life and the ravages caused by strike action in gritty detail. Zola's preparatory dossiers are filled with extensive notes on his trips to French mining villages, political ideas relating to the workers, his observations of a mining strike first-hand and his trip down a pit in person. Living with the Maheu family, Etienne politicises them, promising them a bright future via collective action. The novel traces their near annihilation as a result, while Etienne prospers, leaving the mine to start a new political life for himself with his mentor Pluchart in Paris. Politically descriptive, the novel is also sexually graphic as Etienne falls for and ultimately sleeps with the Maheus' eldest daughter Catherine, a girl in a violent relationship with his rival Chaval. The novel has a rich history in adaptation. It was adapted in silent film in 1913 under the direction of Alberto Capellani, in 1963 again for cinema under the direction of Yves Allégret and in 1993 at the hands of cinema director Claude Berri. This present chapter focuses on the BBC's 1970 version of *Germinal* for television, which has received scant critical attention but which, when read in combination with Lefevere's conceptualisation of the cultural forces shaping translations and adaptations as much if not more than their source texts, offers a powerfully reconfigurative reading of fidelity.

Lefevere's work needs some introduction, absent as it is from the sphere of Adaptation Studies. Translation, for Lefevere, is precisely a type of adaptation as new cultures and eras rewrite a text for their own complex purposes, under the influence of diverse and diffuse cultural prerogatives. He makes clear in *Translation, Rewriting and the Manipulation of Literary Fame* that translation is not merely a linguistic transfer but a cultural process. It is, the introduction to the book argues, a type of rewriting driven by the ideology and poetics of people in power or seeking power.[3] Lefevere's value to Adaptation Studies lies in his detailed and dynamic vision of the multifaceted aspects of culture which shape and author an adaptation or translation as much as, if not more than a source text. Lefevere highlights three cultural forces shaping translations and adaptations which are of particular interest to this chapter: patronage, the dominant poetics and translation ideologies — both that of the translator/adaptor and those of the multiple contexts within which he or she works. Patronage, an elastic category for Lefevere, may be economic, ideological or related to status, but its influence on the shape and form translations and adaptations take, the theorist argues, is pronounced:

> Patronage can be exerted by persons, such as the Medici, Maecenas or Louis XIV, and also by groups of persons, a religious body, a political party, a social class, a royal court, publishers, and, last but not least, the media, both newspapers and magazines and larger television corporations. Patrons try to regulate the

relationship between the literary system and other systems which, together, make up a society, a culture. As a rule they operate by means of institutions set up to regulate, if not the writing of literature, at least its distribution.[4]

The influence, though, of culture is not restricted to the bodies sponsoring or controlling the adaptations and translations in question. According to Lefevere, so too must the formative influence of the 'dominant poetics of a period' be taken into account, poetics which serve 'as the yardstick against which current production is measured' as institutions seek to enforce said poetics.[5] These, like all poetics, tend to change over the years and in different cultures and times. Translators thus translate the same texts very differently in different eras and spaces, shaped as they are by when and where they translate, as well as the demands of the structures via which and for whom they translate. Translation and adaptation, or indeed any act of rewriting for Lefevere, are always innately ideological, shaped by the culture in which they take place. To illustrate this point, Lefevere considers a German translation of *Anne Frank's Diary* shortly after the Second World War, tracing the layers of excisions and amendments made by layers of very different patrons. Otto Frank made changes to Anne Frank's diary in a bid both to sanitise elements of it and to meet the conditions set by the Dutch publishing house Contact. Its German translator, Anneliese Schütz, pushed by the patronage of her German publishing house and the economic patronage of the German market to which it sought to sell, claimed 'a book you want to sell well in Germany [...] should not contain any insults directed at Germans'.[6] She translated Frank's diary of oppression under the Nazis accordingly, shaping it to what she perceived to be the needs and ideology of her target audience. Rewriting, for Lefevere, is frequently an exercise in which politics has a hand. And his core value to Adaptation Studies perhaps lies in his recognition of fidelity precisely as a politically or at least culturally motivated and variable concept. He writes:

> If we accept that translations get published, whether they are 'faithful' or not, and that there is little one can do to prevent an 'unfaithful' translation from projecting its own image of the original, that ought to be an end to the matter. 'Faithfulness' is just one translational strategy that can be inspired by the collocation of a certain ideology with a certain poetics. To exalt it as the only strategy possible, or even allowable, is as utopian as it is futile. Translated texts as such can teach us much about the interaction of cultures and the manipulation of texts. These topics, in turn, may be of more interest to the world at large than our opinion as to whether a certain word has been 'properly' translated or not. In fact, far from being 'objective' or 'value free' as their advocates would have us believe, 'faithful translations' are often inspired by conservative ideology.[7]

Fidelity, Lefevere underscores in a manner which speaks to the findings of Berman in Chapter Four, means different things for different times, places, patrons and individuals. It is an innately shifting, ideologically-shaped construct which cannot be the ultimate arbiter of a translation or adaptation. It is, Lefevere suggests, far more compelling to unpick the cultural bodies and forces which shape and author the very translations and adaptations which then in turn impact on the society, poetics, ideology and culture from which they stem.

If Lefevere is valuable to the field of Adaptation Studies, so too is the BBC as an institution. As the most prolific producer of adaptations in the world across its various arms, it offers an unparalleled range and scope of works stemming from one cultural patron. The BBC offers a compelling test area in which to evaluate Lefevere's theoretical framework, specifically his notions that translations and adaptations are shaped by patronage, a dominant poetics and politics more generally. That the BBC functions as a patron is clear. It commissions and supports new art and artists across its output. Its patronage may have evolved and transformed in cultural and economic terms since the corporation's inception but it has done so in well-documented, arguably traceable ways, as works such as Asa Briggs's gargantuan five-volume history of the BBC underscore.[8] That the BBC has historically occupied the position of a patron is clear. Lance Sieveking dedicated his book *The Stuff of Radio* to Lord Reith, the BBC's Director General who established the tradition of independent public service broadcasting in the UK, overseeing the BBC in its formative years and leaving on it an indelible mark in conceptual terms. Sieveking hailed Reith as a man who:

> Like a patron in the Middle Ages, has made it possible for an art to flourish, by enabling artists and craftsmen to devote their lives to its practice and development in freedom from any limitations save those which seemed, to an ever modifying degree, inherent in it.[9]

Briggs too casts BBC activity in its early years in terms of patronage:

> In the absence of state patronage of the arts, the BBC did much to provide it, subsidizing many cultural activities more generously than many of its more 'philistine' critics wished it to do. The patronage in music, for example, was reflected not only in the taking over of the Promenade Concerts in 1927 — thereby ensuring their survival — but in subsidy to opera and in the commissioning of new works, including an Elgar symphony in 1933. 'Most powerful of all the agencies extending interest in music', Sir Henry Hadow wrote in 1931, 'both in the width of its range and in the concentration of its authority, is the BBC which affords to our composers their due share of opportunity and gives them the whole civilized world for audience.' To the university world also the BBC provided much indirect patronage and far greater opportunities to influence the public than lecturers or professors had ever enjoyed before, either intra-murally or extra-murally.[10]

Patronage, though, extended beyond the early years of the BBC. The corporation has, since the inception of both radio and television, commissioned original and adapted drama, both drawing on the established canon and influencing and altering it by adapting authors from outside said canon with its potentially canonising touch. The range and depth of BBC-adapted work both draws on the dominant poetics of different eras and shapes them in its adaptively experimental moments. The BBC has, as an entity, created its own poetics of adaptation, a poetics which, as a result of the range and depth of its output, has proved influential. Giddings and Selby underline that the BBC's dominance in this area stems from its ability to invest in large-scale historical adaptations which they then sell abroad:

This will inevitably influence the choice of material and even further, the manner of its treatment. Having pioneered the 'British' way of 'doing the classics' the BBC may accidentally have created a prototype. This is seen as the way to do the classics, or to handle history (or even indicate what 'history' actually is).[11]

Moreover, collectively the BBC's adaptive output concurs with Lefevere's assertion that acts of rewriting are always in some senses politically shaped. As a public service broadcaster, the BBC has always, as Asa Briggs's history of it is at pains to point out, been required to be impartial, apolitical and unbiased.[12] Yet, what Briggs's history of the corporation makes clear is the extent to which its very existence is political, shaped by the actions and reactions of successive governments and their abilities to review, fund or cut its finance, shape the competition to it by the breaking of the BBC monopoly in 1954 and debate both its output and mission in parliament.[13] Politics, BBC history makes clear, shapes even outputs which are required to be apolitical.

The association of the BBC with Lefevere's theories is compelling in another yet more important way: it allows us to evaluate his theorisation of fidelity in practice. Fidelity is, as this chapter has already suggested, a shifting, culturally- and politically-shaped construct for Lefevere, whose innate and ideological mutability needs to be recognised. Fidelity has come to be, Giddings and Selby suggest in their work on the classic serial in British radio and television, something of a hallmark of BBC historical adaptation for a complex range of reasons. Using its near synonym, authenticity, they write of the BBC productions which proclaim their fidelity to source explicitly or implicitly: 'The BBC has achieved such a *coup d'état* in our nation's cultural production, that this assertion of the "authentic" is seldom, if ever, challenged'.[14] Yet collectively, the range and scope of BBC output echoes Lefevere's vision of fidelity for the corporation's 'authentic' approach to adaptation has taken different forms in different eras of its existence. In the pre-1950 era of BBC television, the medium was, in terms of budget, organisational structures, staff and consequently its own aesthetic, clearly intertwined with BBC radio.[15] Adaptations in television therefore tended to privilege the spoken word over image, dialogue over visual technique, privileging the authenticity of the source's words. Giddings and Selby write of this era: 'Originally the ambition was faithfully to serve the cause of the literary original. This was promulgated in the late 1930s when the Corporation's radio drama people were actually putting the genre [adaptation] together'.[16] In the 1960s, the BBC, in the words of Lez Cooke, gained a reputation for 'controversial anti-establishment, socially conscious drama' with series such as *Z Cars* and pieces from Ken Loach like *Cathy Come Home*.[17] Authenticity in this context and era took on a different slant, which affected adaptations both new and classical as productions increasingly moved out to film on location and to tackle social and political issues of the contemporary era even in the context of historical period drama. The 1970s and 1980s would come to be dominated precisely by historical period dramas on the BBC for reasons both political and economic. Cooke specifies of the 1970s:

The cultural shift from the 1960s to the 70s, from liberalism to conservatism, from consent to coercion, was reflected in the television drama produced during the decade. The plethora of historical dramas arguably entailed an escape from the increasingly bitter conflicts of 1970s Britain.[18]

Adaptations moved to offer an 'authentic' vision of the past, researched and painstakingly recreated in as much detail as possible as an antidote to the present. Giddings and Selby concur in relation to the 1980s, pointing out that: 'It has been argued that the heritage industry was the only UK industry to thrive under Conservative policies — that modern obsession with finding permanent, solid values in the past, transforming us into diachronic tourists in our own history'.[19] The BBC's quest for 'authentic' historical visions should not, though, be seen solely in a political light. For the phenomenon is also an economic one as the BBC looked to adapted visions of the past to better its own economic future in the face of cuts to its budget, marketing historical dramas and adaptations internationally. The BBC does particularly well in these international markets. Writing of a slightly later adaptation, Giddings and Selby underscore the economic reasons for the 'authenticity' the BBC uses to market its historical adaptations, suggesting:

> The high quality aura is an important factor in their marketability. These productions seem to satisfy particular demands in American viewers. Susan King, television critic of the *Los Angeles Times*, in welcoming 'British Masterpiece' *Jane Eyre*, spoke of the way British television had enchanted viewers 'with its sparkling adaptations of the Austen classics' and assured viewers of its authenticity, having been 'filmed in Hertfordshire and Oxfordshire, England'.[20]

Money, both that to be invested and that to be reaped, shapes adaptations in televisual form. If pre-1950 adaptations privileged authenticity to source text and word, the 1960s authenticity to reality and contemporary issues and the 1970s and 1980s authenticity to a historical past as an antidote to a tempestuous present, the BBC's authenticity in adaptation in the 1990s was cast, Giddings and Selby suggest, in a different form. It was, they argue, shaped by economics and the need to retain viewers in the face of increasing competition. According to Giddings and Selby:

> As the decade progressed, and more and more classic novels were transformed into costume dramas, we began more frequently to hear that 'so and so' has been dramatised 'for the 1990s'. The BBC's education kit to accompany *Middlemarch* actually describes itself on its cover as 'Screening *Middlemarch*: 19th-century Novel to 90s television'. And indeed, among the latest classic novels to appear as this book goes to press [Giddings and Selby's book was published in 2001], there is a strong feeling that modern dramatic situations and conflicts are being superimposed upon novels from the last century.[21]

They conclude: 'There was a noticeable tendency readily to abandon the old BBC tradition of faithfully rendering a classic novel in favour of rewriting, or considerably readjusting, novels to suit the perceived and expected feminist or politically correct requirements of today'.[22] Alive to the contradictions inherent in these adapted works which market themselves as offering an authentic past while adapting themselves to the tastes and needs of their contemporary audience, Giddings and Selby, along with Lez Cooke, trace the evolving shape of authenticity or fidelity in

BBC adaptation over the decades, an evolution at which this current book has tried to gesture in the gap it identifies between the approaches of *The Paradise* (2012) in Chapter One and that of *Germinal* (1970) in this closing chapter. Fidelity, in BBC adaptation, resonates with Lefevere's reading of the phenomenon for it has meant and will continue to mean different things in different eras, moments and markets, shaped as its meaning is by the context which wields it as an interpretative, cultural and economic tool.

If Lefevere's theory needs some introduction in the sphere of Adaptation Studies, so too does the case study television adaptation of this chapter. In January and February 1970 BBC2 aired and repeated a five-part adaptation of Zola's *Germinal*. The adaptation was dramatised by David Turner, produced by David Conroy and directed by John Davies. The five parts of the adaptation each appeared under a different subtitle: 'Miners', 'Mutual Aid', 'Mob Rule', 'Soldiers', 'Trapped'. The reason the adaptation needs introduction lies in its physical absence — the adaptation is no longer publicly available and exists only as a written entry on the BBC Genome online catalogue — and in its critical absence from the annals of critical work on BBC products.[23] Neither Giddings and Selby nor Cooke make extensive mention of it, sitting as it does in the interstice of two very different decades to which both sets of work devote entire chapters, decades filled with larger and more extensive examples of the historic adaptation genre.[24] The BBC's 1970 *Germinal*, though, stands out as a case study for this book as a result of its complex interaction with fidelity as a concept. It allows for the nuancing of the broad brushstroke portrait established in the paragraph above to detail the evolving position of the BBC in relation to authenticity in the pre-1950s, 60s, 70s–80s and 90s. It does so because it contains elements of each of the approaches to authenticity outlined above. If pre-1950 output tended to privilege fidelity to the word and authority of its source text, this 1970 *Germinal* does likewise, carrying dialogue, where it can, directly from Zola's source novel. Etienne in both his novel and television form appeals for the miners' support with the same passionate words: 'The mine should belong to the miner like the sea to the fishermen'.[25] His words in the television adaptation are borrowed directly from the novel, which plays repeatedly on the borrowed nature of its protagonist's words as he reads and recycles the tropes, phrases and rhetoric of his sources. Intriguingly, for the BBC, reading and recycling the tropes, phrases and rhetoric of its Zola source text is a mark of authenticity while the novel implicitly couches the same acts as marks precisely of inauthenticity on the part of its protagonist. The novel repeatedly underlines the way in which Etienne's words are recycled, copied, borrowed, beyond his comprehension and ultimately empty: 'il répétait parfois qu'il fallait bannir la politique de la question sociale, une phrase qu'il avait lue et qui lui semblait bonne à dire, dans le milieu de houilleurs flegmatiques où il vivait'/'Indeed he was full of moderation and illogicality, insisting from time to time that politics had to be kept out of the "social question", an opinion he had read somewhere and which seemed like the right thing to say among the apathetic colliers he worked with' (p. 143/167). Not only does he realise, later, the innate stupidity of his assertion, disavowing it, but his explicitly political stance in contemplating the social question of the mines underlines the meaningless of the words he borrows as he utters them. The urge in the 1960s to probe core social issues and use authenticity in production methods, filming on location where cost and technology allowed, is also visible in this adaptation of *Germinal*. Zola's novel is socially conscious at its core and the novelist pursued authenticity of representation in relation to the mining industry in copious notes and preparatory dossiers. The 1970 television adaptation of it cultivates the authenticity of approach in technical terms which characterised much of the drama on the BBC in the 1960s. Thus, one of the few contemporary reviews of the adaptation, an article appearing in the *Daily Mirror* on 26 January 1970 by Kenneth Eastaugh, hails its social authenticity.[26] Current and former miners largely from Nettlesworth-Drift were recruited to play alongside the adaptation's main actors. In a fascinating statement of the inauthenticity of this authenticity, the newspaper writes:

> The men would troop out of their 'happy little mine' at 3 pm having worked a full shift [...]. They would wash off the real sweat and coal dust, put on artificial grime and by 4 pm would be before the cameras [...] as discontented, downtrodden miners of the nineteenth century.[27]

Rather than mocking up a mine and destroying it as per the novel's narrative, the adaptation used a real decommissioned mine for the same purpose. John Robson, a pitman for forty years, stage-managed the whole thing. According to the *Daily Mirror*, 'in a riot scene the men blow up a coal mine — and it's not faked. A pit due for demolition at nearby Waldridge was actually destroyed'.[28] The sexual freedom of Zola's original novel, a freedom maintained by the adaptation, may have bothered contemporary viewers as Mary Whitehouse's campaign to clean up television suggests, but, when asked about it by the *Daily Mirror*, the miners defended it precisely on the grounds of authenticity: 'there's young lasses going on the fells doing that sort of thing every night of the week'.[29] The BBC left a television set in the local working men's club, which was packed out when the serial aired. Miner John Hall claimed that the serial was 'the only thing on TV for six months that has really gripped us', largely as a result of the authenticity they claimed to see in it.[30] In keeping, though, with the BBC's approach to the authenticity of adaptations in the 1990s whereby classics were adapted and updated to the needs and social mores of the target audience, this television adaptation is an adaptation for its era. Not only is the language, intonation and register largely that of the 1970s, but Catherine's menstrual period is cut, as are the graphic sex scenes in which Zola revels, scenes which would not have helped the BBC in its already bitter battle with Mary Whitehouse and her morality campaign. More interestingly, though, the miners watching this period piece adaptation and participating in this 'authentic' creation of a distant past clearly saw it as speaking to their social and political present. The *Daily Mirror*'s Kenneth Eastaugh writes:

> Fittingly, although the '*Germinal*' miners' oppressed conditions bear no relation to conditions in a modern pit, the Durham men see the serial as a kind of epitaph to themselves as the last of the toil-and-sweat pitmen being ousted by the technical age.[31]

That the BBC's *Germinal* speaks to the present of the real miners involved is clear.

Many, Eastaugh underlines, remember conditions like that of Zola's novel and the overlaps between Zola's novel and this Durham pit are pronounced. Eastaugh writes:

> By coincidence, miners at Nettlesworth revolted against conditions in the same year that Zola set *Germinal* — 1867. In the serial miners revolt at the introduction of tame cheap labour from Belgium. The Nettlesworth miners revolted against the infusion of competitive labour from Cornwall.[32]

Eastaugh clearly identifies the authenticity of the adaptation as working Janus-like, faithfully reflecting back to Zola's past as well as offering the present, albeit a present soon to become a past, of these miners. He states of those acting in the production: 'If indeed these are the last of the "proper miners", the last of a dying breed, then the TV serial is not just a story, it is a tribute and a memorial'.[33] The authenticity innately associated with BBC adaptations not only shifts and evolves over diverse decades, but individual adaptations invoke this authenticity in different and at times contrasting ways.

The television adaptation clearly bears the creative and cultural signature of the BBC as shaping force and patron as much as it bears that of Zola. It is shaped by the trends and tendencies in programme-making which characterised the BBC at its time of production, that is to say by the dominant poetics of the BBC in its era. It sits at the confluence of the 1960s and 1970s and at the intersection of the BBC drama trends dominating these respective decades. The 1960s on BBC television were most notable for the rise of socially realist, socially probing drama. According to Lez Cooke, this trend 'could [...] be said to have begun on 2 January 1962 with [the] first episode of *Z Cars*'.[34] *Z Cars* was a BBC television drama series revolving around a mobile police unit based in the fictional town of Newtown, based on Kirkby in Lancashire. Cooke writes, 'The intention was to set the series in a new town area in the north of England as a way of tapping into social changes taking place in Britain in the early 1960s'.[35] Securing the cooperation of Lancashire Police, the programme can very much be seen as a descendant of the drama documentaries which developed in the 1950s. With its carefully reproduced regional accents, detailed attention to modern policing methods and willingness to show unvarnished violence, *Z Cars* initiated a BBC genre of which the 1970 BBC *Germinal* is something of a descendant. The vocabulary of genetic descent is key to Zola's novel, in which Etienne's violent actions and subsequent life path are dictated by his *fêlure*, by the tainted blood of his forebears. Zola writes:

> Il avait une haine de l'eau-de-vie, la haine du dernier enfant d'une race d'ivrognes, qui souffrait dans sa chair de toute cette ascendance trempée et détraquée d'alcool, au point que la moindre goutte en était devenue pour lui un poison.
>
> [He hated alcohol with the hatred of one who was the last in a long line of drunks and who suffered in his flesh from this wild, drink-sodden inheritance, to such an extent that the merest drop had become the equivalent of poison for him.] (p. 56/47)

His destructive actions at the head of the rampaging mob are directly attributed to the gin he drinks on an empty stomach, gin which liberates the voices of his ancestors. Intriguingly, Zola's notion of heredity, his belief that individuals are shaped by the traits, blood and voices of their forebears, disappears in the BBC adaptation. Yet Zola's notion of the weight of history, of the shaping force of one's predecessors, finds something of an equivalent in the voices of the televisual ancestors to this 1970 BBC *Germinal*, voices which whisper in and inform its production. If *Germinal* builds on the documentary impulses of *Z Cars*, working on real mine locations, with real miners, regional accents and probing social issues, so too is the voice of Ken Loach's canonical 1966 BBC Television play *Cathy Come Home* audible in the adaptation.[36] All names in the BBC's *Germinal* are left in their French form, despite the dialogue being delivered in strong northern-English accents and vocabulary. This creates an intriguing adaptive disconnect in spatial terms. The adaptation is clearly French — it has French character names throughout and the mine-owners talk about their need as French men to undercut English coal-mining markets. Yet it is also impossibly English in language, accents and intonations, which clearly spatially situate the programme in the north of England. This spatial disconnect is, as I have argued elsewhere, something of a hallmark of BBC adaptations, part of BBC adaptive poetics in which characters unproblematically retain their foreignness in works which are clearly almost British.[37] When bidding goodbye to Etienne at the adaptation's close, La Maheude kisses him in a Gallic manner on two cheeks, while addressing him in a broad northern English accent: 'Good bye lad'. In the resolute Frenchness of character names in this 1970 version of *Germinal*, one British character name stands out. Zola's French 'Catherine' becomes a very British 'Cathy' in this BBC adaptation. Her anglicised name triggers a range of associations with Loach's *Cathy Come Home*. Loach's production, as a result of its controversy, marked British culture and reshaped BBC television in many respects, and the overlaps between Loach's play and this adaptation of *Germinal* are pronounced.[38] Both are filmed in a gritty, realistic documentary drama style. Both film on location. Both tackle social issues and the question of family disintegration head on. As the miners watching and helping create the BBC's *Germinal* envisioned the television programme as a documentary of their contemporary lives and imminent professional extinction, *Cathy Come Home* pushed the boundary between drama and news as the programme sought to intervene and change public social policy.[39] Both feature young women leaving overcrowded family homes to move in with their lovers, a proliferation of children and a relentless descent into inescapable poverty. If Etienne is spurred on by the voices of his ancestors echoing through his drunken skull, so this BBC adaptation of *Germinal* audibly has the voices of BBC televisual ancestors echoing through it in the formative influence of programmes such as *Z Cars* and *Cathy Come Home*.

The ancestral voices shaping this 1970 version of *Germinal*, though, do not come exclusively from the BBC. So too is the adaptation formed by the complex and intense rivalry which the corporation had in this era with its competitor ITV. Jamie Medhurst offers an overview of the creation of what came to be ITV: 'The BBC's monopoly on television was effectively broken with the passing of the 1954

Television Act which led to the advertising-funded Independent Television (ITV) broadcasting for the first time via Associated-Rediffusion, the London-based ITV contractor, on 22 September 1955'.[40] By 1962 the regional franchises which made up the ITV system were in place and the 60s saw intense competition between the BBC and Independent Television as they battled for audiences. In 1962, the government-appointed Pilkington Committee charged with considering the shape of broadcasting in the UK reported. It argued that a third channel should be created and that it should go to the BBC. Medhurst writes that this recommendation was based on the strong case the BBC had made for an extra channel. He continues:

> It was also made on the basis that the committee was critical of the quality and range of ITV programming and of the network's apparent disregard for its public service remit. In April 1964, therefore, 28 years after opening its first television service, the Corporation launched a second channel.[41]

When BBC2, the channel on which this chapter's case study *Germinal* was broadcast, was launched in April 1964 it was in many ways a direct response to competition from ITV. The nature of the new channel, reflected in the adaptation discussed in this chapter, might also be read as a response to ITV. Pushed perhaps by the success of ABC (later Thames Television's) Armchair Theatre with their cutting contemporaneity, and by the pull of audiences to the populism of independent television, the BBC began, in the words of Giddings and Selby, 'to treat their classic novels in a more adult fashion'. Thus, when BBC2 was launched, 'a new slot was allocated for classic serial adaptations (of a more adult kind) on Saturday evenings. This allowed for a more sophisticated and sometimes daring choice of novel, and a more adult treatment in longer episodes'.[42] Giddings and Selby write tellingly of the case study at the heart of this chapter, 'With serial versions of Zola's *Germinal* and *Nana* and Flaubert's *Sentimental Education* it was as if we had left the innocent world of *David Copperfield* and *Treasure Island* for good'.[43] The BBC's *Germinal* must then be read not only as an adaptation of Zola's source novel but as an economic and political reflection of the BBC's need to compete with independent television, a force which has a formative influence on this adaptation. That the adaptation is visibly adult is clear. Cathy strips naked in the mine, stifled by the heat which makes her unable to work. Her nudity, though not graphic, is clear. Chaval's forced sex scene with Cathy for bread is uncomfortable in its audibility — as Etienne screws up his eyes to turn away from the brutal sex act, having urged his woman to take the food, we listen with him in the darkness to the non-consensual act. Far from hiding sex, this adaptation revels in it and, to an extent, elevates it in some senses. The adaptation, as this chapter will argue below, is characterised by extreme high-angle shots of the type popular in 1950s American Film Noir, shots which bear down on, entrap and diminish the characters in them. Strikingly, the only elevating shot filmed from a character's feet relates to La Mouquette — the generous, much-loved miner who sleeps with any man who takes her fancy, happily embracing her sexual side as she shares food and her body with anyone in need. When she is having sex with Etienne, a man known for the empty, recycled nature of his words, a man who promises to come back to her but never does, the camera films from La Mouquette's feet. The camera magnifies and almost ennobles her person and sentiments, allowing her to dominate and command the shot as she speaks honestly and truthfully about sex. Etienne asks how she is. She replies:

> MOUQUETTE   As per usual, dying for it [*i.e., sex*].
> Why don't you want me?
> ETIENNE   But I do.
> MOUQUETTE   Get on, you don't want me, not like I want you.
> ETIENNE   Who says I don't?
> MOUQUETTE   It's like that is it? Right we'll have a go then.
> [*after sex*]
> You did it lovely. Was it nice for you as well? Did you like it with me? What's up? Thinking of her? Cathy's the one you'd like it with.
> ETIENNE   It's wrong of me to have pleasure when there are people starving. You're honest, generous, I'll be back.

In the midst of Etienne's posturing and fabricated words, La Mouquette embraces truth in words and in body, and the camera, in its extreme low-angle shot, applauds her for it. Her language, and that of the adaptation as a whole, is graphic. And the miners watching it as a depiction of themselves were uncomfortable with it, hailing it, in the *Daily Mirror* as 'a bit close to the knuckle'.[44] The Maheu family wake for a day's work. They talk of the love triangle going on next door as Levaque sexually services both her husband and the lodger who pays to stay there, spying on them in a tellingly blocked window shot. Zola's novel may seek, in Zola's words, to be a window on the world, but the world of sex cannot be shown graphically on the BBC in 1970. It is however, shown in graphic words. They claim that Madame Levaque works hard, 'husband gets off, lodger gets on', remarking that she will soon be 'bow-legged'.[45] Sexual language is something of a constant through the adaptation in dialogue which clearly aims to have some element of shock. A jealous Chaval berates Cathy violently about her attraction to Etienne, the man he perceives as his rival: 'Get 'im to stuff you,' shouting at her in the family home, 'so you come back 'ere to get him to fill you up'. Cathy and Etienne talk candidly about her having sex with Chaval: 'I just lie there and let him. I hate it'. The adaptation is slightly less candid about Zola's shopkeeper Maigrat's sexual bartering — he allows the women of the mining village to pay him for food with sex. In visual terms it permits none of it to be seen, but it arguably amplifies its shocking nature by bringing to the fore a deliberately difficult and disquieting paedophilia to the exchanges. The youth of his victims is constantly underscored. When La Maheude pleads for credit and food, Maigrat, stuffing his face with the food he withholds from the community, asks, 'How's your little girl coming on? Her needs a bit of developing don't you think', implying that he is just the man to take in hand that development. He revels in the fact that she looks younger than she is. The youth of his victims is constantly emphasised. Later in the action, holding scissors that predict his castration at the hands of the women of the mining village in retaliation for his abuse of their daughters, a castration the adaptation shows, Maigrat explains his gift of a loaf of bread to the Mirouette girl. He gave it to her on account of her being a very 'frolicsome child'. This adaptation, in its adult themes and approach, is the product of not just new departures in BBC drama but also the shaping influence of competition from independent television and its more populist approach, as well as the consequent formation of BBC2. The BBC's 1970 *Germinal* is shaped by where it sits in television history.[46]

So too is it shaped by the personal histories of its creative personnel and their involvement in the social and cultural debates of the time. David Turner and his run-ins with morality campaigner Mary Whitehouse are key to my line of argument here. Television, like any new medium, triggered from its outset concerns about its social impact and utility. There were widespread fears in the early years of the medium that it would be socially harmful, that it would render its audiences passive and sedentary, parasitically reducing audiences for existing art forms.[47] As television audiences grew, so too did the concerns around the medium and, Jamie Medhurst argues, 'It is no coincidence that the launching of Mary Whitehouse's "Clean Up TV" campaign in 1963 occurred at the same time that television set ownership and numbers of viewers were on the increase'.[48] Mary Whitehouse features prominently in the history of British television. Briggs traces Whitehouse's ascent from unknown Shropshire school teacher to prominent morality campaigner.[49] Unhappy in the summer of 1963 at what she described as the BBC's advocacy of the 'New Morality', Whitehouse met with the BBC, complaining about programmes such as *This Nation Tomorrow*, which on 14 July 1963 had shown Dr Alex Comfort defending premarital sex. When the BBC did not take action to adjust their output, Whitehouse turned to campaigning. Briggs writes:

> She believed that the Corporation, instead of listening, seemed quite deliberately to be entering upon 'a trial of strength with its viewers' by 'producing programmes even more likely to affect the good taste of the country.' [...] The campaign began with the drafting of a Manifesto that minced no words. It opened boldly with the affirmation 'We women of Britain believe in a Christian way of life', and in its third clause it referred to 'the propaganda of disbelief, doubt and dirt that the BBC projects into millions of homes through the television screen.' The fifth clause called upon the BBC 'for a radical change of policy'. 'Programmes which build character' should be broadcast in place of programmes which destroy it. They should 'encourage and sustain faith in God and bring Him back to the heart of our family and national life.'[50]

The dramatist behind the BBC's 1970 version of *Germinal*, David Turner, was one of Whitehouse's frequent targets, producing as he did socially, sexually and philosophically challenging pieces.[51] Turner attended the launch of the Whitehouse campaign in a mass meeting in Birmingham Town Hall on 5 May 1964, a meeting Kenneth Bird, the BBC's Midland Regional Information Officer, deemed in a consequent report to be by contrast 'comical', 'sinister' and 'menacing'.[52] Turner, whose BBC plays were often under attack by the Whitehouse campaign, hoped to counter the campaign but was not allowed to speak from the platform. Whitehouse was subsequently to write in her memoirs: 'He had already had ample opportunity to speak not to a mere 2,000 people, but to the whole country — now it was our turn'.[53] Refusing to be put off, Turner interrupted the meeting from the audience, accusing Whitehouse of attacking creative freedoms. He would go on to parody her in one episode of his series *Swizzlewick*, a twice-weekly comedy drama in series of twenty-six episodes which aired in 1964.

Turner's BBC dramas in general, and, for the purposes of this chapter, his 1970 *Germinal* in particular, might be read as part of his continuing response to Mary Whitehouse, uncompromising as they are in their implicit belief that art should probe religious, sexual and philosophical fault lines. The probing of such religious fault lines is visible in Zola's *Germinal*. The anarchist Souvarine advocates the abolition of God and religions and the novelist offers a vision of the abbé Joire who does not care in either spiritual and material terms for the plight of his flock (pp. 200–45/90–92). The miners do not go to church and Zola repeatedly grafts the vocabulary of religion and spirituality onto the mine in its place. Zola describes the mine thus: 'Le reste, la vaste salle, pareille à une nef d'église, se noyait, peuplée de grandes ombres flottantes'/'everything else in the vast, nave-like hall was lost in darkness, and huge shadows seemed to float back and forth' (p. 38/26). In his insistent depiction of the mine as church, Zola perhaps predicts the exchange of vows Etienne and Catherine will make in it, prior to consummating their relationship, a consummation pitched as almost virginal for it is the first sex Catherine has after hitting puberty (p. 394/518). Etienne's words are likened to those of a priest. So too are those of Pluchart. He preaches political and social freedom to the credulous miners, spurred on by his own rhetorical fervour. His assembled congregation drink in his promises of future paradise. Zola writes: 'Jamais religion naissante n'avait fait tant de fidèles'/'No new religion had ever made so many converts so quickly' (p. 205/ 251). When the mining village's new radical priest, l'abbé Ranvier, preaches to the miners, trying to lure them to church with the promise that God will bring revolution, La Maheude thinks she hears Etienne in him: 'La Maheude, qui l'écoutait, croyait entendre Etienne, aux veillées de l'automne, lorsqu'il leur annonçait la fin de leurs maux'/'As she listened, La Maheude thought she could hear Etienne, back on those autumn evenings when he told them that their troubles would soon be over' (p. 307/396). But the novel mocks not just his words but arguably those of the church. Etienne preaches his new religion, but his words, the novel underscores, have no foundation in reality: 'Sur les moyens d'exécution, il se montrait plus vague, mêlant ses lectures, ne craignant pas, devant des ignorants, de se lancer dans des explications où il se perdait lui-même'/'As to how they were to go about it, he was less specific and quoted various things he had read, undaunted by these ignorant people and launching himself into explanations before losing the thread himself' (p. 147/172). His words tellingly appear shortly after a section in which religion is decried as fake, positioning them as promises as empty as those of the church (p. 145/170). Zola will not allow the promises of either creed to be believed. Religion is largely cut from Turner's dramatisation but if Turner does not probe the religious fault lines of Zola's novel, he does, making no concessions whatsoever to Mary Whitehouse, push the sexual and philosophical boundaries outlined above. The sexual challenge to Whitehouse's campaign is clear in the freedom with which the adaptation deals with sex in audible form and naked bodies in visible form, as discussed above. Turner's 1970 *Germinal* also poses a philosophical challenge to Whitehouse's campaign. It does so by promoting and sharing Zola's belief that creative and cultural freedoms must be available to art, whatever its form. In his lifetime Zola's novels were attacked for their filth — Ferragus famously decried them in such terms in Zola's era.[54] Turner embraces the filth of *Germinal* in his adaptation. He does it largely at the level of speech. His colourful language both embraces Zola as source text and enables him simultaneously to offer a creative riposte to Mary Whitehouse. The miners attack the 'new cowing pay structure'. La Maheude rips bread from one of her offspring's mouth, shouting 'we're all cowing hungry'. Chaval attacks Etienne with sexual allusions, screaming 'you bloody ponce you'. Rasseneur attacks Etienne's political beliefs: 'You don't care a sod about socialism. You just want to be their representative in some bloody world parliament'. Chaval throws Catherine out: 'Get out you cow. Take yer fanny somewhere else. Well sod off then'. It is not hard to read Turner's *Germinal* as thumbing its nose at Whitehouse in linguistic terms. But it also, as an adaptation, questions the notions of decency and morality at the core of her campaign. At the start of Turner's dramatisation La Maheude has a clear moral framework. It revolves around fidelity (she condemns her neighbour's sexual servicing of both husband and lover in rotation) and a strong belief that harm must not be done in any form. Yet by the end of the adaptation, she has thrust her daughter into the sexual hands of Chaval in order that credit be extended to her in the company shop. In the novel she merely takes the food from Maigrat, promising falsely that she will send Catherine subsequently to pay him in kind. In the adaptation, La Maheude sends Catherine but has Chaval rage into the shop proclaiming Catherine as his own while scooping up the family food. La Maheude barters her daughter for food, even if it is indirectly, for Chaval will demand sexual payment in Maigrat's place, beginning a violent and abusive relationship with her.[55] Sexual morality proves a privilege beyond La Maheude's financial means. So too is her belief that no harm should be done, ultimately shown by Turner to be a moral framework she simply cannot afford. Battered by the death of children, by poverty, by false words of social hope and freedom, La Maheude in the BBC adaptation urges, demands and enacts violence, threatening those close to her with death if they return to work. In its provocatively colourful language, the BBC's adaptation testifies to the ongoing influence of Turner's spat with Whitehouse, underlining the extra-textual forces shaping it as a creative artefact. But it also, on a deeper level, asks probing questions of the decency and morality Whitehouse espouses.

The forces shaping the BBC's 1970 *Germinal* are not just personal, though, they are also political in a variety of different facets. Key among them, and particularly resonant in relation to a novel precisely about unionisation, is the formative power of the actors' union Equity on both this adaptation and BBC television output of the 1960s and 70s as a whole. Douglas McNaughton, in his strikingly-titled article '"Constipated, studio-bound, wall-confined, rigid": The Influence of British Actors' Equity on BBC Television Drama, 1948–72', underscores the naturalist, theatrical aesthetic or poetics, to use Lefevere's term, which dominated television in this era.[56] McNaughton identifies a conceptualisation of BBC television as a theatrical space, one reliant on 'sustained, dialogue-driven performance showcasing close ups of the face', what Jason Jacobs calls the 'intimate screen'.[57] Troy Kennedy Martin, in his famous criticism of this theatrical aesthetic which privileged dialogue over action, studio production over exterior location shooting and the aural over the visual, was just one of those who called for a 'new drama', for television to develop its own non-theatrical aesthetic.[58] Arguably this theatrical aesthetic dates from early television, when recording technology was not possible and thus performances were live and theatrical in that sense. Yet even after the introduction of recording in 1958, television 'seemed to prefer to think of itself as ephemeral, preserving liveness as an aesthetic long after it existed as a technological constraint'.[59] Head of BBC Drama Michael Barry wrote in 1959:

> Television draws strength from the uninterrupted performance [...] Film making depends upon the edited assembly of minute fragments of performance, put together after that performance has taken place, by an editor who controls almost completely what is finally shown to the public. Television pre-recording must not be allowed to fragment the artist's performance into disjointed moments of effort.[60]

McNaughton attributes the prevalence and resilience of this theatrical aesthetic in television to the stance of the union Equity shaping the aesthetic artefacts in which its members starred. Unpicking the determinants in studio television up to and into the 1970s, McNaughton shows how 'Equity insisted on preserving "theatrical" continuous performance as a specific feature of television drama', resisting at all costs moves to 'rehearse-record studio taping' and delaying the turn to 'all-film drama production at the BBC'.[61] Equity's motivations were complex, partly financial and largely artistic, driven by what McNaughton reads as the 'Benjaminian "aura" of the original performance'.[62] The shaping influence of Equity on drama productions is starkly visible in the agreement they made with commercial companies in 1957. It reads thus:

> <u>Dramatic</u> programmes may be pre-recorded discontinuously provided that this is done within <u>one continuous session</u> and provided also that the total length of the session does not exceed three times the length of the finished programme as ultimately transmitted. If the length of the session exceeds three times the length of the finished programme, additional payment for the excess time is to be made on a basis not yet finally agreed.[63]

McNaughton concludes, 'For financial reasons based around performance payments, therefore, complex editing was still impossible, restricting discontinuous recording to a single recording session entailing all the spatial limitations of live studio drama'.[64] In Zola's *Germinal*, unions and their development shape the core of the writer's narrative. They also shape its delivery in adaptive television form in 1970.

The influence of Equity on the BBC's 1970 adaptation of *Germinal* is legible in subtle ways. It is perhaps most visible in spatial terms. While there are, as this chapter has already suggested, exterior shots of a real mine being collapsed, the majority of the work is confined and constricted, studio-based, dialogue-heavy, with a focus on words and narrative. Far from seeking to expand the spatial constriction of the dominant BBC aesthetics of this era as a result at least in part of Equity's stance, the adaptation works to emphasise it. Zola's novel of vast labyrinthine spaces above and below ground becomes relentlessly claustrophobic in BBC television as the adaptation works to underscore the absolute entrapment of the characters within their socio-economic situation. Spatial constriction is enacted in three ways: obstructed shots, extreme high-angle shots and narrative's tightly woven symmetries and repetitions. Obstructed shots are rife within the adaptation as the camera films dark, claustrophobic, often interior scenes from behind gates, through doors and, most notably, in our first shot of Cathy, through the wrought iron bed-frame bars. The shot through the bed bars symbolises her inevitable entrapment in sexual terms from the outset, before she has lost her virginity. Her mother subsequently barters her to Chaval, commenting on the inevitability of all the local girls ending up in sexual relationships before marriage. She voices her entrapment within the relationship in vocal terms, stating to Etienne, 'I has to do what he wants. He'll give me no peace'. The entrapment she enunciates vocally is mirrored by the use of an extreme high-angle shot as her sexual relationship with Chaval begins. She walks with him after he has saved her from sex with Maigrat, the extreme elevated shot, one redolent of entrapment as it pins spatially-diminished characters in its overarching gaze, indicating the constraints upon her. Though she has escaped the sexual abuse of Maigrat, she is now trapped in a relationship with the violent Chaval as a price for her family having food. The sound of their conversation at the fair is drowned out, for Cathy's words no longer have the power to signal either acquiescence or refusal. Her fate is now decided. Symbolically, as she looks longingly at Etienne at the fair-day celebrations, a bird cage features prominently in the claustrophobic play of gazes between a desiring Etienne, a despairing Cathy and a jealous Chaval. Cathy, in her fair-day finery, has much in common with the pretty bird trapped in its metal enclosure. Etienne cannot or will not speak his desire for Cathy, but the adaptation does it in its images. One of the miners tries to entice Etienne to frequent the knocking shop. As he lists the prostitutes' attractions and the things one can do to them, Etienne looks at Cathy, the miner's lewd comments transcribing both Etienne's desire and Cathy's metaphorical prostitution to ensure her own survival and that of her family. Extreme high-angle shots function as a core part of this adaptation's aesthetic. They feature when the scab Belgian workforce is marched in to break the strike, hinting at the financial necessity these strike breakers find themselves in and gesturing towards the fact that their actions confine the striking miners to their doom, destroying their strike action. This particular elevated shot comes from a barred window, the slats of which confine the shot still further. So too does a similar shot feature when Chaval attends the outdoor strike meeting, despite not being on strike and having every intention of continuing to work. As Etienne denounces him as a traitor, an extreme high-angle shot of Chaval speaks the corner into which Chaval finds himself metaphorically backed, a shot broken only when Chaval promises to persuade workers at his pit to come out in support of the action. Nor is Etienne exempt from such elevated shots, for in the same scene as he preaches social freedom to the workers, urging them to continue to strike in order to break a space for themselves in the world, the adaptation's camera angle makes a mockery of his words. He promises the workers space and financial and political freedom but the camera denies that space, filming him in an extreme elevated shot which both diminishes his stature and traps him beneath the weight of these borrowed, practised and ultimately empty political words. They will come back to haunt him as they trigger misery and death in his followers, unleashing in them a violence which will pull them beyond Etienne's control. Extreme elevated shots return repeatedly at the end of the episode 'Mob Rule', when violence bursts beyond Etienne's control and the marauding mine wives take their revenge on the sexual predator Maigrat. In three almost sequential extreme high-angle shots, Maigrat climbs, struggles on and falls from his shop roof before being castrated at the hands of those whose daughters he abused. Both he and the mine wives are trapped in the same overbearing shots, victims in very different ways of the powerfully constraining forces around them. The overbearing constriction enacted in the machinery of television via extreme high-angle shots is echoed and reinforced by the deliberate doubling and frequent repetitions of the narrative. Souvarine, in a rare confessional moment, describes his love for a woman in Russia, a woman he watched die in the wake of a catastrophic accident resulting from his political inclinations. His tale of this relationship predicts Etienne's consummation of his love for Cathy, a woman he too will watch die in the wake of a catastrophic accident in the mine made possible by Etienne's own political inclinations (his strike has prevented mine maintenance, making it easy for Souvarine to sabotage the mine shaft). Various episodes in the adaptation feature repeat shots of miners filing past the same row of houses to go to the mine, journeys sometimes for work, sometimes in protest, sometimes in concern at an accident. These repeat shots invariably end in a death, their claustrophobic repetition predicting the frequent fatalities with which this adaptation is littered. The adaptation opens with La Maheude trudging to the Grégoire house to beg for charity. It closes with the Grégoires coming to her to offer her charity in a symmetrical scene which underscores the tightly networked nature of this adaptation. Cathy and Chaval may be divided in life by the figure of Etienne — a figure Cathy desires and one Chaval obsessively envies both in political and sexual terms. But the adaptation works to link them in death in a symmetry which marks their fatal enclosure in the mine and its workings, a symmetry which Etienne will escape in physical and professional terms. When trapped in the flooded mine with Etienne, both Chaval and Cathy, shortly before death, hallucinate about being outside the mine, fantasising about space, sex and enjoyment in words which clash cruelly with the dark, confined spaces of the mine which is destroying them. If Chaval and Cathy are fatally doubled in death, marked in their words and dreams by this minescape which will not spare them, Etienne is in contrast doubled with Jeanlin. Both survive the mine, despite being marked by accidents in it. Jeanlin is, Manfred Schmeling suggests in relation to Zola's novel, a dark and uncomfortable double of the novel's protagonist.[65] Both seek refuge in the same space in the mine, both kill and use the mine as a haven for those acts of murder and indeed Etienne thinks explicitly of Jeanlin once he has killed Chaval (p. 388/510). Both are the powerbrokers in love triangles — Etienne's uncomfortable *ménage à trois* with Catherine and Chaval echoes that of Jeanlin with Lydie and Bebert. Jeanlin's prolific thefts resonate with Etienne's life. While Jeanlin steals food and tangible objects, Etienne pilfers words, concepts and other people's voices. He also reads voraciously, if at times uncomprehendingly, and weaves his phrases from a twisted mass of threads drawn from the printed words of others. Etienne steals other people's words and ideas repeatedly, endlessly and ultimately badly. In the BBC adaptation, Jeanlin situates himself as Etienne's double, parroting his ideas and underlining how they authorise his theft and renegade lifestyle as he attacks society with his acts of theft and murder. In the claustrophobic confines of this BBC adaptation, Etienne's words are uttered and re-uttered, returning to him in the circles and cycles of the adaptation.[66]

This adaptation, though, not only adapts the politics of the actors' union Equity at the time of its making, so too does it speak to politics more broadly, enacting Lefevere's claim that acts of rewriting are in many ways political. It anticipates, in unnerving ways, the miners' strikes of 1972 and 1974, resonating with the tensions visible in the industry at the time of its making in 1970. It pits the progressive mine owner seeking to modernise working conditions and improve the lot of his workers against those who view them as fretful children, lucky to have the bread they do and who claim of their mine owner counterpart, 'there's no place for his dreams, not today'. It also echoes or arguably points back to the General Strike of 1926, which, according to Asa Briggs, was an event in which BBC Radio came of age, reporting on the strike and providing, according to Sir Oliver Lodge, a service of national utility.[67] Lodge claimed post-strike:

> The universal feeling is one of gratitude to the BBC for the admirable part their organization has played during the recent happily-ended strife. Had it not been for this possibility of prompt and broadcast communication, the country might have become more uneasy, and been perturbed far more seriously than it has been. By the sending out of trustworthy news, and by the prompt denial of false rumours, the pulse of the country was kept calm and healthy [...]. Both sides of the dispute ought to be grateful to the organizers of this new means of spreading intelligence.[68]

Neither side, though, was. As has been characteristic of much of BBC history, opposing sides of the political spectrum attacked the BBC for what they felt were its political leanings. The miners felt the BBC could have done more to help them and had favoured the government, and the government felt the BBC had been of no political help to them in the situation. BBC guidelines are, and always have been, clear about the need for this public service broadcaster to be politically neutral. Current editorial guidelines are telling in this respect:

> Impartiality lies at the heart of public service and is the core of the BBC's commitment to its audiences. It applies to all our output and services [...]. We must be inclusive, considering the broad perspective and ensuring the existence of a range of views is appropriately reflected. The Agreement accompanying the BBC Charter requires us to do all we can to ensure controversial subjects

are treated with due impartiality in our news and other output dealing with matters of public policy or political or industrial controversy. But we go further than that, applying due impartiality to all subjects.[69]

The BBC's politics of neutrality is manifest within the 1970 adaptation in a variety of ways. A shot of the three political leaders of the adaptation in the local inn is revealing in this respect. Just as BBC programmes are required to acknowledge a range of views and the full political spectrum, the 1970 adaptation, in one shot, profiles the moderate, pragmatic socialist Rasseneur on one side of the screen, the anarchist Souvarine slightly out of focus in the centre background, his haziness a prediction of the unexpected threat he poses, and the ideologically erratic Etienne on the other side of the shot who learns from both men. This triadic shot allows the BBC to represent the three strands of political thought which dominate the adaptation, strands of thought it will subsequently allow the programme to define, depict and represent as Etienne debates them with both men. Crucially, the adaptation allows each political school of thought comparable time and space, implicitly enacting the politics of BBC political neutrality even in its drama output. It is, as a piece of drama, at pains not to endorse any of the ideologies it explores. The upper classes in the adaptation are critiqued. Having refused La Maheude's appeal for money to buy bread, they dine on the finest of foods, writing off the beleaguered miners as petulant children. The Grégoires claim 'we have tightened our belts, why can't they', before inviting, 'Do try some of the Chambertin', pointing out how well it goes with the next course. Their child Cecile implicitly critiques the class from which she comes, engaging in a social rumination with the near mute Bonnemort which implies her growing awareness of social injustice. She states disbelievingly, 'A priest told me that there must always be poor people in the world so that others can exercise charity'. She continues, 'But it's only an accident of birth. If the good lord had willed it so I could have been born here'. The adaptation, though, will not endorse her social opposites — the miners. It details their poverty, offering a moving reading of the motivations for their actions, but shows the full horror of those actions, depicting Bonnemort's strangulation of Cecile immediately after her rumination on justice, social inequality and God. Bonnemort, silent in the novel after his stroke, repeatedly speaks a single word in the murder scene of the adaptation: 'gentry'. Cecile and Cathy die in quick succession in scenes which bear comparison: the children of both classes are killed as a result of the destructive repercussions of the strike. In the confrontation between soldiers and miners, the camera films in what are presumably point-of-view shots, from behind each side of the conflict, physically situating us both in the camp of the forces of law and order and in the camp of the starving miners. The camera will not, it seems, allow us to take sides. If the gentry's world view is set out but not accepted in the adaptation, neither is the ideology of Etienne with its promise of a brave, new socialist world. One scene is particularly telling in this respect. Etienne preaches politics passionately, endlessly and determinedly to the miners who would far rather avail themselves of the prostitutes at the knocking shop. He seeks to persuade them to be part of the creation of a mutual provident fund to provide protection in the event of a strike, promising them power, freedom and justice. The scene cuts immediately to the miners' fair-day celebrations and specifically to an unscrupulous pedlar making extravagant claims for a universal elixir which cures every imaginable ill for just a small initial outlay of cash. The pedlar's words, at which the miners roll their eyes, give the lie to Etienne's passionate words on the mutual provident fund and its ability to protect the miners from every imaginable ill for a similarly small outlay of cash. So too do they undermine his politics, revealing it as a commercial transaction for his own benefit, a transaction which will consume and destroy many of the miners while effectively enabling him to pursue his dreams as a political leader with Pluchart in Paris. The adaptation's conclusion is more politically neutral than that of the novel. Etienne leaves for Paris, having refused the hundred francs compensation from the mine owners for his accident. When asked by Rasseneur why, he replies that he does not know. Rasseneur's sardonic reply underscores how little his strike action has changed: 'Oh that'll teach them, lad!' The miners have returned on the same terms as they left, the terms against which they initially protested, after a strike which has left them depleted, damaged and more downtrodden than ever. La Maheude mouths the words of hope and social revolution in the adaptation's close: 'There's gonna be a day where everything is going to change, I believe that'. But her words test our ability to believe them for she has already, in an earlier episode, reflected on the emptiness of such words, on the necessity of the poor and working classes buying into such words if only to be able to accept their lot: 'Justice, happiness — lies, there's only misery and hunger'.[70] The period nature of the adaptation, moreover, aids its political neutrality, for whilst it draws on political theories of relevance to its 1970 present, it very clearly gives them nineteenth-century faces. La Maheude may revolt against the status quo, may rail against working conditions in the most powerful of terms — 'women have become whores for a loaf of bread. We ain't human, we ain't men and women no more' — but she does so while throwing down and breaking a framed portrait of Napoleon III and his wife. Her political protest, while of relevance to the 1970s, is carefully couched in nineteenth-century terms. Reflecting the politics of neutrality enshrined in its very creation, the BBC produces a political adaptation which is intently and insistently neutral. It adapts the politics of its own existence as well as the details of Zola's source text.

Rewriting, whether it be in the form of translation or adaptation, is always, Lefevere underscores, a complex process in which more than just the source text and its subsequent translation or adaptation need to be taken into account. The BBC's 1970 adaptation of *Germinal* bears out Lefevere's claim and his suggestion that translations and adaptations are culturally valuable documents able to show us the workings of culture, the formative function of people, society, economics and politics on creative artefacts. The BBC embodies, in many ways, core aspects of Lefevere's notion of patronage, for it both commissions, supports and shapes the cultural artefacts it offers the public. The authorial signature of the BBC is legible in its 1970 adaptation of *Germinal* in myriad ways, pushing us to consider the adaptation not just as a reworking of an earlier source novel by Zola, but as an adaptation of contemporary politics, poetics, culture, economics and technological possibilities. The BBC's *Germinal* adapts the dominant poetics of the BBC at the time, reworking in period drama the social realism which had dominated the television which preceded it. It also adapts the BBC's economic context, crafting a distinct BBC2 personality for itself in the face of the economic competition posed by independent television and its populist approach. So too the adaptation is shaped by the corporation's relations with the actors' union Equity, relations which have a material impact on how the adaptation is shot. It adapts the BBC's political history more broadly, reflecting aspects of the corporation's coverage of previous mine strikes but also, and most importantly, the corporation's commitment to political neutrality. In its intent to give a balanced representation of the political spectrum as a whole and in its refusal to endorse or even favour any element of it, the BBC's *Germinal* underlines how works are political even as they seek resolutely not to be so, reacting to a politically driven need not to be politically aligned in any way, shape or form. *Germinal* in many ways adapts the political debates which dogged the BBC and the public funding behind it. It testifies, in drama, to the corporation's need to abstract itself from vagaries and movements of the political system on which it remains so dependent. It also adapts the cultural debates which the BBC has inspired, most notably the personal spat between the adaptation's dramatist, David Turner, and morality campaigner Mary Whitehouse, a spat that feeds legibly into this adaptation which serves as a riposte to Whitehouse's move to restrain artistic freedoms.

The adaptive pairing of the BBC's *Germinal* and Lefevere's theory raises two probing questions for Adaptation Studies in relation specifically to ownership and the fixity of fidelity. Ownership is a recurrent theme in Zola's novel — one of the first questions Etienne asks upon seeing the mine is, to whom does this belong? No one can answer him. The question as to the ownership of the 1970 adaptation is comparably problematic. It belongs in part to Zola, in part to the collaborative creative personnel behind it (dramatist, producer, director, actors etc.). But it also, Lefevere's theory implies, belongs to the BBC, to the patron whose money, culture, politics and moment both make the adaptation possible and shape it in creative ways. Attribution and ownership in adaptation are thorny, multiple concepts, interesting precisely for their plurality. Lefevere and this BBC adaptation also collectively ask questions of the fixity of fidelity. The term has dominated Adaptation Studies but, as Lefevere makes clear, it is a politically motivated, culturally shifting concept which means, has meant and will continue to mean very different things in very different eras. The BBC bears out Lefevere's suggestion as its output, habitually associated with authenticity, has interpreted that authenticity in starkly different ways in diverse eras, producing contrasting artefacts under this residual label of fidelity. Fidelity, this BBC case study underscores in creative and intriguing ways, is no less multiple and plural a concept than that of ownership in the adaptive context. Far from showing a linear translation of Zola's source into television, the BBC's 1970 adaptation of *Germinal* is valuable precisely for the cultural and political influences it makes visible in the process of adaptive rewriting.

Notes to Chapter 5

1. Robert Giddings and Keith Selby, *The Classic Serial on Television and Radio* (Basingstoke: Palgrave, 2001), p. 199.
2. Lefevere, *Translation, Rewriting and the Manipulation of Literary Fame*, p. 42.
3. Ibid., p. 1.
4. Ibid., p. 15.
5. Ibid., p. 19.
6. Anneliese Schütz quoted in Lefevere, *Translation, Rewriting and the Manipulation of Literary Fame*, p. 66.
7. Lefevere, *Translation, Rewriting and the Manipulation of Literary Fame*, p. 51.
8. Asa Briggs, *The History of Broadcasting in the United Kingdom*, 5 vols (London: Oxford University Press, 1961–95).
9. Lance Sieveking quoted in Briggs, *The History of Broadcasting in the United Kingdom*, II, 60.
10. Briggs, *The History of Broadcasting in the United Kingdom*, II, 60.
11. Giddings and Selby, *The Classic Serial on Television and Radio*, p. 199.
12. Briggs, *The History of Broadcasting in the United Kingdom*, I, 328.
13. For further details on the breaking of the BBC television monopoly, see Briggs, *The History of Broadcasting in the United Kingdom*, V.
14. Giddings and Selby, *The Classic Serial on Television and Radio*, p. 199.
15. For further details, see Lez Cooke, *British Television Drama* (London: Bloomsbury, 2003), p. 10.
16. Giddings and Selby, *The Classic Serial on Television and Radio*, p. 140.
17. Cooke, *British Television Drama*, pp. 62–63.
18. Ibid., p. 123.
19. Giddings and Selby, *The Classic Serial on Television and Radio*, p. 58.
20. Ibid., p. 196.
21. Ibid., p. 141.
22. Ibid., p. 191.
23. I am grateful to the BBC for allowing me to consult an archived copy of the adaptation.
24. See Giddings and Selby, *The Classic Serial on Television and Radio*, p. 26.
25. Emile Zola, *Germinal*, in *Œuvres completes*, ed. by Henri Mitterand, 15 vols (Paris: Cercle du Livre Précieux, 1966–69), V, 11–421 (p. 229): 'La mine doit être au mineur, comme la mer est au pêcheur, comme la terre est au paysan... entendez-vous!'/'The mine should belong to the miner as the sea belongs to the fisherman or the land belongs to the peasant' (*Germinal*, trans. by Roger Pearson (London: Penguin, 2004), pp. 285–86). Unless otherwise stated subsequent references are to these editions and will be made in the text.
26. Kenneth Eastaugh, 'Epitaph to the Last of the Miners', *Daily Mirror*, 26 January 1970, p. 13.
27. Ibid.
28. Ibid.
29. Ibid.
30. Ibid.
31. Ibid.
32. Ibid. The duality of time in the adaptation as it looks to the present of its viewers as well as that depicted in Zola's novel in many ways reflects the temporal duality at the core of the novel. Etienne preaches strike, revolution and revolt, offering the miners a utopian fresh start. Yet his words are nothing new, as Bonnemort's reaction to them makes clear. They tap into the circles and cycles of protest and revolt which revolve and endlessly repeat in Bonnemort's reading of the world. When Etienne speaks to the miners' present, Bonnemort is reminded forcibly of the past, of the seemingly eternal cycles of misery against which such words hold no power. Etienne addresses the miners in a clearing in the wood, preaching action and revolt in words borrowed from the books he has read. Bonnemort makes clear that his words are also borrowed from the past, a past which shows their powerlessness. Both the crowd and Etienne try to silence him: 'Pourtant, il ne lâchait pas son idée: ça n'avait jamais bien marché, et ça ne marcherait jamais bien. [...] Il commença le récit d'une autre grève: il en avait tant vu! Toutes aboutissaient sous ces arbres'/'But he kept to his point all the same: things had never been good, and they never

would be. [H]e began to talk about another strike. He had seen so many! It always ended up with them meeting here under the trees' (pp. 232–34/290).
33. Eastaugh, 'Epitaph to the Last of the Miners', p. 13.
34. Cooke, *British Television Drama*, pp. 62–63.
35. Ibid., p. 61.
36. For further analysis of Loach's *Cathy Come Home*, see Cooke, *British Television Drama*, p. 72.
37. For further reading on the curious cultural hybridity of BBC adaptations of foreign sources, see Griffiths, 'Radio and the Space of Adaptation'.
38. Lez Cooke posits it as 'perhaps the most famous *Wednesday Play* of all because of the public response it elicited, both from viewers and the authorities, as a result of the play's success in highlighting [...] the social problems of the day' (Cooke, *British Television Drama*, p. 72).
39. Loach's play did change social policy in that it led to fathers being allowed to stay in homeless shelters with their wives and children, which had previously not been possible. Reaction to the play triggered a publicity campaign on homelessness, and the charities Crisis and Shelter were formed soon after.
40. Jamie Medhurst, 'What a Hullabaloo! Launching BBC Television in 1936 and BBC2 in 1964', *Journal of British Cinema and Television*, 14 (2017), 264–82 (p. 264).
41. Ibid., p. 265.
42. Giddings and Selby, *The Classic Serial on Television and Radio*, p. 26.
43. Ibid.
44. Eastaugh, 'Epitaph to the Last of the Miners', p. 13.
45. The novel does contain a comparable scene of spying on the Levaque household at the same early point in the plot but Zola's treatment of it is less sordid: 'Bon! dit Catherine, Levaque descend, et voilà Bouteloup qui va retrouver la Levaque. [...] Chaque matin, ils s'égayaient ainsi du ménage à trois des voisins, un haveur qui logeait un ouvrier de la coupe à terre, ce qui donnait à la femme deux hommes, l'un de nuit, l'autre de jour'/'As usual! said Catherine. Down goes Levaque, and up comes Bouteloup. La Levaque here we come! [...] Each morning they shared the same joke about the threesome next door, where a hewer was renting a room out to one of the stonemen, which meant that the wife could have two men, one for the night and one for the day' (p. 33/18–19). The BBC adaptation amplifies the sexuality and crudeness of the source in this instance.
46. Moreover, just as the voices of seminal BBC dramas such as *Cathy Come Home* might be seen as part of the ancestry of this 1970 BBC version of *Germinal*, so too might a case be made for identifying traces of the influence of independent television drama. ABC's *Lena, O My Lena* (25 September 1960) is key to my line of argument here. Part of the Armchair Theatre series of which the BBC was so aware or so keen to rival, it displays intriguing overlaps and resonances in both context and approach. Both are set in the industrial north — *Lena, O My Lena* is set in a packing factory in Salford. Both explore the amorous and social relationships that develop when you introduce a man of a different social and educational level into a working-class community, focusing on the transformative power of education, whatever form it takes. Tom (Peter McEnery) is a student who takes a summer job in the warehouse to be near 'real people', just as Etienne, a machinist with some education, works for a short period of time down the mine. Tom develops a relationship with Lena (Billie Whitelaw), a working-class woman in the factory. Through their relationship, the play explores class difference, focusing on Tom's overblown wordiness (Cooke, *British Television Drama*, p. 50). Such words could just as easily apply to Etienne and the overblown, empty rhetoric he recycles to the miners so thirsty for dreams of a brave, new world. *Lena, O My Lena*, like *Germinal*, is structured around a brutal love triangle, albeit one with a slightly different weighting. If Cathy is trapped between Chaval and Etienne, lovers of a different class and level of education, so Lena is using Tom to make her lorry driver boyfriend Glyn (Scott Forbes) jealous. The fights between Chaval and Etienne find something of an equivalent in that between Tom and Glyn, albeit with a different ultimate outcome as Lena tells a bewildered Tom that their relationship was 'just a bit of fun' and echoes her boyfriend's suggestion that Tom should leave the packing factory and go back to his own kind. In both pieces the social and educational interloper leaves at the drama's close.

47. Such fears accompany, in different forms, the majority of new media before they have attained a measure of cultural or artistic ratification. Radio is a case in point, as early critics feared it would render audiences entirely passive. Asa Briggs is compelling in his assessment of this phenomenon. He writes on the cultural and artistic opposition to television, of which there is and was much, 'What is less frequently remembered is the debate about the likely social effects of broadcasting, which has much in common with the later debate about the likely social effects of television. Broadcasting, it was claimed, would not only keep people away from the concert halls, it would stop them from reading books. It would encourage contentment with superficiality' (Briggs, *The History of Broadcasting in the United Kingdom*, I, 13).
48. Medhurst, 'What a Hullabaloo! Launching BBC Television in 1936 and BBC2 in 1964', p. 279.
49. Briggs, *The History of Broadcasting in the United Kingdom*, V, 332.
50. Ibid., p. 333.
51. David Turner (1927–90) had a degree in French from Birmingham University and core elements of his adaptive output for television are French in origin. In addition to the 1970 BBC *Germinal*, he also dramatised, amongst other things, Sartre's *The Roads to Freedom* (1970), *Prometheus: The Life of Balzac* (1975) and Balzac's *Père Goriot* (1968) for the corporation, as well as working for a time as a scriptwriter for BBC Radio on *The Archers*, writing a range of plays more generally.
52. Bird cited in Briggs, *The History of Broadcasting in the United Kingdom*, V, 334.
53. Whitehouse cited in Briggs, *The History of Broadcasting in the United Kingdom*, V, 334, n. 40.
54. See Ferragus, 'La Literature putride'.
55. In the novel, La Maheude has no role in the bringing-together of Catherine and Chaval, but she does accept with resignation the inevitability of a pre-marital sexual relationship for her when La Levaque says of Catherine: 'Laisse donc, elle y passera comme les autres'/'Oh don't you worry. She'll go the same way as all the others' (p. 100/106).
56. Douglas McNaughton, '"Constipated, Studio-bound, Wall-confined, Rigid": The Influence of British Actors' Equity on BBC Television Drama, 1948–72', *Journal of British Cinema and Television*, 11 (2014), 1–22.
57. Ibid., p. 1. Jason Jacobs cited in ibid., p. 2.
58. Troy Kennedy Martin, 'Nats Go Home: First Statement of a New Drama for Television', *Encore* (March-April 1964), 21–33 (cited in McNaughton, '"Constipated, Studio-bound, Wall-confined, Rigid"', p. 2).
59. John Caughie, 'Before the Golden Age: Early Television Drama', in *Popular Television in Britain: Studies in Cultural History*, ed. by John Corner (London: BFI, 1991), pp. 22–41 (p. 34) (cited in McNaughton, '"Constipated, Studio-bound, Wall-confined, Rigid"', p. 2).
60. Michael Barry cited in McNaughton, '"Constipated, Studio-bound, Wall-confined, Rigid"', p. 10.
61. McNaughton, '"Constipated, Studio-bound, Wall-confined, Rigid"', p. 1.
62. Ibid., p. 10.
63. Cited in McNaughton, '"Constipated, Studio-bound, Wall-confined, Rigid"', p. 8.
64. McNaughton, '"Constipated, Studio-bound, Wall-confined, Rigid"', p. 8.
65. Manfred Schmeling, 'Labyinthus subterraneus: *Germinal*', *Cahiers naturalistes*, 84 (2010), 255–88 (p. 271).
66. Zola's novel is tightly networked and spatially claustrophic in its own ways. The symmetries of the novel are striking. It opens with a starving Etienne going down the mine, fearing a cave-in or a flood, sharing a *tartine* with Catherine and discovering her femininity (he initially thinks her a boy). It closes with a starving Etienne trapped in the same mine, subsequent to both a cave-in and a flood, devoured by envy as Chaval withholds and refuses to share his *tartine*, before Etienne kills Chaval and discovers Catherine's femininity in the biblical sense, being the first man to have sex with her after her period. Predictions of the novel's close are woven throughout the narrative from the outset, relentlessly trapping the reader into the flood, fire and blood of its close. The imagery of water, explosion and spilled blood dominates the novel, pointing inexorably to the cave-in which Souvarine's anarchist sabotage will cause, as well as the subsequent explosion of the Maheus' eldest son when the flame of his Davy lamp reacts with a gas pocket as he races to save his trapped sister. Zola's landscape predicts the flood Souvarine

will trigger via its relentless use of the verb 'noyer' [to drown] when contemplating various landscapes inside and outside the mine. The rampaging miners are described in terms which predict the destructive actions of Souvarine: 'On arriva à Gaston-Marie, en une masse grossie encore, plus de deux mille cinq cents forcenés, brisant tout, balayant tout, avec la force accrue du torrent qui roule'/'They arrived at Gaston-Marie in even bigger numbers than before, more than two and a half thousand maniacs bent on destruction and sweeping everything before them with the accumulated energy of a torrent in spate' (p. 268/339). Zola's narrative considers the landscape in a different scene: 'La nuit venait par grandes fumées, noyant les lointains perdus de la plaine. Sur cette mer immense de terres rougeâtres, le ciel bas semblait se fondre en noire poussière. [...] C'était d'une tristesse blafarde et morte d'ensevelissement'/'Night was falling, and great swathes of murk were enveloping the remoter reaches of the plain. The lowering sky seemed to be dissolving into black dust over this immense sea of reddish earth, and not a single breath of wind stirred the darkness at this hour. It was like the scene of some drab and sorry burial' (p. 111/121). The novel's landscape, as the closing lines of the previous quotation suggest, repeatedly predicts the entrapment and death that Catherine and Chaval will experience in the mine at the novel's close. The narrative discusses the miners' future, 'cet horizon de misère, fermé comme une tombe'/'the horizon of poverty that enclosed them like a tomb' (p. 158/185). Blood too spatters the narrative in seemingly innocuous descriptions of the landscape, predicting the slaughter and death which awaits the miners. The fire in the mine is revealing in this respect: 'La salle ne se trouvait éclairée que par ce brasier, dont les reflets sanglants dansaient le long des boiseries crasseuses'/'The only light in the room came from this grate, and blood-red reflections played along the grimy woodwork' (p. 41/29).

67. Briggs, *The History of Broadcasting in the United Kingdom*, I, 351.
68. Sir Oliver Lodge, *Radio Times*, 28 May 1926 (cited in Briggs, *The History of Broadcasting in the United Kingdom*, I, 351).
69. BBC, 'Impartiality', <https://www.bbc.co.uk/editorialguidelines/guidelines/impartiality> [accessed 10 August 2018].
70. Intriguingly, a similar disavowal of La Maheude's words of hope and social justice at the novel's close is to be found in the BBC Radio adaptation of *Germinal* dramatised by Diana Griffiths and produced by Pauline Harris. At the adaptation's close La Maheude claims, 'Next time it'll be the real thing ... Next time we'll be a peaceful army ... and the day will come when we'll find ourselves shoulder to shoulder, millions of workers ... able to seize power and become masters'. But this act of endorsement is undercut in two respects. La Maheude rubbished such words only a few scenes earlier: 'I had my head in the clouds, imagining a life where everyone lived in friendship and equality — but now I know it could never happen. Never!'. Moreover, her dreams of worker solidarity and power are undercut by the brutal interruption of her conversation with Etienne by a fellow worker ordering her, uncaring of her identity, into the prison of the mine: 'Hey, woman. The cage is waiting for you'. For a fuller reading of this scene and the BBC Radio adaptation of *Germinal* see Kate Griffiths and Andrew Watts, *Adapting Nineteenth-century France: Literature in Film, Theatre, Radio, Television and Print* (Cardiff: University of Wales Press, 2013), pp. 25–26.

CONCLUSION

Zola and the Art of Television

The critical silence on British and French television adaptations of the novels of Emile Zola is pretty deafening. This monograph has worked to counter that silence by making visible some of the range and depth of adaptations of the novelist. It has also sought to underscore their creative value. Its core intention, though, has been to tease out the transformative impact that Zola's novels and their television adaptations have on Adaptation Studies and its critical frames when read in association with specific translation theorists. Collectively, Zola and these television adaptations of him allow us to turn back to the frameworks of fidelity which have so often been used to critique and question the artistic value of adaptation, enabling us instead to critique and question fidelity as a concept itself. They push us to reconsider this seemingly static term, 'fidelity', by which we judge adaptations. When read together, they offer a vision of fidelity as a construct which adapts over time, place, context, nation and person. The constancy with which it is used belies, they make clear, the very different possible meanings at the term's core.

That Zola makes adaptive sense in television is clear from the range and variety of works made from him in Britain and France, a range and variety on which this book has sought to shed light. His works span public and commercial channels, as well as eras and televisual trends. Some adaptations, like those discussed in this book's Introduction, modernise the author for the twentieth and twenty-first century, relocating his narratives to the time, look and concerns of the target audience. Others, like *Madame Sourdis*, *L'Œuvre*, *Une page d'amour* and *L'Argent*, the case studies for Chapters Two, Three and Four, clearly position themselves as heritage pieces, as per Sarah Cardwell's reading of the genre.[1] They are works which seek to capture a seemingly authentic past for a history-hungry present. They do so via period costumes and a close focus on period detail. They also do so in aestheticising, lingering, loving, longer shots of period locations which stand out in the otherwise more prevalent close- to mid-length shots which characterise the early to mid-years of television. Both adaptive trends — the move to bring Zola into the present and the intention to take the viewer back to the nineteenth century — are valuable in critical terms. They push us to re-evaluate in critical ways the term 'fidelity', a term which has in many ways shaped the development of adaptation studies. They do so by showing the protean ways in which it can be invoked. Adaptations which modernise Zola might be read as being unfaithful to the Naturalist novelist's urges to document his own nineteenth-century era. Yet the same adaptations might be read as faithfully interpreting Zola's belief that art should comment on its contemporary era. In contrast, those adaptations which seek to recreate Zola's nineteenth-century era in all its authenticity might be interpreted as being just as unfaithful in temporal terms to the novelist. They offer not the realist contemporary vision so central to Zola's project, but a false antique, a fake heritage past created by means of modern technology to meet the supposed needs of modern audiences. In reproducing Zola's past they are unfaithful to his belief that art should reproduce the contemporary reality from which it stems. Such observations are not intended to suggest that adaptations are doomed to be innately and inevitably unfaithful or inauthentic. Rather, they are intended to underscore the critical understanding we need to have of the terms via which we assess adaptations. It is possible to be faithful and authentic in a whole host of fundamentally contradictory ways and, if we ignore the innate multiplicity and multivalency of both terms, we foreclose the creative possibilities of the adaptations offered to us.

This monograph has sought not just visibility for the range and scope of adaptations made for television in Britain and France of Zola's novels. It also seeks, in its constituent chapters, to make a case for their creative value. The adaptations at the heart of this monograph are creatively valuable artefacts in two core respects. First, they evaluate, in the fabric of their fictions, their own adaptive act. Second, aware of the critical framework via which they will be judged, they evaluate the issue of their own artistry. They question the terms of both their existence and their reception. *Madame Sourdis*, the adaptation explored in Chapter Two, is a case in point. Its narrative, like Zola's story, is structured around how one negotiates a creative identity and signature for oneself in collaborative art projects. It explores the complex negotiations of artistic identity when audiences seek a specific artist's name in a work which is actually produced by another. The adaptation's frame narrative functions almost as a metaphor for the adaptive process itself. If *Madame Sourdis* unpicks the complex, interweaving creative signatures at play in the adaptive process, *Une page d'amour*, the case study in Chapter Four, makes televisual art out of the elements of Zola's novel which it cannot adapt. Addressing the borders and fault-lines of adaptation as a process, the telefilm italicises and reflects on what it cannot do in relation to Zola's text. It cannot adapt the repeated frescoes of nineteenth-century Paris which Zola rhythmically places in the foreground in his novel. Nineteenth-century Paris no longer exists in the form Zola knew it and to recreate it would be too expensive. Consequently, the adaptation has its heroine stare at slivers of the Parisian landscape, cropping it just like the Impressionist painters Zola supported did on canvas. The adaptation both proffers and denies the landscape by which Zola was so fascinated, veiling the windows onto it with an almost transparent gauze. The adaptation's windows are important for they reference Zola's intent that his fiction be a window onto a real world.[2] But they also, in their veiled nature, reference the adaptation itself as veil, as a material artefact which both offers us Zola and cannot give him to us in his entirety.

The adaptations at the heart of this monograph, though, do not associate themselves with a sense of lack in relation to Zola. In cropping elements of Zola and his reality, in some senses they take us directly back to Zola. For, as this book has argued, much of the power, artistry and realism of the nineteenth-century novelist's vision of reality stems from his acknowledgement of the fact that ultimately it, as source, necessarily evades him. Zola and the adaptations in this book are powerfully linked by the self-reflexivity of their project. In cropping elements of Zola and his reality, the adaptations also make a claim or space for their own artistry. They do so by adapting the techniques of the Impressionist painters so dear to Zola. It is not, as this book's Introduction suggested, unusual for Zola television adaptations to reference other art forms and the visual arts in particular. Intriguingly, all bar two of this monograph's case study adaptations directly reference the visual arts and painting in particular, situating themselves in relation to them. *The Paradise* adapts paintings in its costumes and setting. *L'Œuvre* ekphrastically reproduces the techniques of the Impressionists, experimenting with *décentrage* and flooding the screen with colour washes to underscore the ability of light and colour to alter the contours and content of objects. It situates the camera as the canvas upon which television paints by having Claude, the artist, paint directly onto the camera lens. The dramatic shot visibly probes the boundary between television adaptation and art. Art is similarly present in *Une page d'amour*. The adaptation reproduces Zola's clear intertextual reference to Fragonard's *L'Escarpolette*, albeit changing the characters involved — Jeanne swings in her mother's place in television in a scene where the system of gazes ignores her as a subject of desire. But the adaptation, as Chapter Four suggested, also inserts and explores a further reference to the visual arts as Rosalie bathes naked in a scene which clearly references Degas and his fascination with the muscularity of the human body. She contorts, naked, to wash herself before a camera fascinated by the play and strength of her muscles. Collectively, the case study adaptations at the heart of this book probe the porous borders between art forms. In so doing they adapt Zola's transmedial artistic interests and inspirations. But, via such references, they simultaneously and self-reflexively address their own potential status as art in a critical system in which they are not always readily accepted as such.

The value of these adaptations, however, lies not just in their self-reflexive status. For they also have a transformative impact on the critical frameworks of Adaptation Studies. When read through the prism of core translation theorists, they push us, as I have already suggested, to reconfigure the debates on fidelity which have dominated Adaptation Studies. They force us to take a new look at the term 'fidelity'. That fidelity discourses have dominated large areas of Adaptation Studies is clear. That key powerful critical and theoretical voices have sought to revise and move away from fidelity discourses is equally clear. This book has sought to feed into those revisionary critical and theoretical debates, but it has not argued that we should reject fidelity as a concept. Artworks which profess themselves to be adaptations will necessarily be assessed at least in part by their relation to their chosen source. Rather, the revisionary dialogue generated by Zola's novels, their television adaptations and key translation theorists, forces us to consider how we use the term 'fidelity', the multiple things we might mean by it. They suggest that a two-fold re-evaluation of fidelity is necessary. First, they make the case for the innate mutability of this core concept which has dominated critical assessments of translation and adaptation (either in their rejection of or acceptance of the concept). The fixity of the use of the term 'fidelity' belies the shifting meanings of its invocation, meanings which collectively these adaptations will not allow us to ignore. Second, these novels, adaptations and theorists collectively underscore that fidelity discourses foreclose and block off the interpersonal networks of creative identities generating adaptive art by insisting on a text-to-text framework as a source text is sought in its adaptive recreation.

The recognition of the innate mutability of fidelity in different eras and contexts has powerful implications for the reception and assessment of adaptations. Though the use of fidelity is something of a constant in the critical frames within which adaptations are assessed, its meaning or rather meanings are anything but constant. Fidelity is itself an adaptive and adapting concept, a notion which has meant, currently means and will perhaps always mean different things in different eras, nations, artefacts and subjective frameworks, as the theory of Antoine Berman suggested in Chapter Four. It is also not a neutral term, as Andre Lefevere argued in Chapter Five. It is a term fashioned by and translated through the prisms of the culture, politics and personalities of the instances in which it is used. Each of the adaptations chosen for the chapters of this book is a faithful adaptation, but each interprets fidelity differently. In Chapter One, *The Paradise* is faithful to the needs and requirements of a 2012 UK market, translating and updating Zola's look and values for its contemporary audience, while privileging a sense of the 'authentic' so core to BBC adaptation collectively. In Chapter Five, *Germinal* is faithful to the dominant poetics of the BBC and its charter, to the accepted televisual and cultural mores of the 1970s, underscoring that adaptations at times need, in order to exist, to be faithful to more than just their source text. Thus both *The Paradise* and *Germinal* offer themselves as faithful reproductions of Zola's era and source novel. But the vision of the past, the vision of Zola that they offer us is starkly different. And that difference matters. Their visions are different because they were made in different eras with different creative teams, values, technological possibilities, acting cast, poetics and politics. The association of these two very different BBC adaptations, linked both by their intent to be faithful and their much-vaunted BBC 'authenticity', allows for an understanding of fidelity and authenticity as evolving concepts both within and de facto beyond the BBC. Collectively the adaptations reveal fidelity to be a temporally-conditioned concept, a notion Janus-like in its invocation as it looks back to its source text but adjusts to the time of its target text. Fidelity, these adaptations make clear, means and looks very different in very different eras and different cultural contexts.

The recognition, via these adaptations and their source texts, of the need to read adaptations in terms of relationships between people and not just those between texts is, arguably, equally impactful on Adaptation Studies. Fidelity discourses focus on the intertextual relationship between source text and subsequent adaptive artefact. But to focus on adaptation in terms of text-to-text relations is, as Chapters Two and Three suggest in relation to the theories of Lawrence Venuti and Christiane Nord, to ignore the people at the heart of the process. Venuti's value to Adaptation

Studies lies both in his insistence that Translation and Adaptation Studies should talk to each other in more sustained theoretical terms and in his focus on the creative identities mediating reproductive artworks. Venuti focuses in largely binary terms on the relationship between the source author or text and the reproductive artist — in his case the translator, but for the purposes of this book, those adapting for television. Nord multiplies the personal relationships behind reproductive texts beyond Venuti's more binary approach. She suggests that fidelity as a system of thought falls short in its focus on the movement of one text into another text. She argues that translation is a process done by people for people and Chapter Three extended her thought to adaptation, arguing that we limit the utility of 'fidelity' as a term if we ignore the interpersonal nature of adaptive genesis. Thus, the chapter reads Jacques Rouffio's *L'Argent* not just for its relationship with Zola's source novel but in interpersonal creative terms, unpicking the influence of the teams behind the adaptation, whether they be the source author, his historical colleagues, the dramatist, the producer, the director, actors, the sound specialist, and the list goes on. Adaptations are personal and subjective in their creation, refracted products born at the interstice of multiple creative personalities. So too are they personal and subjective in their reception as different people read and judge them differently. Fidelity is a shifting, mutating, personal concept which means different things at different times. It is not, and cannot be, an all-encompassing fixed critical stick with which to beat adaptations which do not meet our own subjective expectations of what adaptation should be.

Far from taking us away from Zola, this re-evaluative reading of fidelity as a subjective, shifting concept takes us directly to him. That fidelity is a key concept for Zola's mission is clear. When evaluating realism in an early letter to the poet Antony Valabrègue in 1864, he couches it in terms reminiscent of the discourses of fidelity. He characterises its prose as a pane of transparent glass via which reality as source may be glimpsed in all its detail and truth. He claims:

> L'Ecran réaliste est un simple verre à vitre, très mince, très clair, et qui a la prétention d'être si parfaitement transparent que les images le traversent et se reproduisent ensuite dans toute leur réalité. L'écran réaliste nie sa propre existence.[3]
>
> [The realist screen is a pane of glass. Both thin and clear, it aims to be so transparent that images cross perfectly through it and are reproduced in their innate realness. The realist screen pretends not even to be there.]

Zola's words may seem to embrace fidelity as an unproblematic concept, but his terms not only anticipate Venuti's canonical vision of the invisibility of translation in the modern world, they also lead to a more nuanced vision of the very possibility of fidelity, a nuancing which speaks to the work of the translation theorists cited in this book. Zola continues:

> Il est, certes, difficile de caractériser un Ecran qui a pour qualité principale celle de n'être presque pas; je crois, cependant, le bien juger, en disant qu'une fine poussière grise trouble sa limpidité. Tout objet, en passant par ce milieu, y perd son éclat, ou, plutôt s'y noircit légèrement.[4]

[It is, without question, difficult to define a screen whose core quality is almost not to be present. I think it fair to say though that a delicate grey dust affects its clarity. Each object passing through it loses some of its impact or rather is darkened by it.]

Reproductive art cannot deliver its source in its integrity and entirety, rather it renders it absent even while making it present. Zola's focus on the imagery of dust in the context of reproductive art is far from incidental. It echoes that analysed in Chapter Four as Zola embedded dust, the symbol of presence becoming an absence or materiality becoming dematerialised, at the heart of his adaptations of the contemporary landscape whose transcription symbolises the nineteenth-century novelist's realist intent. Zola's fiction promises to translate the presence of reality faithfully but it recognises that all it can offer us is fragments of said source. Zola is a writer who contemplates the limits and fault-lines of fidelity, enacting them in his fiction and making art out of them. Art, for Zola, as well as truth and beauty, lie precisely in such a recognition. He states:

> Toutes mes sympathies, s'il faut le dire, sont pour l'Ecran réaliste; il contente ma raison, et je sens en lui des beautés immenses de solidité et de vérité. Seulement, je le répète, je ne peux l'accepter tel qu'il veut se presenter à moi; je ne puis admettre qu'il nous donne des images vraies et j'affirme qu'il doit avoir en lui des propriétés particulières qui déforment les images, et qui, par conséquent, font des ces images des œuvres d'art.[5]

[If I must come down on one side, I am all for the realist screen. It suits my way of thinking and I find in it immense beauty in the solidity and truth it offers. But I must reiterate that I cannot take it at face value. I cannot accept that its images are entirely true. Its particular properties deform images and, as a result, make these images into art.]

Part of the reason for this deforming tendency is that art, for Zola, is always refracted through the artist as person, as shaping consciousness. He, in a manner which maps onto the critical frameworks of Venuti and Nord, situates fidelity in a subjective context. The adaptation of reality that Zola's novels offer us is, he makes clear, personal, hermeneutic and subjective. Zola's theoretical writing questions and nuances the very possibility of fidelity. When read in association with his creative works, they mark him as a key case study for Adaptation Studies.

Zola's power as a case study for Adaptation Studies is magnified when the nineteenth-century novelist is considered in the medium of television. The reasons why Zola is adapted for television so frequently are perhaps as diverse as the televisual offerings made of him. Moving beyond the commonly-stated belief that nineteenth-century novels work well on television because their original feuilleton or serial publication can be echoed in the serial medium of television (many of the adaptations listed above are one-off adaptations), this monograph looks for the link between Zola and television elsewhere. It finds it in a variety of places: a shared spatial paradox, an intriguing aesthetic which is more intricate than it is often given credit for and an innate mutability of medium. The link between Zola and television in terms of space is clear. Historically, television in the early and mid-years of its development, years from which the majority of this book's case studies stem, was characterised by a spatially restrained aesthetic in its dramatic output. The medium in this era of its development offered studio-based productions, heavy in dialogue, close-ups and mid-shots, filmed in a boxy 3:4 ratio. The historical spatially restrained approach offers, in its smallness, something of a paradox in this medium whose range and reach in terms of audience and broadcast span is vast. This spatial paradox resonates with the spatial aesthetics of Zola. His works are vast in their geographical frescoes, which attempt to see and show all in narratives which focus on the claustrophobic lives of his characters. Zola's narratives pin his characters beneath their dissecting gaze, trapping them in tiny, inexorable lives beneath the shaping forces of race, milieu and moment or heredity, environment and era.[6] The link between Zola and television is also clear in terms of the critical reception of their respective aesthetics. The novelist, in his lifetime and arguably beyond, was attacked by critics such as Ferragus for his lack of aesthetic, for his portrayal of reality in unvarnished, in-artistic form. Television, with frequently smaller budgets than its cinema counterparts, was, in the era of television history assessed in this book, habitually associated with a stripped-back aesthetic, with a *mise en scène* which was functional and non-distracting. Nussbaum, cited in the introduction to this book, when evaluating how television became art with the turn of the millennium, characterises that era precisely as the moment when television's *mise en scène* began to change and to experiment in formal terms in innovative ways. This book's case studies suggest, though, that formal experimentation has always been a feature of television as a medium, just as it was a feature of Zola's work. Cardinal's *L'Œuvre* (1967) has the actors paint on the camera screen and works to flood the screen with colour washes, as Chapter Two explored. The repeated extreme high-angle shots of the BBC's *Germinal* (1970) in Chapter Five explore, in aesthetic terms, the visual entrapment of the striking miners in their socio-economic fate. In the spheres of space and aesthetics, Zola and television adaptation have clear points of contact.

Zola in televisual form also offers Adaptation Studies a platform from which to ask what television is, compelling us to consider television not just as a medium of adaptation but actually as a medium which itself adapts and mutates, shapeshifting in intriguing ways. This monograph has focused on the mid-years of television, 1967–88 (with the exception of its opening chapter on a 2012 BBC production, *The Paradise*). Within this period, television was an arguably comparably static experience as members of the family, singly or collectively, gathered to watch television within set time-slots according to pre-defined programming schedules. The invention of video recording, a technology which became available in the 1970s and more commercially accessible in the 80s, initiated the shapeshifting which has come to characterise television perhaps more than any other medium. It enabled viewers to capture adaptations, own them as tangible artefacts, watch them in their own time and shape them to their own requirements, fast-forwarding and pausing scenes for their own personal impact. The VCR changed television as a medium but it also changed viewers' relationship to the medium and their viewing patterns and habits.

The technological advances which postdate the majority of the adaptations in this monograph, advances which merit further consideration, have only accelerated these changes both to television and to the way it is consumed. Smart televisions, connected to the internet with a range of online features, offering on-demand content, access to streaming services and the ability to connect to devices such as smartphones, are a case in point. Viewers may now watch what they want, when they want, how they want. They may watch Zola on television in the house, on the go, on a range of appliances, pausing live television, editing the viewing experience with their remote or even their voice in the case of voice-activated technology. Different viewing platforms shape the Zola adaptations on offer, offering different visions and experiences of the novelist and his adaptation. So too do the social media which at times shape and valuably document the viewing experience. This monograph has gestured to the changes to television viewing practices triggered by the use of social media such as Twitter. Twitter allows disparate viewers an online viewing community around contemporary Zola adaptations which is in some ways akin to the communal viewing of television in its earliest days as families gathered around the family's set to watch and discuss together. Twitter archives both audience commentary and viewing habits. But Twitter is far from the only social media and its counterparts' relationship with television viewing practices might valuably be considered. Television's shapeshifting may offer us different Zolas on different technological platforms, Zolas consumed differently in different social media, but it does not take us away from Zola. In its shapeshifting, television in fact leads us back to Zola. He was, as a novelist, adapted and re-adapted into hosts of different media both within his lifetime and beyond it. He presided over his own adaptation and re-adaptation into different media. He adapted and re-adapted different authors, sources and media in his work. Shapeshifting lies at the core of both Zola's novels and the adaptations made of them in the mutating medium of television.

If both Zola and television shapeshift, this monograph has also sought to shift the shape of Zola studies by assessing the fertile relationship between the nineteenth-century novelist and the medium of television. So too has it intended a comparable impact on Adaptation Studies and the frameworks of fidelity which have shaped so many debates within it. Fidelity is, as a concept, as shapeshifting as Zola's novels and television as a medium. For all the constancy of the term in debates on adaptation, the concept itself is innately inconstant, meaning very different things in very different moments, places and contexts. It is also an innately subjective word, a word which means different things for different people at different times. The Zola novels, television adaptations and theorists discussed in this monograph collectively underline that to seek merely Zola's source text in a reproductive artefact is to occlude the interpersonal nature of these Zola adaptations. Such adaptations are created by people for people, and the myriad layers of creative identities who contribute to them in visible and less visible ways all bring artistic value. The Zola adaptations in this book are not passively subject to theoretical frameworks of adaptation, rather they interact with them. Like their source author, they probe the terms of their own existence, underscoring the limits and fault-lines of their endeavour, italicising the different layers of identities so core to their genesis. But in so doing they find creative power. In so doing they make art.

Notes to the Conclusion

1. Cardwell, *Adaptation Revisited: Television and the Classic Novel*, pp. 122–23.
2. See Naomi Schor, 'Zola from Window to Window', *Yale French Studies*, 42 (1969), 38–51 (pp. 35–51).
3. Emile Zola, letter to Antony Valabrègue, 1864, <http://www.cahiers-naturalistes.com/pages/ecrans.html> [accessed 21 September 2018].
4. Ibid.
5. Ibid.
6. The spatial codes of television both are evolving and have evolved. While television drama and comedy has habitually relied on a three-camera set-up to encompass the action, modern quality US drama for example is amongst that which has innovated in the use of a single-camera set-up in an output which has become in many ways more filmic both in its spatial expansiveness and meaning-laden *mise en scène* (see for example *True Detective* and *Treme*).

BIBLIOGRAPHY

AHEARN, EDWARD J., 'Monceau, Camondo, *La Curée*, *L'Argent*: History, Art, Evil', *French Review*, 73.6 (2000), 1100–15

ANTOINE, ANDRÉ, *Mes souvenirs sur le Théâtre-libre* (Paris: Arthème Fayard, 1921)

ARBEAU, THOINOT, 'Belle qui tiens ma vie', 'Beautiful One Who Holds my Life', <https://lyricstranslate.com/en/belle-qui-tiens-ma-vie-beautiful-one-who-holds-my-life.html> [accessed 10 October 2018]

ATTAL, DOMINIQUE, and DOMINIQUE BARON, 'Entretien avec Caroline Huppert', <www.groupe25images.fr/up/files/gazette/LC32CHUPPERT.pdf> [accessed November 2014]

BAGULEY, DAVID, *Napoleon III and his Regime: An Extravaganza* (Baton Rouge: Louisiana State University Press, 2000)

—— 'Zola devant la critique de langue anglaise (1877–1970)', *Cahiers naturalistes*, 43 (1972), 105–23

BARON, A.-M., 'Zola sur petit et grand écran, de la sagesse au délire', *Cahiers naturalistes*, 84 (2010), 391–92

BARTHES, ROLAND, *S/Z* (Paris: Seuil, 1970)

—— *S/Z*, trans. by Richard Miller (New York: Noonday Press, 1993)

BASSNETT, SUSAN, *Translation Studies* (London: Routledge, 2002)

BBC, 'Impartiality', <https://www.bbc.co.uk/editorialguidelines/guidelines/impartiality> [accessed 10 August 2018]

BELL, DAVID F., *Models of Power: Politics and Economics in Zola's Rougon-Macquart* (Lincoln, NE: University of Nebraska Press, 1988)

BELLALOU, GAËL, '*Nadia Coupeau, dite Nana*: A Modern Adaptation of Zola's Eponymous Work', *Bulletin of the Emile Zola Society*, 30 (2004), 16–22

BERG, WILLIAM J., *The Visual Novel: Emile Zola and the Art of his Times* (University Park, PA: Pennsylvania State University Press, 1992)

BERG, WILLIAM J., and LAUREY KRAMER MARTIN, *Emile Zola Revisited* (New York: Twayne, 1992)

BERMAN, ANTOINE, *L'Epreuve de l'étranger: culture et traduction dans l'Allemagne romantique* (Paris: Gallimard, 1984)

—— *La Traduction et la lettre ou L'Auberge du lointain* (Paris: Seuil, 1999)

—— 'Translation as the Trial of the Foreign', trans. by Lawrence Venuti, in *The Translation Studies Reader*, ed. by Lawrence Venuti (London: Routledge, 2000), pp. 233–50

BITZER, MICHEL, 'Du bagne à la sûreté', *Le Républicain lorrain*, 18 August 2012, <https://www.republicain-lorrain.fr/actualite/2012/08/12/du-bagne-a-la-surete> [accessed 2 October 2018]

BLUESTONE, GEORGE, *Novels into Film* (Berkeley & London: University of California Press, 1957)

BOWLBY, RACHEL, *Just Looking: Consumer Culture in Dreiser, Gissing and Zola* (London: Methuen, 1989)

BOYER, ROBERT, 'Who's the Comeback Kid? France, Germany, Italy', *The International Economy* (2003), 8–11, <www.international-economy.com/TIE_F03_Euro3.pdf> [accessed 21 March 2014]

BRADY, PATRICK, *L'Œuvre de Emile Zola: roman sur les arts, manifeste, autobiographie, roman à clef* (Geneva: Droz, 1967)

BRIGGS, ASA, *The History of Broadcasting in the United Kingdom*, 5 vols (London: Oxford University Press, 1961–95)

BRUNSDON, CHARLOTTE, *Screen Tastes: Soap Opera to Satellite Dishes* (London: Routledge 1997)

BURKE, PETER, *Eye Witnessing: The Uses of Images as Historical Evidence* (London: Reaktion, 2001)

BUSS, ROBIN, 'J'accuse', *Guardian*, 28 September 2002, <https://www.theguardian.com/books/2002/sep/28/classics.emilezola> [accessed 29 April 2017]

BYRD, ALMA W., *The First Generation Reception of the Novels of Emile Zola in Britain and America: An Annotated Bibliography of English Language Responses to his Work, 1877–1902* (Lampeter: Edwin Mellen Press, 2007)

BYRNE, KATHERINE, *Edwardians on Screen* (London: Palgrave, 2015)

CARDWELL, SARAH, *Adaptation Revisited: Television and the Classic Novel* (Manchester: Manchester University Press, 2002)

CARTER, LAWSON A., *Zola and the Theater* (New Haven, CT: Yale University Press, 1963)

CATTRYSSE, PATRICK, 'Film (Adaptation) as Translation: Some Methodological Proposals', *Target*, 4 (1992), 53–70

CAUGHIE, JOHN, 'Before the Golden Age: Early Television Drama', in *Popular Television in Britain: Studies in Cultural History*, ed. by John Corner (London: BFI, 1991), pp. 22–41

CHAPLIN, TAMARA, *Turning on the Mind: French Philosophers on Television* (Chicago: University of Chicago Press, 2007)

CONCHON, GEORGES, *Le Sucre* (Paris: Broché, 1977)

COOKE, LEZ, *British Television Drama* (London: Bloomsbury, 2003)

COUSINS, RUSSELL, 'Adapting Zola for TV: The Example of Jacques Rouffio's *L'Argent*', *Excavatio*, 12 (1999), 153–61

CUMMINS, A., 'Emile Zola's Cheap English Dress: The Vizetelly Translations, Late-Victorian Print Culture and the Crisis of Literary Value', *Review of English Studies*, 60 (2009), 108–32

DELBAERE-GARANT, JEANNE, *Henry James* (Liège: Presse universitaire de Liège, 1970)

DOOLEY, ROBERT A., 'Style and Acceptability: The Guarani New Testament', *Notes on Translation*, 3 (1989), 49–57

DOUSTEYSSIER-KHOZE, CATHERINE, *Zola et la littérature naturaliste en parodies* (Paris: Eurédit, 2004)

EASTAUGH, KENNETH, 'Epitaph to the Last of the Miners', *Daily Mirror*, 26 January 1970

FENWICK, 'Our Story. Our Heritage', <https://www.fenwick.co.uk/our-story.html> [accessed 3 September 2018]

FERNANDEZ-ZOÏLA, ADOLFO, 'Le Système écriture-peinture et le figural dans *L'Œuvre*', *Cahiers naturalistes*, 66 (1992), 91–103

FERRAGUS, 'La Littérature putride', *Le Figaro*, 23 January 1868

GAUTEUR, CLAUDE, and GINETTE VINCENDEAU, *Jean Gabin: anatomie d'un mythe* (Paris: Nouveau Monde, 2006)

GIDDINGS, ROBERT, KEITH SELBY, and CHRIS WENSLEY, *Screening the Novel: The Theory and Practice of Literary Dramatization* (London: Palgrave, 1990)

GIDDINGS, ROBERT, and KEITH SELBY, *The Classic Serial on Television and Radio* (Basingstoke: Palgrave, 2001)

GIDDINGS, ROBERT, and ERICA SHEEN, eds, *The Classic Novel: From Page to Screen* (Manchester: Manchester University Press, 2000)

GILLE, PHILIPPE, '*L'Argent*, par Émile Zola', *Le Figaro*, 13 March 1891

GORDON, RAE BETH, *Ornament, Fantasy and Desire in Nineteenth-century French Literature* (Princeton: Princeton University Press, 1992)
GRIFFITHS, KATE, *Emile Zola and the Artistry of Adaptation* (Oxford: Legenda, 2009)
—— 'Mythical Returns: Televising *Thérèse Raquin*', *Nineteenth-Century French Studies*, 39 (2011), 285–95
—— 'Radio and the Space of Adaptation: Diana Griffiths's *Madame Bovary* (Radio 4, 2006)', *Dix-Neuf*, 18 (2014), 211–23
—— '*Thérèse Raquin* and the Anxieties of Adaptation', in *Adapting the Canon*, ed. by Ann Lewis and Silke Arnold-de Simine (Oxford: Legenda, forthcoming)
—— 'Visions and Revisions: Pierre Cardinal's *L'Œuvre*', in *The Art of Text*, ed. by Susan Harrow (Cardiff: University of Wales Press, 2013), pp. 171–85
GRIFFITHS, KATE, and ANDREW WATTS, *Adapting Nineteenth-century France: Literature in Film, Theatre, Radio, Television and Print* (Cardiff: University of Wales Press, 2013)
GUIEU, JEAN-MAX, and ALISON HILTON, eds, *Emile Zola and the Arts* (Washington, DC: University of Georgetown Press, 1988)
GURAL-MIGDAL, ANNA and ROBERT SINGER, eds, *Zola and Film: Essays in the Art of Adaptation* (Jefferson, NC: McFarland, 2005)
GUTT, ERNST-AUGUST, *Translation and Relevance: Cognition and Context* (Manchester: St Jerome, 2000)
HARROW, SUSAN, *Zola, The Body Modern: Pressures and Prospects of Representation* (Oxford: Legenda, 2010)
HERMANS, THEO, *Conference of the Tongues* (Manchester: St Jerome, 2007)
HERTZ, HENRI, 'Emile Zola, témoin de la vérité', *Europe*, 30 (1952), 83–84
HIGSON, ANDREW, 'The Heritage Film and British Cinema', in *Dissolving Views: Key Writings on British Cinema*, ed. by Andrew Higson (London, Cassell: 1996), pp. 232–49
HUNT, LYNN, and VANESSA R. SCHWARTZ, 'Capturing the Moment: Images and Eyewitnessing in History', *Journal of Visual Culture*, 9 (2010), 259–71
HUTCHEON, LINDA, *A Theory of Adaptation* (London: Routledge, 2006)
JOHNSON, DAVID T., 'Adaptation and Fidelity', in *The Oxford Handbook of Adaptation Studies*, ed. by Thomas Leitch (Oxford: Oxford University Press, 2017), pp. 87–100
JULLIEN, DOMINIQUE, 'Cendrillon au grand magasin: *Au Bonheur des dames* et *Le Rêve*', *Cahiers naturalistes*, 67 (1993), 97–105
KENNEDY MARTIN, TROY, 'Nats Go Home: First Statement of a New Drama for Television', *Encore* (March-April 1964), 21–33
KLEINECKE-BATES, I., *Victorians on Screen: The Nineteenth Century on British Television 1994–2005* (London: Palgrave, 2014)
KOLLER, WERNER, *Einführung in die Übersetzungswissenschaft* (Heidelberg: Quelle & Meyer, 1983)
KRANOWSKI, NATHAN, *Paris dans les romans d'Emile Zola* (Paris: Presses universitaires de France, 1968)
KRANZ, DAVID. L., and NANCY C. MELLERSKI, eds, *In/Fidelity: Essays on Film Adaptation* (Newcastle upon Tyne: Cambridge Scholars Publishing, 2008)
KREBS, KATJA, ed., *Translation and Adaptation in Theatre and Film* (London: Routledge, 2013)
KUBLER, CORINNE, 'Intertextualités zoliennes', *Cahiers naturalistes*, 63 (1989), 168–81
KULCZYCKA-SALONI, M. J., 'Zola en Pologne', *Cahiers naturalistes*, 25 (1963) 24–25
LAWSON, MARK, '*The Paradise*: Do Viewers Really Need More Period Drama?', *The Guardian*, 25 September 2012, <https://www.theguardian.com/tv-and-radio/tvandradioblog/2012/sep/25/the-paradise-another-period-drama> [accessed 9 August 2017]
LECOMTE-HILMY, ANNE, 'L'Artiste de tempérament chez Zola et devant le public: essai d'analyse lexicologique et sémiologique', in *Emile Zola and the Arts*, ed. by Jean-Max

Guieu and Alison Hilton (Washington, DC: Georgetown University Press, 1988), pp. 85–99

LEFEVERE, ANDRÉ, *Translation, Rewriting and the Manipulation of Literary Fame* (London: Routledge 1992)

LEITCH, THOMAS, 'Adaptation Studies at a Crossroads', *Adaptation*, 1 (2008), 63–77

LEITCH, THOMAS, ed., *The Oxford Handbook of Adaptation Studies* (Oxford: Oxford University Press, 2017)

LETHBRIDGE, ROBERT, 'L'Accueil critique à l'œuvre de Zola avant *L'Assommoir*', *Cahiers naturalistes*, 54 (1980), 214–23

——— 'L'Accueil critique des premières œuvres de Zola (1864–1869): vers une bibliographie intégrale', *Cahiers naturalistes*, 53 (1979), 124–31

——— 'Zola et Haussmann: une expropriation littéraire', in *La Curée de Zola ou 'La Vie à outrance'*, ed. by David Baguley (Paris: Sedes, 1987), pp. 85–96

LODGE, SIR OLIVER, *Radio Times*, 28 May 1926

LURY, KAREN, *Interpreting Television* (London: Bloomsbury, 2005)

MACCABE, COLIN, KATHLEEN MURRAY and RICK WARNER, eds, *True to the Spirit: Film Adaptation and the Question of Fidelity* (Oxford: Oxford University Press, 2011)

MARCUS, SHARON, *Apartment Stories: City and Home in Nineteenth-century Paris and London* (Berkeley: University of California Press, 1999)

MATVIICHYNE, V., 'Emile Zola en Ukraine', *Cahiers naturalistes*, 33 (1967), 68–72

MCFARLANE, BRIAN, *Novel to Film: An Introduction to the Theory of Adaptation* (Oxford: Clarendon Press, 1996)

MCNAUGHTON, DOUGLAS, '"Constipated, Studio-bound, Wall-confined, Rigid": The Influence of British Actors' Equity on BBC Television Drama, 1948–72', *Journal of British Cinema and Television*, 11 (2014), 1–22

MEDHURST, JAMIE, 'What a Hullabaloo! Launching BBC Television in 1936 and BBC2 in 1964', *Journal of British Cinema and Television*, 14 (2017), 264–82

MESEGUER, P., 'Traducción y reescritura ideológica bajo el franquismo: *La Faute de l'abbé Mouret* de Emile Zola', *Cedille*, 11 (2015), 389–412

MITTERAND, HENRI, 'Le Musée dans le texte', *Cahiers naturalistes*, 66 (1992), 13–22

MOREL, CHANTAL, 'La Fortune de Zola en Angleterre: les œuvres illustrées', *Cahiers naturalistes*, 66 (1992), 195–208

MUNDAY, JEREMY, *Introducing Translation Studies: Theories and Applications* (London: Routledge, 2008)

NELSON, BRIAN, 'Désir et consummation dans au Bonheur des dames', *Cahiers naturalistes*, 70 (1996), 19–34

——— 'The Politics of Style', *Meanjin*, 64 (2005), 90–98

NIESS, ROBERT J., *Zola, Cézanne and Manet: A Study of L'Œuvre* (Ann Arbor: University of Michigan Press, 1968)

NORD, CHRISTIANE, 'Function Plus Loyalty: Ethics in Professional Translation', *Génesis: Revista Cientifica do ISAG* (2006–07), 7–17

——— 'Manipulation and Loyalty in Functional Translation', *Current Writing*, 14 (2002), 32–44

——— *Translating as a Purposeful Activity: Functionalist Approaches Explained* (Manchester: St Jerome, 1997)

NUSSBAUM, EMILY, 'When TV Became Art', *New York Entertainment*, 4 December 2009, <http://nymag.com/arts/all/aughts/62513/> [accessed 15 May 2017]

OITTINEN, RITTA, *Translating for Children* (London: Routledge, 2000)

OPEN UNIVERSITY, 'End of a Cultural Era — But OU on TV Evolution Continues', 11 December 2006, <https://www3.open.ac.uk/media/fullstory.aspx?id=9898> [accessed 27 May 2017]

PALAIS GALLIERA, 'Marie Brignole-Sale, Duchesse de Galliera', <http://www.palaisgalliera.paris.fr/fr/palais-galliera/le-palais/marie-brignole-sale-duchesse-de-galliera> [accessed 16 December 2018]

RAMAZANI, VAHEED, 'Gender, War and the Department Store: Zola's Au Bonheur des dames', *SubStance*, 36.2 (2007), 126–46

RAW, LAURENCE, 'The Skopos of a Remake: Michael Winner's *The Big Sleep* (1978)', *Adaptation*, 4 (2011), 199–209

ROTHMAN, JOSHUA, and ERIN OVERBEY, 'How TV Became Art', *New Yorker*, 28 August 2017, <https://www.newyorker.com/culture/culture-desk/how-tv-became-art> [accessed 18 October 2018]

ROZAT, PASCAL, 'Television History: The French Exception' (2011), <http://www.inaglobal.fr/en/television/article/television-history-french-exception> [accessed 31 May 2017]

SAMINADAYAR-PERRIN, CORINNE, 'Fiction de la bourse', *Cahiers naturalistes*, 2004 (78), 41–62

SANDERS, JULIE, *Adaptation and Appropriation* (London & New York: Routledge, 2006)

SCHLEIERMACHER, FRIEDRICH, 'On the Different Methods of Translating', in *The Translation Studies Reader*, ed. by Lawrence Venuti (London: Routledge, 2000), pp. 43–63

SCHMELING, MANFRED, 'Labyinthus subterraneus: *Germinal*', *Cahiers naturalistes*, 84 (2010), 255–88

SCHOR, NAOMI, 'Zola: From Window to Window', *Yale French Studies*, 42 (1969), 38–51

SCHULTE, RAINER, and JOHN BIGUENET, eds, *Theories of Translation: A Collection of Essays from Dryden to Derrida* (Chicago: Chicago University Press, 1992)

SCOTT, WALTER, *Ivanhoe* (Ware: Wordsworth Editions, 2000)

SIGAUX, G., 'Les *Rougon-Macquart* en 1962', *Cahiers naturalistes*, 22 (1962), 241–48

SMITH, IAIN ROBERT, *The Hollywood Meme: Transnational Adaptations in World Cinema* (Edinburgh: Edinburgh University Press, 2017)

THOMPSON, HANNAH, *Naturalism Re-dressed: Identity and Clothing in the Novels of Emile Zola* (Oxford: Legenda, 2004)

VENUTI, LAWRENCE, 'Adaptation, Translation, Critique', *Journal of Visual Culture*, 6 (2007), 25–43

——— 'Genealogies of Translation Theory: Jerome', *Boundary 2*, 37.3 (2010), 5–28

——— *Translation Changes Everything: Theory and Practice* (London: Routledge, 2013)

——— *The Translator's Invisibility: A History of Translation* (London: Routledge, 2009)

VENUTI, LAWRENCE, ed., *The Translation Studies Reader* (London: Routledge, 2012)

VIZETELLY, ERNEST ALFRED, 'Preface to *Fecundity*', <http://www.gutenberg.org/files/10330/10330-h/10330-h.htm#link2H_4_0001> [accessed 13 September 2018]

——— 'Preface to *The Fortune of the Rougons*', <https://www.gutenberg.org/files/5135/5135-h/5135-h.htm#link2H_INTR> [accessed 13 September 2018]

——— 'Preface to *The Fat and the Thin*', <https://www.gutenberg.org/files/5744/5744-h/5744-h.htm#link2H_INTR> [accessed 13 September 2018]

——— 'Preface to *Rome*', <https://www.gutenberg.org/files/8726/8726-h/8726-h.htm#link2H_PREF> [accessed 13 September 2018]

——— *With Zola in England*, <http://onlinebooks.library.upenn.edu/webbin/book/lookupname?key=Vizetelly%2C%20Ernest%20Alfred%2C%201853–1922> [accessed 5 September 2017]

WALTER, RODOLPHE, 'Emile Zola et Claude Monet', *Cahiers naturalistes*, 26 (1964), 51–61

WHITE, ARMOND, 'Film is Art. Television is a Medium', *New York Times*, 3 April 2014, <https://www.nytimes.com/roomfordebate/2014/04/03/television-tests-tinseltown/film-is-art-television-is-a-medium> [accessed 1 May 2017]

WILLIAMS, RAYMOND, *Television* (London: Routledge, 1975)

WILSON, STEVEN, 'Nana, Prostitution and the Textual Foundations of Zola's *Au Bonheur des dames*', *Nineteenth-Century French Studies*, 41 (2012), 91–104

WOODHEAD, LINDY, *Shopping, Seduction and Mr Selfridge* (London: Profile, 2012)

ZOLA, EMILE, *L'Argent*, in *Œuvres complètes*, ed. by Henri Mitterand, 15 vols (Paris: Cercle du Livre Précieux, 1966–69), VI, 311–675

—— *Money*, trans. by Ernest Alfred Vizetelly (New York: Mondial, 2007)

—— *Au Bonheur des dames*, in *Œuvres complètes*, ed. by Henri Mitterand, 15 vols (Paris: Cercle du Livre Précieux, 1966–69), IV, 699–1053

—— *The Paradise*, trans. by Ernest Alfred Vizetelly (London: Penguin, 2013)

—— *Contes et nouvelles* (Paris: Gallimard, 1976)

—— *The Attack on the Mill*, trans. by Douglas Parmée (Oxford: Oxford University Press, 1984)

—— *Correspondance*, ed. by B. H. Bakker, 10 vols (Montreal: Presses de l'Université de Montréal; Paris: CNRS, 1978–95)

—— *Ecrits sur l'art*, ed. by Jean-Pierre Leduc-Adine (Paris: Gallimard, 1991)

—— *Germinal*, in *Œuvres complètes*, ed. by Henri Mitterand, 15 vols (Paris: Cercle du Livre Précieux, 1966–69), V, 11–421

—— *Germinal*, trans. by Roger Pearson (London: Penguin, 2004)

——, letter to Valabrègue, 1864, <http://www.cahiers-naturalistes.com/pages/ecrans.html> [accessed 21 September 2018]

—— 'Le Moment artistique', *L'Evénement*, 4 May 1866

—— *Nana*, in *Œuvres complètes*, ed. by Henri Mitterand, 15 vols (Paris: Cercle du Livre Précieux, 1966–69), IV, 11–363

—— *L'Œuvre*, in *L'Œuvres complètes*, ed. by Henri Mitterand, 15 vols (Paris: Cercle du Livre Précieux, 1966–69), IV, 423–747

—— *His Masterpiece*, trans. by Ernest Alfred Vizetelly, Project Gutenberg ebook, <http://www.gutenberg.org/files/15900/15900.txt> [accessed September 7 2017]

—— *The Masterpiece*, trans. by Roger Pearson (Oxford: Oxford University Press, 1993)

—— *Œuvres complètes*, ed. by Henri Mitterand, 15 vols (Paris: Cercle du Livre Précieux, 1966–69)

—— *Les Rougon-Macquart*, ed. by Henri Mitterand, 5 vols (Paris: Gallimard 1960–67)

—— *Une page d'amour*, in *Œuvres complètes*, ed. by Henri Mitterand, 15 vols (Paris: Cercle du Livre Précieux, 1966–69), III, 959–1220

—— *A Love Episode*, trans. by Ernest Alfred Vizetelly (London: Hutchinson and Co, 1895)

—— *A Love Story*, trans. by Helen Constantine (Oxford: Oxford University Press, 2017)

INDEX

ABC, Armchair Theatre series 133
  Lena, O My Lena (1960) 146 n. 46
actors 15, 70–71, 81–83; *see also* unions
Adaptation Studies/theory 1, 3, 11–12, 124, 149, 154–55, 156
  and fidelity 3–4, 5, 24, 51, 72, 77, 101–02, 125, 144, 149–50, 151–52
  and Translation Studies/theory 1–3, 52, 72 151–52, 153
  and visibility 54, 72
  see also Berman, Antoine; Gutt, Ernst-August; Nord, Christiane; Venuti, Lawrence
L'Affaire Dreyfus (France 2, 1995) 14
Ahearn, Edward J. 80
'L'Air du muguet' (Tournier) 12
Allégret, Yves, *Germinal* (1963) 124
Allen, Melanie 26
anti-Semitism 85, 94, 98 n. 18
Apollinaire, 'Le Matelot d'Amsterdam' 12
Arbeau, Thoinot, 'Belle qui tiens ma vie' 114–16
Arbres de vie (Antenne 2, 1985) 22 n. 52
archives, television 7–9, 13
L'Argent 17, 77, 78–81, 87–93, 96, 149
  Cercle du Livre Précieux edition 78, 80–81, 84, 90, 98 n. 17
  English translation of (E. A. Vizetelly) 17
  French television adaption of (Antenne 2, 1988) 1, 7, 11, 17, 77, 81–87, 88, 91–92, 93–96, 153
Armchair Theatre series (ABC, 1960) 133, 146 n. 46
art 5, 37–39, 151
  definitions of 9, 10–11, 36, 57–58
  television as 4–5, 9–11, 29–30, 155, 156–57
  artists/painters 65
  female 65–67, 68–70
  Impressionist 57, 61–62, 71, 72, 111–12, 151
  in television adaptations 67–70, 71, 72
  in Zola's literary works 53, 59–62, 64–67, 72, 74 n. 30
  see also under individual artists' names
Arzner, Dorothy, *Nana* (1934; BBC1, 1974) 14
Associated-Rediffusion 133
Au Bonheur des dames 1, 23, 24–26, 27–29, 30, 32, 34–39, 40, 44–46
  British television adaption of, *see Paradise, The*
Au siècle de Maupassant (France 2, 2009) 12
audiences 30–33
  television adaptations tailored to 96, 102, 150, 152

see also consumption (of television); relevance theory; viewing experiences
authenticity 27, 150
  and BBC television productions 18, 26, 123, 127–31, 144, 152
  and French television productions 85, 103, 149
  see also fidelity; period adaptations

Bach, Johann Sebastian, Cello Suites 1–6: 106, 116–17
Bakhtin, Mikhail 110
Barry, Michael 138
Barthes, Roland 37
BBC (British Broadcasting Corporation) 6, 126–27
  adaptive output 6–7, 12, 13–15, 21 n. 51, 123, 126–28; *see also under individual programme titles*
  archives of 8
  channels/platforms 8, 13–14, 31
  charter 123, 141–42, 152
  competition with independent television channels 30, 41, 123, 132–35, 146 n. 46
  creative influence (on adaptations) 18, 26–27, 131, 135, 143–44
  and economics/funding 29–30, 123, 128, 132–33, 144
  and historical 'authenticity' (in adaptations) 127–31
  politics shaping output 123, 127, 132–35, 141–44, 152
  programming conventions 13, 26, 31
  technology 8, 31, 123
BBC Knowledge 13–14
BBC Sounds 8
BBC1 13, 14, 23
BBC2 13, 14, 129, 133, 135, 144
'Belle qui tiens ma vie' (Arbeau) 114–16
Berg, William 121 n. 21
Berman, Antoine 1, 13, 103, 107, 109–10, 118–19, 152
  and Adaptation Studies 17, 101–02
  La Traduction et la letter ou L'Auberge du lointain 109–10
  and translation theory 1, 101, 114
Berri, Claude, *Germinal* (1993) 14, 124
Bête humaine, La 7, 11, 14, 15
  British television adaption of (BBC, 1996) 7, 11
  film adaptations of 14, 15
Bête humaine, La (Renoir, 1938) 14, 15
Bird, Kenneth 135
Bismarck, Otto von 80, 81, 92

Bluestone, George, *Novels into Film* (1957) 3
Bluwal, Marcel:
　Dom Juan ou Le Festin de Pierre (1965) 82
　Le Jeu de l'amour et du hazard (1967) 82
　Les Nouvelles Aventures de Vidocq (ORTF, 1971) 82–83
body, the:
　artistic/painterly 60–61, 64–72
　female 28–29, 55, 59, 60, 63, 71, 113–14, 151
　in Zola's literary works 39, 58–63, 89–90
Bon Marché, Paris 36, 47 n. 7, 47 n. 8
Bouton de rose, Le:
　French television adaption of (Première Chaîne, 1971) 7, 11
Bowlby, Rachel 29
Boyer, Robert 94–95
Brasseur, Claude 82–83
Briggs, Asa 126, 127, 135, 141, 147 n. 47
Brunsdon, Charlotte 29–30
　'Can the Jew be Innocent?' ('In My Defence', BBC2, 1991) 14

Capellani, Alberto, *Germinal* (1913) 124
capitalism 27, 30, 89; *see also* consumerism/consumer culture
Cardinal, Pierre, *L'Œuvre* (Deuxième Chaîne, 1967) 7, 10, 53–57, 60, 71–72, 151, 155
Cardwell, Sarah 149, 99 n. 31
Carné, Michel, *Thérèse Raquin* (1953) 14
Castaldi, Jean-Pierre 118
Cathy Come Home (Loach, 1966) 132
Cattrysse, Patrick 3
Cau, Jean, 'Un viol' 12
Ce cochon de Morin (Heynemann, 2008) 70–71
Cello Suites 1–6 (Bach) 106, 116–17
Cézanne, Paul 61, 74 n. 30
Chaplin, Tamara 54
Chouraqui, Elie, *Une page d'amour* (FR3, 1980) 1, 7, 11, 17, 101, 102–06, 107–08, 113–18, 151
cinema/cinematic adaptations 2–3, 4, 7, 9, 26, 124
　television screenings of 14–15, 21 n. 51, 138
　see also telefilms
Cisife, Jean-Paul 53–54
class system, the 27, 30, 42, 47 n. 18, 142–43, 146 n. 46
'Clean Up TV' campaign (1963) 135, 136–37
Clémenti, Pierre 71
Comfort, Dr Alex 135
Conchon, Georges, *Le Sucre* (1977) 83, 98 n. 17
Conroy, David 129
consumerism/consumer culture 25, 26, 29, 30–32; *see also* retail/shopping
consumption (of television) 8, 9, 11, 26, 31, 33
Cooke, Lez 127–28, 129, 131
Coppée, François, 'Le Louis d'or' 12
costume 26–27, 149, 151
costume dramas, *see* period adaptations

Couture, Thomas 74 n. 30
creative artists/networks:
　personalities shaping re-creative art 17, 82, 87, 91–92, 96, 102, 152, 156
　and television adaptations 4, 9, 18, 77, 78, 88, 91–92, 96, 152, 156
　and theatrical adaptations 5–6
　and translations 4, 16, 17, 77–78
creative identities/personalities:
　and the BBC 18, 26–27, 131, 135, 143–44
　and collaboration 5–6, 67–70, 88, 135, 150, 153, 156; *see also* creative artists/networks
　and television adaptations 4, 54, 67–70, 77, 88, 135, 150, 153, 156
　and translators/translations 4, 15–16, 77–78
　in Zola's literary works 53, 59–60, 64–67
　see also artists/painters;
Cultural Turn 3–4, 18; *see also* Berman, Antoine; Lefevere, André; Venuti, Lawrence
Curée, La 40, 83, 90
　film adaptations of 14
Curée, La (Vadim, 1966) 14

Dacqmine, Jacques 81–82
Daily Mirror 130–31, 134
Davies, John 129
deformation 101–02, 103–05, 109, 118–19
Degas, Edgar 113–14, 121 n. 22, 151
Dans un café (L'Absinthe) (1876) 71
Delacroix, Eugène, *La Mort de Sardanapale* (1827) 37–38
department stores 25, 26, 30–32, 34–37, 38–39, 40, 41, 42, 44, 47 n. 7, 47 n. 8
Dieterle, William, *Life of Emile Zola, The* (1937) 14
directors, creative identities of 15, 54, 70, 83, 85–87, 91–92; *see also* creative artists/networks
Dom Juan ou Le Festin de Pierre (Bluwal, 1965) 82
Dooley, Robert A. 24
Downton Abbey (BBC, 2010) 48 n. 40
Dreyfus affair 14, 63
Dryden, John 73 n. 8
DVD, viewing television on 21 n. 50, 31, 83
DVR, viewing television on 31, 48 n. 23

Eastaugh, Kenneth 130–31
Eatwell, Joanne 26
Elliott, Marianne, *Thérèse Raquin* (2006) 121 n. 21
Equity 137–39, 140, 141, 144
equivalence 3, 24, 43, 44, 52
　Fat and the Thin (E. A. Vizetelly) 63–64, 76 n. 41
　Faute de l'abbé Mouret, La 22 n. 52

Fécondité:
　English translation of 75 n. 38
　Fecundity (E. A. Vizetelly) 75 n. 38
female gaze, the 27–29

femme innocente, Une (TF1, 1987) 7, 11, 12
Fenwick, John James 47 n. 7
Fernandel 15
Fernandez-Zoïla, Adolfo 62
Ferragus 10–11, 137, 155
Ferrer, José, *I Accuse* (1958) 14
fidelity 1, 15, 17, 18, 102–03, 109, 110, 124, 151
   and Adaptation Studies/theory 1–3, 5, 24, 51, 72, 77–78, 101–02, 125, 144, 151–53, 156
   and the BBC 127, 128–29, 144
   and deformation 101, 118–19
   and context 11–14, 123–24, 149, 152, 154, 156
   and Translation Studies/theory 2–4, 5, 24, 51, 52, 77–78, 101, 151–53
   Zola's reflections on 5–6, 153–54
film, *see* cinema/cinematic adaptations
filming locations 103, 127, 130, 132, 138, 149
filming techniques 56–57, 71–72, 103, 140, 151
   dialogue over visuals 118, 127
   high camera angles 85, 133, 139–40, 155
   theatrical 138
Fitzgerald, Edward 73 n. 8
Flaubert, Gustave, *Sentimental Education*:
   television adaptation of 133
Fortune des Rougon, La:
   French television adaption of (TF1, 1980) 7, 11
Fourier, Charles 48 n. 19
'fourth wall', the 33, 95
Fragonard, Jean-Honoré, *The Swing* (1767) 113, 151
Frank, Anne:
   diary of 125
Functionalist theory 3–4, 15, 18, 23–24, 78, 93–94; *see also* Gutt, Ernst-August; Nord, Christiane

Gallagher, Bill 26
Gauteur, Claude 15
Gautier, Théophile, 'Omphale' 12
gender stereotypes 27, 41–42, 65–66
General Strike (1926) 141
Genome archive (BBC) 8
Germinal 11, 40, 123, 124, 129–30, 131–32, 136–37, 140–41
   British television adaption of (BBC, 1970) 1, 6–7, 13–14, 18, 123, 129–44, 155
   film adaptions of 124
   French television adaption of (FR3, 1976) 7
   radio adaptation (BBC, 2007) 148 n. 70
Giddings, Robert 2, 12, 28, 123, 126–27, 128, 129, 133
Gilbert, Pierre-Henri 83, 84
Gill, André 61, 74 n. 30
Gille, Philippe 79
Gordon, Rae Beth 44
Griffiths, Diana 148 n. 70
Gros plan (series) 54
Gural-Migdal, Anna 7
Gutt, Ernst-August 1, 3, 4, 5, 14, 18

   and Adaptation Studies 24, 41
   and relevance theory 15, 23–25, 30–31, 36, 43, 45–46, 51
   and Translation Studies/theory 15, 23–24

Hall, John 130
Harris, Pauline 148 n. 70
Harrow, Susan 58
Haussmann, Baron 35, 36
heritage 26, 27, 40, 103, 127–31, 149
L'Héritage (Heynemann, 2007) 70
Heynemann, Laurent, *Chez Maupassant* (series) 70–71
   Ce cochon de Morin (2008) 70–71
L'Héritage (2007) 70
   His Masterpiece (E. A. Vizetelly) 53, 59, 62–64
   'Histoire d'un fou' 11, 12
   French television adaptations of (TF1, 1987) 7, 11, 12
Human Desire (Lang, 1954) 14
Humboldt, Wilhelm von 109–10
Huppert, Caroline 70, 71

I Accuse (Ferrer, 1958) 14
Impressionism 5, 10, 38, 56, 57, 61–62, 111–12
   painting techniques 71–72, 108, 151
   see also under individual artists' names
Inathèque (INA), Bibliothèque nationale de France 7, 8
independent television 30, 40–41, 123, 132–35, 146 n. 46
iPlayer (BBC) 8, 31
ITV (Independent Television):
   competition with BBC 30, 41, 123, 132–35
   creation of 132–33
Ivanhoe (Scott) 110–11

Jacobs, Jason 138
James, Henry 11
Jeu de l'amour et du hazard, Le (Bluwal, 1967) 82
Johnson, David T. 2
Joie de vivre, La 7, 11
   French television adaptions of (France 2, 2011) 7, 11
Jullien, Dominique 39, 40

Kassel, Vincent 98 n. 14
Kleinecke-Bates, I. 13
Kranowski, Nathan 111
Kranz, David L. 2
Krebs, Katja 2, 3

Lang, Fritz, *Human Desire* (1954) 14
Lawson, Mark 26
Leboursier, Raymond:
   Naïs (1945) 15
Lefevere, André 1, 3, 4, 5, 13, 17–18, 77–78, 143, 152
   and Adaptation Studies 124–25, 144

Translation, Rewriting and the Manipulation of Literary Fame 124
and Translation Studies/theory 123
Lena, O My Lena (ABC, 1960) 146 n. 46
Liberté de Marie, La (France 3, 2002) 7, 12
Life of Emile Zola, The (Dieterle, 1937) 14
Loach, Ken, *Cathy Come Home* (1966) 132
Lodge, Sir Oliver 141
'Le Louis d'or' (Coppée) 12
Love Episode, A (E. A. Vizetelly) 113
Lury, Karen 31

MacCabe, Colin 2
'Madame Sourdis' 1, 11, 16, 51–52, 53, 64–67, 70, 72, 149, 150
  French television adaption of (Antenne 2, 1979) 1, 7, 11, 16, 51, 67–71, 72
make-up 26–27
Manet, Edouard 57, 61, 62, 74 n. 30, 97 n. 13
  Bar aux Folies-Bergère 73 n. 13, 97 n. 13
  Déjeuner sur l'herbe (1862–63) 71
  Nana (1876) 10
  Olympia (1865) 56
Martin, Troy Kennedy 138
Marx, Karl 89
'Le Matelot d'Amsterdam' (Apollinaire) 12
Maupassant, Guy de 61
'Miss Harriet', television adaptation of (Rouffio, 2007) 83, 84–85, 86
McFarlane, Brian 2
McKay, Malcolm 7
McNaughton, Douglas 137–38
Medhurst, Jamie 132–33, 135
Mellerski, Nancy C. 2
Mirage dangereux (TF1, 1987) 7, 11, 12
Mirès, Jules 90
Miss Harriet (Rouffio, 2007) 83, 84–85, 86
Mitterand, Henri 37, 61
Molière 82
Moll Flanders (1996) 99 n. 31
Monet, Claude 61–62, 74 n. 30, 111
Money (E. A. Vizetelly) 17
Morisot, Berthe, *Femme et enfant au balcon* (1874) 121 n. 21
Mr Selfridge (ITV, 2013) 30, 40–41
Muller, Robert 6
Murray, Kathleen 2
music 106, 114–17
Musset, Alfred de, *Un caprice* (1837) 104

Nadia Coupeau, dite Nana (France 2, 2001) 7, 12–13
Nais (Leboursier/Pagnol, 1945) 15
Nais, film adaptions of 15
Nana 11, 12–13, 40, 80, 92
British television adaptions of (BBC, 1968) 6, 133
film adaptations of 14
French television adaptions of: Antenne 2 (1981) 7, 10; France 2 (2001) 7, 12–13
Nana (Arzner, 1934) 14
Napoleon Bonaparte 64, 91
Napoleon III, Emperor of France 80, 91, 143
Nelson, Brian 35
Nord, Christiane 1, 3, 4, 5, 14, 15, 88–91, 93, 153
  and Adaptation Studies 77–78, 96
  and Translation Studies/theory 17, 77–78, 96
nostalgia 12, 26, 27
Nouvelles Aventures de Vidocq, Les (Bluwal, 1971) 82–83
Novels into Film (Bluestone, 1957) 3
Nussbaum, Emily 9, 155

Œuvre, L' 1, 16, 51, 53, 57–62, 149
  English translation of (E. A. Vizetelly) 53, 59, 62–64
  French television adaption of (Deuxième Chaîne, 1967) 1, 7, 10, 16, 51, 53–57, 60, 71–72, 151, 155
  Œuvre, L' (Cardinal, 1967) 7, 10, 53–57, 60, 71–72, 151, 155
Offenbach, Jacques 92
  La Périchole 99 n. 25
on-demand content 8, 13, 31, 156
'Omphale' (Gautier) 12
Open University (OU) 13, 21 n. 21

page d'amour, Une 1, 11, 17, 101, 102, 103–09, 110–13, 149, 150
  English translation of (E. A. Vizetelly) 113
  French television adaptions of:
    FR3 (Chouraqui, 1980) 1, 7, 11, 17, 101, 102–06, 107–08, 113–18, 151
    FR3 (1995) 7
painting/paintings:
  in television adaptations 9–10, 54, 55, 56, 67–69, 71, 151
  in Zola's literary works 5, 37–39, 53, 59–60, 64, 97 n. 13, 111–13, 121 n. 21, 151
  see also artists; Impressionism; *and under individual artists' names*
Paradise, The (BBC, 2012) 1, 7, 15, 18, 23, 25–27, 30–35, 38, 39–46, 123, 151
Paris 25, 35, 36, 45, 62, 63–64
  department stores 25, 36–37, 47 n. 7, 47 n. 8
  landscapes of 44, 55, 59, 103, 104–09, 111–13, 150
  patronage 18, 123, 124–26, 131, 143
Pearson, Roger 63
Périchole, La (Offenbach) 99 n. 25
period adaptations 28
  British television 12, 26, 30, 40–41, 127–28, 143–44, 152
  French television 81, 85, 103–06, 149
Pot-Bouille 11
  French television adaption of (Deuxième Chaîne, 1972) 7, 11

'Pour une nuit d'amour' 11, 12
French television adaption of (TF1, 1987) 7, 11, 12
  public service broadcasting 6, 126, 141–42; *see also* BBC
  public/private spaces:
  shifting boundaries of 34–36, 37
  women's access to 35–36, 37

radio 126, 127, 141, 147 n. 47, 148 n. 70
Ramazani, Vaheed 36
Raw, Laurence 3
re-creative works, personalities shaping 4, 15–16, 17, 72, 77–78, 82, 87, 91–92, 96, 102, 152, 156; *see also* translations
recording technology 8, 31, 48 n. 23, 138, 155
Reith, Lord 126
relevance theory 15, 23
  and audiences 4, 14, 15, 24–25, 30–31, 45–46
  see also Gutt, Ernst-August
Renoir, Jean, *La Bête humaine* (1938) 14, 15
retail/shopping 30, 31–32, 34–36, 38–39, 40, 44–45; *see also* department stores
Rêve, Le 40
reviews 32–33, 130, 134
Robson, John 130
Rome (E. A. Vizetelly) 75 n. 38
Rothschild, James de 80–81
Rouffio, Jacques 83–84
  L'Argent (1988) 1, 7, 11, 17, 77, 81–87, 88–89, 93, 94, 153
  Miss Harriet (2007) 83, 84–85, 86
  Le Sucre (1978) 83–84
Rougon-Macquart (series) 37, 40, 63, 83, 90, 92, 103; *see also under individual titles*

Saminadayar-Perrin, Corinne 92
Sanders, Julie 2, 39, 118
Schleiermacher, Friedrich 11–12
Schmeling, Manfred 140
Schütz, Anneliese 125
Scott, Walter, *Ivanhoe* 110–11
Selby, Keith 12, 28, 123, 126–27, 128, 129, 133
Sentimental Education (BBC) 133
set designs 26
Shearer, Marella 27
Sheen, Erica 2
Sieveking, Lance, *The Stuff of Radio* (1934) 126
Singer, Robert 7
smart televisions 156
smartphones 13, 31, 156
Smith, Samuel 10
social media 32–33, 156
streaming services 156
Stuff of Radio, The (Sieveking, 1934) 126
Sucre, Le (Conchon, 1977) 83, 98 n. 17
Sucre, Le (Rouffio, 1978) 83–84

Swizzlewick (Turner, 1964) 136

telefilms 12, 53–55, 70, 82, 103, 150
television 7–9, 55–56
  as art 4–5, 9–11, 29–30, 155, 156–57
  early years of 8, 9, 154–55
  see also archives, television
Television Act (1954) 132–33
television adaptations:
  anthology 12
  archiving 7–8
  as 'art' 4–5, 11, 29–30, 151, 156–57
  British 6–9, 11–12, 13–14; *see also under individual titles*
  creative identities involved in 4, 54, 77, 88, 150, 153, 156
  and education 13
  French 6, 7, 8, 9, 11–13; *see also under individual titles*
  and integrity to original text 6, 16, 53, 54–55, 78; *see also* fidelity
  and modernisation 12–13, 149–50
  and period/heritage settings 12, 26, 28, 40–41, 103, 149
  reviews of 32–33, 130, 134
  and subjectivity 1, 78, 153–54
television platforms:
  digital/online 8, 13, 31, 31, 156
  diversification of 8, 13, 31–33, 156
  on-demand 8, 13, 31, 156
Terre, La, English translation of (H. Vizetelly) 63
theatre/theatrical adaptations 3, 5, 120 n. 9, 121 n. 21
Thérèse Raquin 6, 7, 11, 12, 13
  British television adaptions of: BBC (1950) 6, 8; BBC (1980) 6
  film adaptations of 14
  French television adaptions of: France 3 (*La Liberté de Marie*, 2002) 7, 12, 13; Première Chaine (1957) 7
theatre adaptation (Elliott, 2006) 121 n. 21
Thérèse Raquin (Carné, 1953) 14
This Nation Tomorrow (1963) 135
Thompson, Hannah 42
Tissot, James 26, 38
Tournier, Michel, 'L'Air du muguet' 12
translation Studies/theory 2, 3, 16–17, 65–66, 149
  and Adaptation Studies/theory 1–3, 52, 151
  and fidelity 2, 3, 4, 24, 51, 52, 101, 151
  and Functionalism 15, 18, 23–24, 93–94
  see also Berman, Antoine; Gutt, Ernst-August; Lefevere, André; Nord, Christiane; Venuti, Lawrence
translations 1, 63, 124–25, 126
  and audiences 4, 24, 52
  and fidelity 101–02, 151–52
  as interpersonal transactions 4, 17, 51, 77, 88–91, 93, 96, 153; *see also* translators

translators 24, 73 n. 8, 125
    and television adaptions 6, 16, 17, 77, 88–91, 93, 96, 153
    visibility of 4, 15–16, 51–52, 59, 62–64, 67, 72, 88
Turn of the Century (BBC, 1960) 14
Turner, David 123, 129, 135–37, 144
Twitter 32–33, 156

Un caprice (Musset, 1837) 104
unions (actors') 137–39, 140, 141, 144

Vadim, Roger, *La Curée* (1966) 14
VCR, viewing television on 13, 155, 156
Ventre de Paris, Le 60, 63–64
    English translation of, *see Fat and the Thin*
Venuti, Lawrence 1, 5, 11–12, 14, 25, 51–57, 59, 67, 88
    and Adaptation Studies 51–52, 72, 152–53
    'Adaptation, Translation, Critique' (2007) 2
    and Translation Studies/theory 2, 3–4, 15–16, 52, 62, 153
Vidal, Gore 14
viewing experiences (television):
    in archives 8, 13
    communal 32–33, 155, 156
    diversification of 8, 13, 31, 48 n. 23, 155–56
    and social media 32–33, 156
    technological change affecting 13, 31–33, 48 n. 23, 155–56
    viewing figures 29, 30
Vincendeau, Ginette 15
'Un viol' (Cau) 12
Vizetelly, Ernest Alfred 16, 17, 53, 62–64
    Fat and the Thin (English translation of *Le Ventre de Paris*) 63–64, 76 n. 41
    Fecundity (English translation of *Fécondité*) 75 n. 38
    His Masterpiece (English translation of *L'Œuvre*) 53, 59, 62–64
    A Love Episode (English translation of *Une page d'amour*) 113
    Money (English translation of *L'Argent*) 17
    Rome (English translation of *Rome*) 75 n. 38
    With Zola in England 63
Vizetelly, Henry 16, 63, 75 n. 38
Voyage au bout de la nuit (D8) 22 n. 52

Walter, Rodolphe 111
Warner, Rick 2
Wensley, Chris 12, 28
White, Armond 9, 11
Whitehouse, Mary 130, 135–37, 144

Wilson, Steven 40
windows 28–29
    as a literary device 68, 103, 105–06, 111, 112, 119 n. 8, 150
With Zola in England (E. A. Vizetelly) 63
women:
    as artists 65–67, 68–70
    and access to public spaces 35–36, 37
    see also body, the

Z Cars (BBC, 1962) 131
Zola, Émile 14, 62–63, 92–93
    and art (definition of) 5–6, 11, 36, 51, 57–59, 150, 154
    and fidelity 5, 153–54
    and the Impressionists 57, 111–12, 151
    and Naturalist philosophy 46, 105–06, 108–09
    and photography 46
    as translator 5, 60–62, 151
Zola, Émile, works of:
    L'Argent 17, 77, 78–81, 87–93, 96, 149
    La Bête humaine 7, 11, 14, 15
    Au Bonheur des dames 1, 23, 24–26, 27–29, 30, 32, 34–39, 40, 44–46
    Le Bouton de rose 7, 11
    La Curée 14, 40, 83, 90
    La Faute de l'abbé Mouret 22 n. 52
    Fécondité 75 n. 38
    La Fortune des Rougon 7, 11
    Germinal 11, 40, 123, 124, 129–30, 131–32, 136–37, 140–41
    'Histoire d'un fou' 11, 12
    La Joie de vivre 7, 11
    'Madame Sourdis' 1, 11, 16, 51–52, 53, 64–67, 70, 72, 149, 150
    Naïs 15
    Nana 11, 12–13, 40, 80, 92
    L'Œuvre 1, 16, 51, 53, 57–62, 149
    Pot-Bouille 11
    'Pour une nuit d'amour' 11, 12
    Le Rêve 40
    Rome 75 n. 38
    Rougon-Macquart (series) 37, 40, 63, 83, 90, 92, 103; *see also under individual titles*
    Thérèse Raquin 6, 7, 11, 12, 13
    Une page d'amour 1, 11, 17, 101, 102, 103–09, 110–13, 149, 150
    Le Ventre de Paris 60, 63–64
    for adaptations and translations, *see under individual title entries*

www.ingramcontent.com/pod-product-compliance
Lightning Source LLC
LaVergne TN
LVHW061252060426
835507LV00017B/2033